Statistical Methods for Annotation Analysis

Synthesis Lectures on Human Language Technologies

Editor
Graeme Hirst, *University of Toronto*

Synthesis Lectures on Human Language Technologies is edited by Graeme Hirst of the University of Toronto. The series consists of 50- to 150-page monographs on topics relating to natural language processing, computational linguistics, information retrieval, and spoken language understanding. Emphasis is on important new techniques, on new applications, and on topics that combine two or more HLT subfields.

Statistical Methods for Annotation Analysis
Silviu Paun, Ron Artstein, and Massimo Poesio
2021

Validity, Reliability, and Significance: Empirical Methods for NLP and Data Science
Stefan Riezler and Michael Hagmann
2021

Pretrained Transformers for Text Ranking: BERT and Beyond
Jimmy Lin, Rodrigo Nogueira, and Andrew Yates
2021

Automated Essay Scoring
Beata Beigman Klebanov and Nitin Madnani
2021

Explainable Natural Language Processing
Anders Søgaard
2021

Finite-State Text Processing
Kyle Gorman and Richard Sproat
2021

Semantic Relations Between Nominals, Second Edition
Vivi Nastase, Stan Szpakowicz, Preslav Nakov, and Diarmuid Ó Séagdha
2021

Statistical Language Models for Information Retrieval
ChengXiang Zhai
2008

Statistical Methods for Annotation Analysis

Silviu Paun, Ron Artstein, and Massimo Poesio

ISBN: 978-3-031-03753-5   paperback
ISBN: 978-3-031-03763-4   PDF
ISBN: 978-3-031-03773-3   hardcover

DOI 10.1007/978-3-031-03763-4

A Publication in the Springer series
SYNTHESIS LECTURES ON HUMAN LANGUAGE TECHNOLOGIES

Lecture #54
Series Editor: Graeme Hirst, *University of Toronto*
Series ISSN
Print 1947-4040   Electronic 1947-4059

Statistical Methods for Annotation Analysis

Silviu Paun
Queen Mary University of London

Ron Artstein
University of Southern California

Massimo Poesio
Queen Mary University of London and Turing Institue

SYNTHESIS LECTURES ON HUMAN LANGUAGE TECHNOLOGIES #54

ABSTRACT

Labelling data is one of the most fundamental activities in science, and has underpinned practice, particularly in medicine, for decades, as well as research in corpus linguistics since at least the development of the Brown corpus. With the shift towards Machine Learning in Artificial Intelligence (AI), the creation of datasets to be used for training and evaluating AI systems, also known in AI as corpora, has become a central activity in the field as well.

Early AI datasets were created on an *ad-hoc* basis to tackle specific problems. As larger and more reusable datasets were created, requiring greater investment, the need for a more systematic approach to dataset creation arose to ensure increased quality. A range of statistical methods were adopted, often but not exclusively from the medical sciences, to ensure that the labels used were not subjective, or to choose among different labels provided by the coders. A wide variety of such methods is now in regular use. This book is meant to provide a survey of the most widely used among these statistical methods supporting annotation practice.

As far as the authors know, this is the first book attempting to cover the two families of methods in wider use. The first family of methods is concerned with the development of labelling schemes and, in particular, ensuring that such schemes are such that sufficient agreement can be observed among the coders. The second family includes methods developed to analyze the output of coders once the scheme has been agreed upon, particularly although not exclusively to identify the most likely label for an item among those provided by the coders.

The focus of this book is primarily on Natural Language Processing, the area of AI devoted to the development of models of language interpretation and production, but many if not most of the methods discussed here are also applicable to other areas of AI, or indeed, to other areas of Data Science.

KEYWORDS

statistics, corpus annotation, agreement, coefficients of agreement, probabilistic annotation models, variational autoencoders, latent models, neural models for learning from the crowd

In memory of Janyce Wiebe

Contents

Preface

When, almost 15 years ago, two of us (Massimo and Ron) completed what was to become our (Artstein and Poesio, 2008) paper, we felt elated at reaching a milestone after three years of hard work. But we were also aware that the stage we had reached, on the one hand, left a number of open questions, particularly about the interpretability of coefficients of agreement. On the other hand, it failed to cover important areas of research within the field of statistical methods for annotation analysis, such as latent models of agreement or probabilistic annotation models, which we felt could make important contributions to data creation and use within Computational Linguistics even though, at the time, it had only begun being experimented with in such pioneering work as Beigman Klebanov and Beigman (2009), Bruce and Wiebe (1999), Carpenter (2008), and Reidsma and Carletta (2008). 2008 was also the year of the seminal paper by Snow et al. (2008) that started the crowdsourcing revolution in Natural Language Processing (NLP), in which such methods were to play an essential role. We were therefore delighted when, many years later, Graeme Hirst and Mike Morgan offered us the opportunity to make further progress along the path begun in that paper. This book is the result of that progress.

As the 2008 paper covered the material in its scope—coefficients of agreement—in a, we thought, reasonably thorough way; and, as even more thorough works covering that material have appeared since, such as Gwet (2014), we didn't attempt to expand our coverage of that topic much in this book. We merely aimed to incorporate some material that had been left out in the original paper and to update the presentation to take into account more recent proposals, e.g., on unitizing. Our effort focused instead primarily on covering methods that had not been covered at all in the 2008 paper, also because meanwhile those techniques have become much more widespread in NLP. We hope this book offers as accessible an introduction to latent models of agreement, probabilistic models of aggregation, and learning directly from multiple coders, as the 2008 paper did for coefficients of agreement.

Silviu Paun, Ron Artstein, and Massimo Poesio
September 2021

Acknowledgements

We are extremely grateful to Graeme Hirst and Mike Morgan for offering us the opportunity to continue our work in this area, and to the many colleagues who collaborated with us on this effort at various stages and/or offered their comments and support. We would especially like to thank Bob Carpenter, Jon Chamberlain, Janosch Haber, Dirk Hovy, Tommaso Fornaciari, Udo Kruschwitz, Chris Madge, Becky Passonneau, Barbara Plank, Edwin Simpson, Alexandra Uma, and Juntao Yu, for much inspiration, feedback, and help over the years. We would also like to thank Jacopo Amidei, Lora Aroyo, Valerio Basile, Beata Beigman-Klebanov, Raffaella Bernardi, Alex Braylan, Chris Callison-Burch, Jean Carletta, Chris Cieri, Barbara di Eugenio, Anca Dumitrache, James Fiumara, Iryna Gurevych, Nancy Ide, Klaus Krippendorff, Walter Lasecki, Matt Lease, Mark Liberman, Yann Mathet, Sabine Schulte im Walde, Yannick Versley, Renata Vieira, Aline Villavicencio, and Janyce Wiebe.

Silviu Paun and Massimo Poesio were supported by the DALI project, ERC Advanced Grant 695662 to Massimo Poesio.

Ron Artstein was sponsored by the U.S. Army Research Laboratory (ARL) under contract number W911NF-14-D-0005. Statements and opinions expressed and content included do not necessarily reflect the position or the policy of the government, and no official endorsement should be inferred.

Silviu Paun, Ron Artstein, and Massimo Poesio
September 2021

CHAPTER 1

Introduction

Labelling data is one of the most fundamental activities in science, and has underpinned practice, e.g., in medicine and psychology (Agresti, 2003, Siegel and Castellan, 1988) for decades, but also research in content analysis (Krippendorff, 2004a) and corpus linguistics (McEnery and Wilson, 2019). With the shift in Artificial Intelligence (AI) toward Machine Learning, the creation of datasets/corpora to be used for training and evaluating AI systems has become a central activity in the field as well, including in the area of AI with which we are primarily concerned, Natural Language Processing (NLP) (Ide and Pustejovsky, 2017).

Early AI datasets were created on an ad-hoc basis to tackle specific problems, but as larger and more reusable datasets were created, requiring greater investment, the need for a more systematic approach to dataset creation arose, that would ensure a better quality (Ide and Pustejovsky, 2017). A range of statistical methods were adopted to ensure that the labels used were not subjective (Artstein and Poesio, 2008, Carletta, 1996, Cohen, 1960, Gwet, 2014, Krippendorff, 1980, 2004a, Scott, 1955, Siegel and Castellan, 1988) or to choose among different labels provided by the coders (Carpenter, 2008, Dawid and Skene, 1979, Hovy et al., 2013, Passonneau and Carpenter, 2014, Paun et al., 2018a, Whitehill et al., 2009). A wide variety of such methods is now in regular use in NLP and in AI more generally. This book is meant to provide an in-depth introduction to the most widely used among these statistical methods supporting annotation practice.

As far as we know, this is the first book attempting to cover the two families of methods in wider use. The first family of methods is concerned with the development of labelling schemes, and in particular, with ensuring that such schemes are such that sufficient agreement can be observed among the coders (Artstein and Poesio, 2008, Carletta, 1996, Cohen, 1960, Gwet, 2014, Krippendorff, 1980, 2004a, Scott, 1955, Siegel and Castellan, 1988). Our chapters on this topic cover well-known **coefficien of agreement** such as π, κ, and their variants (Carletta, 1996, Cohen, 1960, Scott, 1955, Siegel and Castellan, 1988), or α (Krippendorff, 1980, 2004a, Passonneau, 2004) that have been extensively used in NLP and AI, more generally (Chapter 2 and 3). We also cover work addressing the known limitations of these methods by recasting agreement analysis in probabilistic terms (Aickin, 1990, Bruce and Wiebe, 1999, Guggenmoos-Holzmann, 1996, Uebersax and Grove, 1990) (Chapters 4).

The second family includes methods developed to analyze the output of coders once the scheme has been agreed upon, in particular although, not exclusively, to identify the most likely label for an item among those provided by the coders. These methods have been used more and more in NLP after **crowdsourcing** became widespread (Alonso, 2019, Snow et al., 2008). The part of the book dedicated to these methods covers, in detail, not only the best-known **probabilistic aggregation methods** (Carpenter, 2008, Dawid and Skene, 1979, Hovy et al., 2013, Passonneau and Carpenter, 2014, Paun et al., 2018a, Whitehill et al., 2009) (in Chapter 5), but also more recent neural approaches to aggregation (Chu et al., 2021, Li et al., 2020, Rodrigues and Pereira, 2018, Yin et al., 2017). In addition, we discuss more recent proposals to bypass the aggregation step entirely to **learn directly from annotator labels** (Albarqouni et al., 2016, Chu et al., 2021, Fornaciari et al., 2021, Guan et al., 2018, Peterson et al., 2019, Raykar et al., 2010, Rodrigues and Pereira, 2018, Uma et al., 2020, 2021b) (Chapter 6).

The book focuses primarily on NLP, the area of AI devoted to the development of models of language interpretation and production, but many if not most of the methods discussed here are applicable to other areas of AI as well, such as Computer Vision, or indeed to Data Science in medicine, from which many of these methods originate.

1.1   RELIABILITY AND VALIDITY, AND OTHER ISSUES

One theme than runs through this book is the relation between **reliability** (or **agreement**)—the extent to which coders agree with themselves and each other—and **validity**—the extent to which the annotations are 'correct'. Part of the issue is that the type of data labelling carried out in different disciplines has different degrees of objectivity. In the medical sciences, labelling is often related to diagnosis: the coders are doctors or other medical experts, judging whether, e.g., an x-ray indicates a patient has a certain disease. As a result, the objective of the analysis of such labelling exercises is often to identify the 'true' label of an item, and/or the validity of certain judgments (see, e.g., Uebersax (1988)). In the social sciences, by contrast, judgments are often subjective, and therefore it makes less sense of talking about validity in the sense above—the more limited objective is to ensure that the judgments on which the findings of a study are based are **replicable**.

The type of annotation carried out in NLP, and in AI more generally, occupies an intermediate position in between these two extremes. Much of the early corpus creation work was concerned with the annotation of the linguistic interpretation of a certain expression at a particular level—e.g., the part of speech of a word (Francis and Kucera, 1982), or the syntactic interpretation of a sentence (Marcus et al., 1993)—which was assumed to be objective. In this context, it made sense to be concerned with recovering the 'true', or **gold**, interpretation. But this assumption was found to be problematic as soon as the attention of the community shifted to annotating more complex judgments, such as word senses (Bruce and Wiebe, 1999, Passonneau et al., 2012) or discourse phenomena (Carletta et al., 1997, Passonneau and Litman, 1997, Poesio and Artstein, 2005). The gold assumption has become even more problematic after the shift in NLP toward the study of subjective judgments (Bruce and Wiebe, 1998, Wiebe et al., 2005), where we do not expect a particular interpretation to be 'true' by definition, hence the notion of validity is not truly applicable (Basile, 2020, Uma et al., 2021b). We will return to this point several times throughout the book (see in particular Section 2.2).

1.2   A VERY SHORT GUIDE TO THE PROBABILISTICALLY MORE ADVANCED CONTENT IN THE BOOK

While the earliest chapters of this book only require basic notions of probability, some of the later chapters assume familiarity with some key concepts used in the literature on statistical modelling. We briefly mention in this section some of the concepts that are needed to fully understand the discussion, and provide further intuitions in the form of boxes in the chapters, but we recommend readers without the required background to consult books starting with the excellent introductory book by Cohen (2016) in this series. For a more in-depth introduction, see the books by Kruschke (2015) or Gelman et al. (2013). The book by Bishop (2016) is another great resource but maybe for the more advanced readers.

Generative Process   We typically describe the models in this book following what it is referred to as their generative process, i.e., an imaginary process about the way the observed data is believed to have been generated. The process consists of all the assumptions the model makes to explain the phenomenon it is modelling. The role of the inference is then to recover the parameters of the model that best explain the observed data under the specified generative process.

Inference   The details about the estimation of the parameters for the probabilistic models we present go beyond the scope of this book. Luckily, existing software make it easy to fit these models on a dataset without requiring any technical details about optimization. The inference is taken care of by the software. All that the reader is required to know to put these models to practice is how to specify them, and this book goes at length to offer sufficient details to facilitate that. In addition to detailed descriptions of the models we also include practical sections where we experiment with publicly available implementations or our own implementations using an off-the-shelf software. All of this should hopefully make it easier for the reader to kick-start their own experiments. For an easy-to-use statistical modelling and inference platform, regularly updated and with a vibrant community, we recommend checking out Stan (Carpenter et al., 2017).

Fitness Tests   The goodness of fit of a probabilistic model refers to how well the model fits the observed data, i.e., how well the set of assumptions that makes up the model captures the behaviour of the observed data. The test for assessing the goodness of fit measures the discrepancy between the observed data and the data that is expected under the model. If there is significant difference between the observed and the expected data then the model is misspecified and its assumptions need to be reconsidered. There are many ways to assess the fitness of a model depending exactly on how the aforementioned discrepancy in quantified. For example, in Chapter 4 goodness of fit is measured using Chi-squared tests, commonly employed when working with categorical data (as the annotations typically are). Gelman et al. (2013) has an excellent chapter on model checking where you can read more on this topic.

Choice of Priors   There are many aspects that guide the selection of priors for a probabilistic model. Probably the most obvious one is to specify the priors to allow us to incorporate our prior beliefs about the phenomenon that is being modelled, be that any documented evidence we have available, or our own intuitions. Another typical reason for a particular choice of priors is mathematical convenience, e.g., when we want to ensure conjugacy so we can apply a particular inference theory. Or other times the priors will be selected to stabilize the inference on a particular dataset, e.g., by using weakly informative priors, not too strong to rule out meaningful parameter values, but not too broad either to have the inference wander around inefficiently. In general, we let the readers make their own judgements about what are the right priors for their application. We include priors only as to give an example, and these will typically be non-informative, useful to regularize the parameters at inference time, or weakly informative for stability as we mentioned before. The exception when we discuss in more detail a particular selection of priors is when we want to convey an important message, e.g., in Chapter 5.7 we discuss how to model sequential data and there it is important for the reader to understand how to encode unwanted transitions into the prior.

Expressing Probabilities   When expressing probabilities we sometimes use the sampling notation, as in $c \sim \mathsf{Categorical}(\pi)$, to specify the probability distribution for a particular random variable. In our small example the random variable c is distributed according to a $\mathsf{Categorical}$ distribution with parameter vector π whose elements encode the probability of this variable taking on different categories. We typically use this notation when we describe the generative process of a model, i.e., to describe how various variables are generated under the assumptions made by the model. Other times, when we want to focus on a particular probability for an event, we use the more classic notation; for example, we use $p(c = k | \pi) = \pi_k$ to inform the reader that the probability of the random variable c taking on category k is π_k. The reader should be aware of these two different notations as we will often switch between them in the book. Also, for brevity, but at the expense of notation rigour, we sometimes drop some parameters and constants when expressing conditional dependencies. For example, we sometimes write $p(c_i = k) = \pi_k$ instead of $p(c_i = k | \pi) = \pi_k$. You can still see the full list of dependencies but by examining the right-hand side expression.

1.3   THE COMPANION WEBSITE

A companion website was created for this book at:

https://sites.google.com/view/stats-annotation-analysis/

Readers can find additional information there, such as links to resources like software and datasets discussed in the text.

PART I

Analysing Agreement

CHAPTER 2

Coefficien of Agreement

2.1 INTRODUCTION AND MOTIVATIONS

Ever since the mid-1990s, increasing effort has gone into putting semantics and discourse research on the same empirical footing as other areas of Computational Linguistics (CL). This soon led to worries about the subjectivity of the judgments required to create annotated resources, much greater for semantics and pragmatics than for the aspects of language interpretation of concern to the first resource creation efforts such as the creation of the Brown corpus (Francis and Kucera, 1982), the British National Corpus (Leech et al., 1994), or the Penn Treebank (Marcus et al., 1993). Problems with early proposals for assessing coders' agreement on discourse segmentation tasks (such as Passonneau and Litman, 1993) led Carletta (1996) to suggest the adoption of the K coefficient of agreement, a variant of Cohen's κ (Cohen, 1960), as this had already been used for similar purposes in **content analysis** for a long time.[1] Carletta's proposals were enormously influential, and K quickly became the de-facto standard for measuring agreement in CL not only in work on discourse (Carletta et al., 1997, Carlson et al., 2003, Core and Allen, 1997, Di Eugenio, 2000, Hearst, 1997, Poesio and Vieira, 1998, Stolcke et al., 1997) but also for other annotation tasks (e.g., Bruce and Wiebe, 1998, Craggs and McGee Wood, 2004, Mieskes and Strube, 2006, Nenkova and Passonneau, 2004, Stevenson and Gaizauskas, 2000, Véronis, 1998). During this period, however, a number of questions have also been raised about K and similar coefficients—some already in Carletta et al.'s own work (Carletta et al., 1997)—ranging from simple questions about the way the coefficient is computed (e.g., whether it is really applicable when more than two coders are used), to debates about which levels of agreement can be considered 'acceptable' (Craggs and McGee Wood, 2005, Di Eugenio, 2000) to the realization that K is not appropriate for all types of agreement (Di Eugenio, 2000, Marcu et al., 1999, Poesio and Vieira, 1998, Stevenson and Gaizauskas, 2000). Di Eugenio (2000) raised the issues of the effect of **skewed distributions** on the value of K and pointed out that the original κ developed by Cohen (1960) is based on very different assumptions about coder bias from

---

[1]As we will see below, there are lots of terminological inconsistencies in the literature. Carletta uses the term kappa for the coefficient of agreement, referring to Krippendorff (1980) and Siegel and Castellan (1988) for an introduction, and using Siegel and Castellan's terminology and definitions. However, Siegel and Castellan's statistic, which they call K, is actually Fleiss' generalization to more than two coders of Scott's π, not of the original Cohen's κ; to confuse matters further, Siegel and Castellan use the term κ to indicate the parameter which is estimated by K (i.e., a function of K with an approximately normal distribution which can be used to estimate the significance of the value of K obtained). In what follows, we will use the term κ to indicate coefficients that calculate chance agreement by looking at individual coder marginals—Cohen's original coefficient and its generalization to more than two coders—and use the term K for the coefficient discussed by Siegel and Castellan.

K of Siegel and Castellan (1988), which is typically used in CL. This issue of annotator bias was further debated in Di Eugenio and Glass (2004) and Craggs and McGee Wood (2005). Di Eugenio and Glass (2004) pointed out that the choice of calculating chance agreement by using individual coder marginals (κ) or pooled distributions (K) can lead to reliability values falling on different sides of the dreaded 0.67 threshold, and recommended reporting both values. Craggs and McGee Wood (2005), by contrast, argued, following Krippendorff (2004a,b), that measures like Cohen's κ are inappropriate for measuring agreement. Finally, Passonneau has been advocating the use of Krippendorff's α (Krippendorff, 1980, 2004a) for coding tasks in CL which do not involve nominal and disjoint categories, including anaphoric annotation, wordsense tagging, and summarization (Nenkova and Passonneau, 2004, Passonneau, 2006, Passonneau et al., 2006, Passonneau, 2004).

Content analysis

Content analysis, in the broad definition from Wikipedia, is "research using the categorization and classification of speech, written text, interviews, images, or other forms of communication". (For a more systematic but equally broad definition, see Krippendorff (2019).) Under this rather general definition, content analysis clearly overlaps to a significant extent with corpus linguistics (which, however, is primarily interested in the categorization and classification of linguistic phenomena), but also with computational linguistics after its 'empirical turn' and its more recent broadening of the types of classification of interest beyond the linguistic to include, e.g., categories of interest to the clinical and social sciences as in hate speech detection, for instance. One characteristic that used to distinguish content analysis from computational linguistics was the focus on manual analysis as opposed to computational analysis, but this has changed. So we would say that the true distinguishing feature of content analysis in comparison with corpus linguistics in particular is the focus on the *how* to analyze, as opposed to *what*—i.e., on the methodology to be used to be able to draw scientifically testable conclusions from the analyzed data, as illustrated in particular by Krippendorff's textbook.

These and other issues were considered in our own survey (Artstein and Poesio, 2008). In that article we first discussed in some detail the mathematics and underlying assumptions of the coefficients used or mentioned in the CL or the content analysis literature. Second, we also covered in some detail Krippendorff's α, whose use in CL literature had been pioneered by Passonneau. Third, we reviewed the first ten years of experience with coefficients of agreement in CL, reconsidering the issues that have been raised also from a mathematical perspective. This chapter and the next mostly cover similar ground to Artstein and Poesio (2008), but the discussion has been updated to mention some of the progress made in recent years.

2.2   COEFFICIENTS OF AGREEMENT

2.2.1   AGREEMENT, RELIABILITY, AND VALIDITY

The intent of coefficients of agreement is to infer the reliability of an annotation effort. Typically, agreement coefficients are calculated on a sample of the data, and if the process is deemed reliable then large-scale annotation may proceed. The following section is a quick recap of what agreement studies can and cannot achieve, inspired by Krippendorff (2004a, Section 11.1).

Researchers who wish to use hand-coded data, that is, data in which **items** are labeled with **categories**, whether to support an empirical claim or to develop and test a computational model, need to show that such data are **reliable**. The fundamental assumption behind the methodologies discussed in this chapter is that data are reliable if coders can be shown to **agree** on the categories assigned to items to an extent determined by the purposes of the study (Craggs and McGee Wood, 2005, Krippendorff, 2004a). If different coders produce consistently similar results, then we can infer that they have internalized a similar understanding of the annotation guidelines, and we can expect them to perform consistently under this understanding.

Reliability is thus a prerequisite for demonstrating the **validity** of the coding scheme— that is, to show that the coding scheme captures the 'truth' of the phenomenon being studied, in case this matters: if the annotators are not consistent then either some of them are wrong or else the annotation scheme is inappropriate for the data. (Just as in real life, the fact that witnesses to an event disagree with each other makes it difficult for third parties to know what actually happened.) However, it is important to keep in mind that achieving good agreement cannot ensure validity: two observers of the same event may well share the same prejudice while still being objectively wrong.

The last point to keep in mind is that the term 'reliability' can be used in three different ways, depending on how agreement is tested. First of all, we may want to test **stability** or **intra-coder agreement**: the extent to which the coding process yields the same results when repeated over time, typically measured by observing how much the same coder agrees with her or his previous coding at a distance of time. A stronger test is measuring **reproducibility**: the degree to which different coders achieve the same coding when working independently. This is the type of test required for large annotation efforts employing multiple coders. Finally, **accuracy** is the degree to which a coding process yields the results specified by a gold standard, when one such exists.

2.2.2   A COMMON NOTATION

A reliability study for a simple annotation scheme involves a set of **items** (markables) to be annotated, a set of **categories** (labels) to be applied to items, and a set of **coders** (annotators) who assign to each item a unique category label. (In a more elaborate scheme, items and categories may have structures that are more complex than a set, and identification of the items may be part of the annotation task.) The discussions in the literature often use different notations to express these concepts. We will introduce a uniform notation, which we hope will make the relations between the different coefficients of agreement clearer.

- The set of **items** is $\{ i \mid i \in I \}$ and is of cardinality **i**.

- The set of **categories** is $\{ k \mid k \in K \}$ and is of cardinality **k**.

- The set of **coders** is $\{ c \mid c \in C \}$ and is of cardinality **c**.

Confusion also arises from the use of the letter P, which is used in the literature with at least three distinct interpretations, namely "proportion", "percent", and "probability". We will use the following notations uniformly throughout the chapter.

- We will use the notation A_o for observed agreement and D_o for observed disagreement.

- The notation A_e and D_e will be used to indicate expected agreement and expected disagreement, respectively. The relevant coefficient will be indicated with a superscript when an ambiguity may arise (for example, A_e^π is the expected agreement used for calculating π, and A_e^κ is the expected agreement used for calculating κ).

- The notation $P(\cdot)$ will be reserved for the probability of a variable, and $\hat{P}(\cdot)$ will be used for an estimate of such probability from observed data.

Finally, we will use **n** with a subscript parameter to indicate the number of judgments of a particular type.

- n_{ik} is the number of annotations where item i is assigned to category k; since each coder labels each item at most once, this is the same as the number of coders who assigned item i to category k.

- n_{ck} is the number of annotations where coder c assigns category k to some item; since each coder labels each item at most once, this is the same as the number of items assigned by coder c to category k.

- n_k is the total number of annotations assigned to category k.

2.2.3   THE NEED FOR DEDICATED MEASURES OF AGREEMENT

Why are custom coefficients to measure agreement necessary? Couldn't existing measures such as percentage agreement or traditional statistics like χ^2 do the job? Although this question has already been addressed a number of times in the literature, it is useful to consider it again, in part for completeness' sake, but also to clarify the problems that kappa-like measures are meant to solve.

Table 2.1: A simple example of agreement on dialogue act tagging

		Coder A		
		Stat	IReq	Total
Coder B	Stat	20	20	40
	IReq	10	50	60
	Total	30	70	100

Percentage Agreement   The simplest measure of agreement between two coders is **percentage of agreement** or **observed agreement**, defined for example by Scott (1955, page 323) as "the percentage of judgments on which the two analysts agree when coding the same data independently". This is the number of items on which the coders agree divided by the total number of items. More precisely, and looking ahead to the discussion below, observed agreement is the arithmetic mean of the **agreement value** agr_i for all items $i \in I$, defined as follows:

$$\text{agr}_i = \begin{cases} 1 & \text{if the two coders assign } i \text{ to the same category} \\ 0 & \text{if the two coders assign } i \text{ to different categories} \end{cases}$$

Observed agreement over the values agr_i for all items $i \in I$ is then:

$$A_o = \frac{1}{i} \sum_{i \in I} \text{agr}_i$$

For example, let us assume we have a very simple annotation scheme for dialogue acts in information-seeking dialogues making a binary distinction between the categories "statement" (Stat) and "information request" (IReq), as in the DAMSL dialogue act scheme (Allen and Core, 1997), and that 2 coders classify 100 utterances according to this scheme, as shown in Table 2.1. Percentage agreement for this data set is obtained by summing up the cells on the diagonal and dividing by the total number of items: $A_o = (20 + 50)/100 = 0.7$.

Observed agreement enters in the computation of all the measures of agreement we consider, but on its own it does not yield values that can be compared across studies, since some agreement is due to chance, and the amount of chance agreement is affected by two factors that vary from one study to the other. First of all, as Scott (1955, page 322) points out, "[percentage agreement] is biased in favor of dimensions with a small number of categories". In other words, given two coding schemes for the same phenomenon, the one with fewer categories will result in higher percentage agreement just by chance. If two coders randomly classify utterances in a uniform manner using the scheme of Table 2.1, we would expect an equal number of items to fall in each of the four cells in the table, and therefore pure chance will cause the coders to agree on half of the items (the two cells on the diagonal: $\frac{1}{4} + \frac{1}{4}$). But suppose we want to refine the simple binary coding scheme by introducing a new category, a "check" or request for confirmation (Chck), as in the MapTask coding scheme (Carletta et al., 1997). If two coders randomly classify utterances in a uniform manner using the three categories in the second scheme, they would only agree on a third of the items ($\frac{1}{9} + \frac{1}{9} + \frac{1}{9}$). The second reason percentage agreement can not be trusted is that is does not correct for the distribution of items among categories: we expect a higher percentage agreement when one category is much more common than the other. This problem, already raised by Hsu and Field (2003, page 207), among others, can be illustrated using the following example (Di Eugenio and Glass, 2004, example 3, pages 98–99). Suppose 95% of utterances in a particular domain are Stat, and only 5% are IReq. We would then expect by chance that $0.95 \times 0.95 = 0.9025$ of the utterances would be classified as Stat by both coders, and $0.05 \times 0.05 = 0.0025$ as IReq, so the coders would agree on 90.5% of the utterances. Under such circumstances, a seemingly high observed agreement of 90% is actually worse than expected by chance.

The conclusion reached in the literature is that in order to get figures that are comparable across studies, observed agreement has to be adjusted for chance agreement. We will not look at the variants of percentage agreement used in CL work on discourse before the introduction of kappa, such as percentage agreement with an expert and percentage agreement with the majority; see Carletta (1996) for discussion and criticism. We will review various ways of correcting percentage agreement for chance, starting in Section 2.2.4. But first, we will look at other chance-adjusted measures and show why they are inadequate for measuring agreement—hence the need to develop specific agreement coefficients.

Measures of Association   The χ^2 statistic is also inappropriate as a measure of agreement. As pointed out by Cohen (1960, page 39), χ^2 is a measure of association rather than agreement—which means that we get a high value of χ^2 whenever a particular cooccurrence of judgments is different from the expected value. This may happen not just when we find good agreement, but also when we have systematic disagreement. The agreement matrix in Table 2.2 reports the results of an annotation experiment (unrelated to the one in Table 2.1) in which two coders classify utterances as either Stat, IReq, or Chck. The value of χ^2 for this table is 64.59, which is highly significant, but this strong association does not indicate agreement. The χ^2 statistic measures how actual values differ from predicted values in all cells of the table. Indeed, the highest contribution to the χ^2 value comes from the utterances classified by A as IReq and by B as Chck, where the observed value 0.15 is much higher than the expected value 0.06—a case of disagreement.

Correlation Coefficien   A point perhaps not sufficiently emphasized in the CL literature on agreement is that κ and related measures of agreement such as α or π are not primarily statistics in the sense of t, χ^2, or F, which are (functions associated with) probability distributions whose value specifies the significance of the result obtained. The title of Cohen's classic article is very illuminating in this respect: π, κ, α, etc. are 'coefficient(s) of agreement for nominal

Table 2.2: High association but low agreement (adapted from Cohen, 1960)

| | | Coder A | | | |
		Stat	IReq	Chck	Total
	Stat	0.25	0.13	0.12	0.50
Coder B	IReq	0.12	0.02	0.16	0.30
	Chck	0.03	0.15	0.02	0.20
	Total	0.40	0.30	0.30	1.00

Table 2.3: Correlation need not indicate agreement

| | Exp 1 | | Exp 2 | |
Item	A	B	C	D
a	1	1	1	2
b	2	2	2	4
c	3	3	3	6
d	4	4	4	8
e	5	5	5	10
	$r = 1.0$		$r = 1.0$	

scales'. What this means is that they are coefficients taking values between -1 and $+1$, just like Pearson's product-moment coefficient r or Spearman's rank-correlation coefficient r_s, but intended for nominal scales, and for measuring agreement rather than association. Thinking of the kappa-like measures of agreement as coefficients is illuminating in certain respects, as they have some of the formal properties of correlation coefficients (Krippendorff, 1970a), and the problem of deciding whether a particular value of, say, κ indicates a sufficient degree of agreement is similar to the problem of determining whether a particular value of r expresses a strong enough association. However, neither product-moment correlation r nor rank order correlation r_s are good measures of agreement (Bartko and Carpenter, 1976, page 309). This is not just because these coefficients are specified for real values rather than nominal scales; correlation is not the same thing as agreement, and a strong correlation may exist even when coders disagree. The problem is illustrated by Table 2.3 (adapted from Bartko and Carpenter, 1976). Suppose we have a coding scheme according to which coders give each item a rating between 1 and 10 (this might be a marking scheme for student essays, for example), and we ran two experiments to test the scheme. In the first experiment, coders A and B (whose marks are shown in the second and third columns) are in complete agreement, while in the second, coders C and D (whose marks are shown in the fourth and fifth columns) disagree on all items, but assign marks that are linearly correlated. Exactly the same product-moment value will be obtained in both experiments, even though there is perfect agreement between A and B, but no agreement at all between C and D.[2]

2.2.4 CHANCE-CORRECTED COEFFICIENTS FOR MEASURING AGREEMENT BETWEEN TWO CODERS

We now present the specialized agreement coefficients, as found in the literature. For expository purposes, we start with the simplest case of calculating agreement, namely agreement between two coders assigning a single label from a fixed set of labels to each of a pre-defined set of items. Subsequently, we will show how these coefficients can be generalized by relaxing some of these conditions: multiple coders (Section 2.2.5), different kinds of labels (Section 2.2.6), partial annotations or missing data (Section 2.3), and items that are not determined in advance (Section 2.4).

At the heart of all of the coefficients discussed in this chapter is the concept of expected agreement (A_e), a value that reflects the amount of agreement we would expect to see if the coders were making arbitrary label choices. This value is used to perform chance correction on the observed agreement (A_o): The value $1 - A_e$ measures how much agreement over and above chance is attainable; the value $A_o - A_e$ tells us how much agreement beyond chance was actually found; and the ratio between $A_o - A_e$ and $1 - A_e$ tells us which proportion of the possible agreement beyond chance was actually observed. This idea is expressed by the following formula:

$$\phi = \frac{A_o - A_e}{1 - A_e} \text{ where } \phi \text{ stands for a coefficient like } S, \pi, \text{ or } \kappa$$

The three best-known coefficients, S (Bennett et al., 1954), π (Scott, 1955), and κ (Cohen, 1960), and their generalizations, all use this formula, whereas Krippendorff's α is based on a related formula expressed in terms of disagreement (see Section 2.2.6). All three coefficients therefore yield values of agreement between $-A_e/1 - A_e$ (no observed agreement) and 1 (observed agreement = 1), with the value 0 signifying chance agreement (observed agreement = expected agreement). Note also that whenever agreement is less than perfect ($A_o < 1$), chance-corrected agreement will be strictly lower than observed agreement, since some amount of agreement is always expected by chance.

Observed agreement A_o is easy to compute, and is the same for all three coefficients—the proportion of items on which the two coders agree. But the notion of chance agreement, or the probability that two coders will classify an arbitrary item as belonging to the same category by chance, requires a model that specifies (or operationalizes) the notion of arbitrary agreement. All

---

[2]In a recent paper, Amidei et al. (2019) argued that correlation is appropriate for tasks like Natural Language Generation (NLG) in which judgments (e.g., about the acceptability of sentences generated by an NLG system) are typically ordinal (e.g., on a Likert scale), and in which expecting judges to always choose the exact same score may be unrealistic, but their judgments may still covary.

three coefficients assume *independence* of the two coders—that is, that the chance of c_1 and c_2 agreeing on any given category k is the product of the chance of each of them assigning an item to that category: $P(k|c_1) \cdot P(k|c_2)$ (the independence assumption has been the subject of much criticism, for example by John S. Uebersax).[3] Expected agreement is then the probability of c_1 and c_2 agreeing on any category, that is, the sum of the above product over all categories:

$$A_e^S = A_e^\pi = A_e^\kappa = \sum_{k \in K} P(k|c_1) \cdot P(k|c_2)$$

Models of Chance Agreement

The difference between S, π, and κ lies in the assumptions leading to the calculation of $P(k|c_i)$, the chance that coder c_i will assign an arbitrary item to category k (Hsu and Field, 2003, Zwick, 1988).

S: This coefficient models arbitrary assignment of labels as driven by a uniform distribution, i.e., for any two coders c_m, c_n and any two categories k_j, k_l, $P(k_j|c_m) = P(k_l|c_n)$. (Put another way: arbitrary assignment does not distinguish between categories and coders.)

π: Arbitrary assignment is driven by a single distribution that is shared among all the coders: for any two coders c_m, c_n and any category k, $P(k|c_m) = P(k|c_n)$. (That is, arbitrary assignment distinguishes between categories, but not coders.)

κ: Arbitrary assignment is driven by separate distribution for each coder: chance distinguishes between both categories and coders.

A further complication, explained perhaps most clearly by Krippendorff (1980), is a problem that is all too familiar in CL: the lack of independent prior knowledge of the distribution of items among categories. The distribution of categories (for π) and the priors for the individual coders (for κ) therefore have to be estimated from the observed data. We begin here by giving detailed examples on how the coefficients are calculated for two coders; we will discuss a variety of proposed generalizations starting in Section 2.2.5.

All Categories Are Equally Likely: S The simplest way of discounting for chance is the one adopted to compute the coefficient S, also known in the literature as C, κ_n, G, and RE (see Hsu and Field, 2003, Zwick, 1988). As said above, the computation of S is based on an interpretation of chance as a random choice of category from a uniform distribution—that is, all categories are equally likely. If coders classify the items into **k** categories, then the chance $P(k|c_i)$ of any coder assigning an item to category k under the uniformity assumption is $\frac{1}{k}$; hence, the total

---

[3]https://www.john-uebersax.com/stat/kappa.htm.

agreement expected by chance is

$$A_e^S = \sum_{k \in K} \frac{1}{k} \cdot \frac{1}{k} = k \cdot \left(\frac{1}{k}\right)^2 = \frac{1}{k}$$

For example, the value of S for the coding example in Table 2.1 is as follows (where $A_o = 0.7$, see above).

$$A_e^S = 2 \times \left(\frac{1}{2}\right)^2 = 0.5$$

$$S = \frac{0.7 - 0.5}{1 - 0.5} = 0.4$$

The coefficient S is problematic in many respects. The value of the coefficient can be artificially increased simply by adding spurious categories which the coders would never use (Scott, 1955, pages 322–323). In the case of CL, for example, S would reward designing extremely fine-grained tagsets, provided that most tags are never actually encountered in real data. Additional limitations are noted by Hsu and Field (2003). It has been argued that uniformity is the best model for a chance distribution of items among categories if we have no independent prior knowledge of the distribution (Brennan and Prediger, 1981). However, a lack of prior knowledge does not mean that the distribution cannot be estimated post-hoc. A uniform distribution is not a very plausible model for annotation in CL, as in pretty much all tagging tasks, from parts-of-speech (Bruce and Wiebe, 1998, Fellbaum et al., 1997, Véronis, 1998) to dialogue acts (Carletta et al., 1997, Core and Allen, 1997) we find substantial differences in the distribution of tags. For these reasons the S coefficient has never really found much use in CL, and studying it does not contribute to the points we develop in this chapter, so we will not discuss it further.

A Shared Distribution: π   All of the other methods for discounting chance agreement we discuss in this chapter attempt to overcome the limitations of S's strong uniformity assumption using an idea first proposed by Scott (1955): use the actual behavior of the coders to estimate the prior distribution of the categories. As said above, Scott based his characterization of π on the assumption that arbitrary assignment of categories to items, by any coder, is governed by the distribution of items among categories in the actual world; the best estimate of this distribution is $\hat{P}(k)$, the observed proportion of items assigned to category k by both coders.[4]

$$P(k|c_1) = P(k|c_2) = \hat{P}(k)$$

$\hat{P}(k)$, the observed proportion of items assigned to category k by both coders, is the total number of assignments to k by both coders n_k, divided by the overall number of assignments, which in the two-coder case is twice the number of items i:

$$\hat{P}(k) = \frac{n_k}{2i}$$

---

[4]The same method is used to compute the K coefficient discussed by Siegel and Castellan (1988), which is why we consider K to be a generalization of π rather than κ; this has already been pointed out by Di Eugenio and Glass (2004).

Given the assumption that coders act independently, expected agreement is computed as follows.[5]

$$A_e^\pi = \sum_{k \in K} \hat{P}(k) \cdot \hat{P}(k) = \sum_{k \in K} \left(\frac{\mathbf{n}_k}{2\mathbf{i}} \right)^2 = \frac{1}{4\mathbf{i}^2} \sum_{k \in K} \mathbf{n}_k^2$$

The value of π for the experiment in Table 2.1 is calculated as follows.

$$P(\text{Stat} \mid \text{Coder A}) = P(\text{Stat} \mid \text{Coder B}) = \hat{P}(\text{Stat}) = 0.35$$

$$P(\text{IReq} \mid \text{Coder A}) = P(\text{IReq} \mid \text{Coder B}) = \hat{P}(\text{IReq}) = 0.65$$

$$A_e^\pi = 0.35^2 + 0.65^2 = 0.1225 + 0.4225 = 0.545$$

$$\pi = \frac{0.7 - 0.545}{1 - 0.545} = \frac{0.155}{0.455} \approx 0.341$$

It is easy to show that for any set of coding data, $A_e^\pi \geq A_e^S$ and therefore $\pi \leq S$, with the limiting case (equality) obtaining when the observed distribution of items among categories is uniform.

Individual Coder Distributions: κ The method proposed by Cohen (1960) to calculate expected agreement A_e in his κ coefficient assumes that arbitrary assignment of categories to items is governed by prior distributions that are unique to each coder, and which reflect **individual annotator bias**. An individual coder's prior distribution is estimated by looking at her actual distribution: $P(k|c_i)$, the probability that coder c_i will classify an arbitrary item into category k, is estimated by using $\hat{P}(k|c)$, the proportion of items actually assigned by coder c_i to category k; this is the number of assignments to k by c, $\mathbf{n}_{ck}$, divided by the number of items $\mathbf{i}$.

$$P(k|c_i) = \hat{P}(k|c_i) = \frac{\mathbf{n}_{c_i k}}{\mathbf{i}}$$

As in the case of S and π, the probability that the two coders c_1 and c_2 assign an item to a particular category $k \in K$ is the joint probability of each coder making this assignment independently. For κ this joint probability is $\hat{P}(k|c_1) \cdot \hat{P}(k|c_2)$; expected agreement is then the sum of this joint probability over all the categories $k \in K$.[6]

$$A_e^\kappa = \sum_{k \in K} \hat{P}(k|c_1) \cdot \hat{P}(k|c_2) = \sum_{k \in K} \frac{\mathbf{n}_{c_1 k}}{\mathbf{i}} \cdot \frac{\mathbf{n}_{c_2 k}}{\mathbf{i}} = \frac{1}{\mathbf{i}^2} \sum_{k \in K} \mathbf{n}_{c_1 k} \mathbf{n}_{c_2 k}$$

---

[5]We should note that A_e^π is a **biased estimator** which overestimates the expected agreement. This is because A_e^π is calculated from a single sample, and items in a sample tend to be somewhat closer together than items in the entire population (which amounts to the loss of one "degree of freedom"). Thus, while $\hat{P}(k)$ is an unbiased estimator of the distribution of items in the entire population, A_e^π is a biased estimator of the expected agreement in the entire population; an unbiased estimator would be $(2\mathbf{i}A_e^\pi - 1)/(2\mathbf{i} - 1)$, as used for Krippendorff's α (Section 2.2.6).

[6]Since A_e^κ is calculated from two independent samples, it is an **unbiased estimator** of the expected agreement of the two specific coders on the entire population of items.

The value of κ for the experiment in Table 2.1 is as follows.

$$P(\text{Stat} \mid \text{Coder A}) = 0.3 \quad P(\text{Stat} \mid \text{Coder B}) = 0.4$$

$$P(\text{IReq} \mid \text{Coder A}) = 0.7 \quad P(\text{IReq} \mid \text{Coder B}) = 0.6$$

$$A_e^\kappa = 0.3 \times 0.4 + 0.6 \times 0.7 = 0.12 + 0.42 = 0.54$$

$$\kappa = \frac{0.7 - 0.54}{1 - 0.54} = \frac{0.16}{0.46} \approx 0.348$$

In this example, the values of π and κ turn out to be fairly close, with π slightly lower than κ (0.341 compared to 0.348). It is easy to show that for any set of coding data, $A_e^\pi \geq A_e^\kappa$ and therefore $\pi \leq \kappa$, with the limiting case (equality) obtaining when the observed distributions of the two coders are identical. The relationship between κ and S is not fixed.

What Is Measured by Pi and Kappa The difference between π and κ has been the subject of much contention in the literature, both in CL (Craggs and McGee Wood, 2005, Di Eugenio and Glass, 2004) and in other fields where it constitutes a long-standing debate (Byrt et al., 1993, Fleiss, 1975, Krippendorff, 1978, 2004b). We will discuss this difference in more detail in Section 2.5.1, where we also prove that the values of π and κ get closer as the number of coders grows. At this point we only wish to point out that by averaging the individual distributions, π reflects our expectations for arbitrary coders, whereas κ relates specifically to the coders who performed the annotation (since it takes their individual distributions as a basis for calculating chance agreement). When generalization is desired (as in most reliability studies), π is therefore more appropriate. Arbitrary coders are expected to display additional variability beyond what is found among the known coders, so it is not surprising that $\pi \leq \kappa$ for any particular set of data, with equality obtaining when the coders are indistinguishable.

A Numerical Comparison of S, Pi, and Kappa Zwick (1988) provides a particularly clear illustration of the effect of differences between the coders' observed distributions (**coder marginals**) on the values of S, κ, and π. We reproduce one of her examples here, recasting it in a CL setting.

Let us assume a dialogue act classification scheme, again adapted from DAMSL, with four categories for a forward-looking function: statement (`Stat`), information request (`IReq`), influencing addressee future action (`Iafa`), and committing speaker future action (`Csfa`). Let us again assume we have two coders, coder A and coder B. In Table 2.4, we find three illustrations of the three situations that may arise, in all of which the observed agreement A_o is 0.60.

Case 1 is an example of the case in which the coders assign equal proportions of items to all categories; in this case, all three coefficients of agreement have the same value. Case 2 exemplifies the situation in which coder A and coder B, while not assigning equal proportions of items to all categories, still end up assigning items to categories in identical proportions: both judge 40% of items to be `Stat`, 20% to be `IReq`, and so forth. In this situation, κ and π still have the same value. Finally, Case 3 is an example of the situation in which Coder A and Coder B do

Table 2.4: The effect of coder marginals on coefficient values

Case 1: Marginals Uniform
$S = 0.467, \pi = 0.467, \kappa = 0.467$

		Coder A				
		Stat	IReq	Iafa	Csfa	Total
	Stat	0.20	—	—	0.05	0.25
	IReq	—	0.10	0.15	—	0.25
Coder B	Iafa	—	0.15	0.10	—	0.25
	Csfa	0.05	—	—	0.20	0.25
	Total	0.25	0.25	0.25	0.25	1.00

Case 2: Marginals Equal But Not Uniform
$S = 0.467, \pi = 0.444, \kappa = 0.444$

		Coder A				
		Stat	IReq	Iafa	Csfa	Total
	Stat	0.20	0.10	0.10	—	0.40
	IReq	0.10	0.10	—	—	0.20
Coder B	Iafa	0.10	—	0.10	—	0.20
	Csfa	—	—	—	0.20	0.20
	Total	0.40	0.20	0.20	0.20	1.00

Case 3: Marginals Unequal
$S = 0.467, \pi = 0.460, \kappa = 0.474$

		Coder A				
		Stat	IReq	Iafa	Csfa	Total
	Stat	0.20	0.05	0.05	0.10	0.40
	IReq	—	0.10	0.05	0.05	0.20
Coder B	Iafa	—	0.05	0.10	0.05	0.20
	Csfa	—	—	—	0.20	0.20
	Total	0.20	0.20	0.20	0.40	1.00

not even agree on the proportion of items belonging to a given category: in this case, κ and π have different values. Notice also that in Case 2 we get lower values of κ and π than in Case 3—that is, when observed agreement is held constant, agreement on the marginals results in lowered coefficient values (Cicchetti and Feinstein, 1990, Di Eugenio and Glass, 2004, Feinstein and Cicchetti, 1990).

2.2.5   MORE THAN TWO CODERS

In corpus annotation practice, measuring reliability with only two coders is seldom considered enough, except for small-scale studies. The coefficients π and κ, presented above with their original definitions for two coders, can be generalized to reliability studies with more than two coders. Due to a historical accident, the terminology here becomes confusing. Fleiss (1971) proposed a coefficient of agreement for multiple coders and called it κ, even though it calculates expected agreement based on the cumulative distribution of judgments by all coders and is thus better thought of as a generalization of Scott's π. This unfortunate choice of name was the cause of much confusion in subsequent literature: often, studies which claim to give a generalization of κ to more than two coders actually report Fleiss's coefficient (e.g., Bartko and Carpenter, 1976, Di Eugenio and Glass, 2004, Siegel and Castellan, 1988). Since Carletta (1996) introduced reliability to the CL community based on the definitions of Siegel and Castellan (1988), the term "kappa" has been usually associated in this community with Siegel and Castellan's K, which is in effect Fleiss' coefficient, that is a generalization of Scott's π.

We will call Fleiss' coefficient multi-π, reserving the name multi-κ for a proper generalization of Cohen's κ (Davies and Fleiss, 1982). We will drop the multi-prefixes when no confusion is expected to arise.

Fleiss' Multi-π   With more than two coders, the observed agreement A_o can no longer be defined as the percentage of items on which there is agreement, since inevitably there will be items on which some coders agree and others disagree. The solution offered by Fleiss is to measure *pairwise agreement*: Fleiss (1971) defines the amount of agreement on a particular item as the proportion of agreeing judgment pairs out of the total number of judgment pairs for that item. Thus, for example, when two coders agree a label for an item and a third coder disagrees, agreement is $\frac{1}{3}$ (one agreeing pair and two disagreeing pairs).

Multiple coders also pose a problem for the visualization of the data. When the number of coders **c** is greater than two, judgments cannot be shown in a contingency table like Table 2.1 or 2.2, because each coder has to be represented in a separate dimension. Fleiss (1971) therefore uses a different type of table, which lists each item with the number of judgments it received for each category; Siegel and Castellan (1988) use a similar table, which Di Eugenio and Glass (2004) call an **agreement table**. Table 2.5 is an example of such an agreement table, in which the same 100 utterances from Table 2.1 are labeled by 3 coders instead of 2. Di Eugenio and Glass (2004, page 97) note that compared to contingency tables like Tables 2.1 and 2.2, agreement tables like Table 2.5 lose information because they do not say which coder gave which judg-

Table 2.5: Agreement table with three coders

	Stat	IReq
Utt_1	2	1
Utt_2	0	3
$\vdots$		
Utt_{100}	1	2
Total	90 (0.3)	210 (0.7)

ment. This information is not used in the calculation of π, but is necessary for determining the individual coders' distributions in the calculation of κ. (Agreement tables also add information compared to contingency tables, namely the identity of the items that make up each contingency class, but this information is not used in the calculation of either κ or π.)

Let $\mathbf{n}_{ik}$ stand for the number of times an item i is classified in category k (i.e., the number of coders that make such a judgment): for example, given the distribution in Table 2.5, $\mathbf{n}_{\text{Utt}_1\text{Stat}} = 2$ and $\mathbf{n}_{\text{Utt}_1\text{IReq}} = 1$. Each category k contributes $\binom{\mathbf{n}_{ik}}{2}$ pairs of agreeing judgments for item i; the amount of agreement agr_i for item i is the sum of $\binom{\mathbf{n}_{ik}}{2}$ over all categories $k \in K$, divided by $\binom{c}{2}$, the total number of judgment pairs per item.

$$\text{agr}_i = \frac{1}{\binom{c}{2}} \sum_{k \in K} \binom{\mathbf{n}_{ik}}{2} = \frac{1}{\mathbf{c}(\mathbf{c}-1)} \sum_{k \in K} \mathbf{n}_{ik}(\mathbf{n}_{ik} - 1)$$

For example, given the results in Table 2.5, we find the agreement value for Utterance 1.

$$\text{agr}_1 = \frac{1}{\binom{3}{2}} \left(\binom{\mathbf{n}_{\text{Utt}_1\text{Stat}}}{2} + \binom{\mathbf{n}_{\text{Utt}_1\text{IReq}}}{2} \right) = \frac{1}{3}(1+0) \approx 0.33$$

The overall observed agreement is the mean of agr_i for all items $i \in I$.

$$A_o = \frac{1}{\mathbf{i}} \sum_{i \in I} \text{agr}_i = \frac{1}{\mathbf{i}\mathbf{c}(\mathbf{c}-1)} \sum_{i \in I} \sum_{k \in K} \mathbf{n}_{ik}(\mathbf{n}_{ik} - 1)$$

(Notice that the above definition of observed agreement is equivalent to the mean of the two-coder observed agreement values from Section 2.2.4 for all coder pairs.)

If observed agreement is measured on the basis of pairwise agreement (the proportion of agreeing judgment pairs), it makes sense to measure *expected* agreement in terms of pairwise comparisons as well, i.e., as the probability that any pair of judgments for an item would be in agreement—or, said otherwise, the probability that two arbitrary coders would make the same judgment for a particular item by chance. This is the approach taken by Fleiss (1971).

Like Scott, Fleiss interprets 'chance agreement' as the agreement expected by a shared distribution which reflects the combined judgments of all coders, meaning that expected agreement is calculated using $\hat{P}(k)$, the overall proportion of items assigned to category k, which is the total number of such assignments by all coders $\mathbf{n}_k$ divided by the overall number of assignments. The latter, in turn, is the number of items $\mathbf{i}$ multiplied by the number of coders $\mathbf{c}$.

$$\hat{P}(k) = \frac{1}{\mathbf{ic}} \mathbf{n}_k$$

The probability that two arbitrary coders assign an item to a particular category $k \in K$ is assumed to be the joint probability of each coder making this assignment independently, that is $(\hat{P}(k))^2$. The expected agreement is the sum of this joint probability over all the categories $k \in K$.[7]

$$A_e^\pi = \sum_{k \in K} \left(\hat{P}(k) \right)^2 = \sum_{k \in K} \left(\frac{1}{\mathbf{ic}} \mathbf{n}_k \right)^2 = \frac{1}{(\mathbf{ic})^2} \sum_{k \in K} \mathbf{n}_k^2$$

Multi-π is the coefficient that Siegel and Castellan (1988) call K.

Multi-κ   It is fairly straightforward to adapt Fleiss' proposal to generalize Cohen's κ proper to more than two coders; the development below is our own, but an identical proposal can be found in Davies and Fleiss (1982).

For multi-κ, we calculate a separate probability distribution for each annotator: the probability of assigning an item to category k by coder c is the observed proportion of such assignments $\hat{P}(k|c)$, which is the number of such assignments $\mathbf{n}_{ck}$ divided by the number of items $\mathbf{i}$.

$$\hat{P}(k|c) = \frac{1}{\mathbf{i}} \mathbf{n}_{ck}$$

The probability that two arbitrary coders assign an item to a particular category $k \in K$ is the joint probability of each coder making this assignment independently. The joint probability for two particular coders c_m and c_n is $\hat{P}(k|c_m)\hat{P}(k|c_n)$, and since all coders judge all items, the joint probability for an arbitrary pair of coders is the arithmetic mean of $\hat{P}(k|c_m)\hat{P}(k|c_n)$ over all coder pairs c_m, c_n. Again, the expected agreement is the sum of this joint probability over all the categories $k \in K$.

$$A_e^\kappa = \sum_{k \in K} \frac{1}{\binom{c}{2}} \sum_{m=1}^{c-1} \sum_{n=m+1}^{c} \hat{P}(k|c_m)\hat{P}(k|c_n)$$

It is easy to see that A_e^κ for multiple coders is the mean of the two-coder A_e^κ values from Section 2.2.4 for all coder pairs.

---

[7]As in the two-coder case, multiple-coder A_e^π is a biased estimator calculated from a single sample; an unbiased estimator would be $(\mathbf{ic}A_e^\pi - 1)/(\mathbf{ic} - 1)$.

2.2.6   KRIPPENDORFF'S ALPHA AND OTHER WEIGHTED AGREEMENT COEFFICIENTS

A serious limitation of both π and κ is that all disagreements are treated equally. But especially for semantic and pragmatic features, disagreements are not all alike. Even in the relatively simple case of dialogue act tagging, a disagreement between an `accept` and a `reject` interpretation of an utterance is clearly more serious than a disagreement between an `IReq` and a `Chck`. For tasks such as anaphora resolution, where reliability is determined by measuring agreement on sets (coreference chains), allowing for degrees of disagreement becomes essential (see Section 3.4.1). Under such circumstances, π and κ are not very useful. Instead, what is needed are coefficients that can take into account the magnitude of the disagreements.

In this section we discuss two coefficients that make it possible to differentiate between types of disagreements: α (Krippendorff, 1980, 2004a, 2013, 2019), which is a coefficient defined in a general way that is appropriate for use with multiple coders, different magnitudes of disagreement, and also missing values, and is based on assumptions similar to those of π; and weighted kappa κ_w (Cohen, 1968), a generalization of κ.

Krippendorff's α

The coefficient α (Krippendorff, 1980, 2004a) is an extremely versatile agreement coefficient. It is based on assumptions similar to π, namely that expected agreement is calculated by looking at the overall distribution of judgments without regard to which coders produced these judgments. It applies to multiple coders, and it allows for different magnitudes of disagreement. When all disagreements are considered equal it is nearly identical to multi-π, correcting for small sample sizes by using an unbiased estimator for expected agreement (cf. footnote 5 on page 19). In this section we will present Krippendorff's α and relate it to the other coefficients discussed in this chapter, but we will start with α's origins as a measure of **variance**, following a long tradition of using variance to measure reliability (see citations in Krippendorff, 1970b, Rajaratnam, 1960).

Variance is a useful concept if the coders assign numerical values to the items (as in magnitude estimation tasks). We follow the standard definition of a sample's variance s^2 as the sum of square differences from the mean $SS = \sum(x - \bar{x})^2$ divided by the degrees of freedom df. Each item in a reliability study can be considered to be a separate level in a single-factor analysis of variance: the smaller the variance around each level, the higher the reliability. In order to be comparable across studies, the variance within the levels (s^2_{within}) needs to be scaled with respect to the expected variance, which is estimated by the overall variance of the data (s^2_{total}). The ratio s^2_{within}/s^2_{total} has the following properties.

- $s^2_{within}/s^2_{total} = 0$ when agreement is perfect (no variance within the levels).

- $s^2_{within}/s^2_{total} = 1$ when agreement is the result of chance.

- $s^2_{within}/s^2_{total} > 1$ when there is systematic disagreement.

Subtracting the ratio s^2_{within}/s^2_{total} from 1 gives a coefficient with the same "anchors" as the ones from the previous sections, namely the value 1 signifies perfect agreement while 0 signifies chance agreement.

$$\alpha = 1 - \frac{s^2_{within}}{s^2_{total}} = 1 - \frac{SS_{within}/df_{within}}{SS_{total}/df_{total}}$$

We also note that the ratio s^2_{within}/s^2_{total} cannot exceed 2: $SS_{within} \leq SS_{total}$ by definition, and $df_{total} < 2\,df_{within}$ because each item has at least two judgments. The lower bound for α is therefore -1.

We can unpack the formula for α to bring it to a form which is similar to the other coefficients we have looked at, and which will allow generalizing α beyond simple numerical values. The first step is to get rid of the notion of arithmetic mean which lies at the heart of the measure of variance. We observe that for any set of numbers $x_1, \ldots, x_N$ with a mean $\bar{x} = \frac{1}{N}\sum_{n=1}^{N} x_n$, the sum of square differences from the mean SS can be expressed as the sum of square of differences between all the (ordered) pairs of numbers, scaled by a factor of $1/2N$.

$$SS = \sum_{n=1}^{N}(x_n - \bar{x})^2 = \frac{1}{2N}\sum_{n=1}^{N}\sum_{m=1}^{N}(x_n - x_m)^2$$

For calculating α we considered each item to be a separate level in an analysis of variance; the number of levels is thus the number of items $\mathbf{i}$, and since each coder marks each item, the number of observations for each item is the number of coders $\mathbf{c}$. Within-level variance is the sum of the square differences from the mean of each item $SS_{within} = \sum_i \sum_c (x_{ic} - \bar{x}_i)^2$, divided by the degrees of freedom $df_{within} = \mathbf{i}(\mathbf{c}-1)$. We can express this as the sum of the squares of the differences between all of the judgments pairs for each item, summed over all items and scaled by the appropriate factor. We use the notation x_{ic} for the value given by coder c to item i, and $\bar{x}_i$ for the mean of all the values given to item i.

$$s^2_{within} = \frac{SS_{within}}{df_{within}} = \frac{1}{\mathbf{i}(\mathbf{c}-1)}\sum_{i \in I}\sum_{c \in C}(x_{ic} - \bar{x}_i)^2 = \frac{1}{2\mathbf{i}\mathbf{c}(\mathbf{c}-1)}\sum_{i \in I}\sum_{m=1}^{\mathbf{c}}\sum_{n=1}^{\mathbf{c}}(x_{ic_m} - x_{ic_n})^2$$

The total variance is the sum of the square differences of all judgments from the grand mean $SS_{total} = \sum_i \sum_c (x_{ic} - \bar{x})^2$, divided by the degrees of freedom $df_{total} = \mathbf{i}\mathbf{c} - 1$. This can be expressed as the sum of the squares of the differences between all of the judgments pairs without regard to items, again scaled by the appropriate factor. The notation $\bar{x}$ is the overall mean of all the judgments in the data.

$$s^2_{total} = \frac{SS_{total}}{df_{total}} = \frac{1}{\mathbf{i}\mathbf{c} - 1}\sum_{i \in I}\sum_{c \in C}(x_{ic} - \bar{x})^2 = \frac{1}{2\mathbf{i}\mathbf{c}(\mathbf{i}\mathbf{c} - 1)}\sum_{j=1}^{\mathbf{i}}\sum_{m=1}^{\mathbf{c}}\sum_{l=1}^{\mathbf{i}}\sum_{n=1}^{\mathbf{c}}(x_{i_j c_m} - x_{i_l c_n})^2$$

Now that we have removed reference to means from our formulas, we can abstract over the measure of variance. We define a distance function $\mathbf{d}$ which takes two numbers and returns the square of their difference.

$$\mathbf{d}_{ab} = (a - b)^2$$

We also simplify the computation by counting all the identical value assignments together. Each unique value used by the coders will be considered a category $k \in K$. We use $\mathbf{n}_{ik}$ for the number of times item i is given the value k, that is the number of coders that make such judgment. For every (ordered) pair of distinct values $k_a, k_b \in K$ there are $\mathbf{n}_{ik_a}\mathbf{n}_{ik_b}$ pairs of judgments of item i, whereas for non-distinct values there are $\mathbf{n}_{ik_a}(\mathbf{n}_{ik_a} - 1)$ pairs. We use this notation to rewrite the formula for the within-level variance. D_o^α, the observed disagreement for α, is defined as twice the variance within the levels in order to get rid of the factor 2 in the denominator; note also that the formula below incorrectly counts the number of pairs of identical judgments, but there's no need to correct for this because $\mathbf{d}_{kk} = 0$ for all k.

$$D_o^\alpha = 2\,s_{within}^2 = \frac{1}{\mathbf{ic}(\mathbf{c} - 1)} \sum_{i \in I} \sum_{j=1}^{k} \sum_{l=1}^{k} \mathbf{n}_{ik_j}\mathbf{n}_{ik_l}\mathbf{d}_{k_j k_l}$$

We do the same simplification for the total variance, where $\mathbf{n}_k$ stands for the total number of times the value k is assigned to any item by any coder. The expected disagreement for α, D_e^α, is twice the total variance.

$$D_e^\alpha = 2\,s_{total}^2 = \frac{1}{\mathbf{ic}(\mathbf{ic} - 1)} \sum_{j=1}^{k} \sum_{l=1}^{k} \mathbf{n}_{k_j}\mathbf{n}_{k_l}\mathbf{d}_{k_j k_l}$$

Since both expected and observed disagreement are twice the respective variances, the coefficient α retains the same form when expressed with the disagreement values.

$$\alpha = 1 - \frac{D_o}{D_e}$$

Now that α has been expressed without explicit reference to means, differences, and squares, it can be generalized to a variety of coding schemes in which the labels cannot be interpreted as numerical values: all one has to do is to replace the square difference function $\mathbf{d}$ with a different distance function. Krippendorff (1980, 2004a) offers distance metrics suitable for nominal, interval, ordinal, and ratio scales. Of particular interest is the function for nominal categories, that is a function which considers all distinct labels equally distant from one another.

$$\mathbf{d}_{ab} = \begin{cases} 0 \text{ if } a = b \\ 1 \text{ if } a \neq b \end{cases}$$

It turns out that with this distance function, the observed disagreement D_o^α, is exactly the complement of the observed agreement of Fleiss' multi-π, $1 - A_o^\pi$, and the expected disagreement D_e^α differs from $1 - A_e^\pi$ by a factor of $(\mathbf{ic} - 1)/\mathbf{ic}$; the difference is due to the the fact that

π uses a biased estimator of the expected agreement in the population whereas α uses an unbiased estimator. The following equation shows that given the correspondence between observed and expected agreement and disagreement, the coefficients themselves are nearly equivalent.

$$\alpha = 1 - \frac{D_o^\alpha}{D_e^\alpha} \approx 1 - \frac{1 - A_o^\pi}{1 - A_e^\pi} = \frac{1 - A_e^\pi - (1 - A_o^\pi)}{1 - A_e^\pi} = \frac{A_o^\pi - A_e^\pi}{1 - A_e^\pi} = \pi$$

For nominal data, the coefficients π and α approach each other as either the number of items or the number of coders approaches infinity (this is noted already by Krippendorff 1980, page 138).

Krippendorff's α will work with any distance metric, provided that identical categories always have a distance of zero ($d_{kk} = 0$ for all k). Another useful constraint is symmetry ($d_{ab} = d_{ba}$ for all a, b). Krippendorff (2010, 2013, 2019) provides distance metrics for several kinds of data: nominal, ordinal, interval, ratio, polar, and circular. This flexibility affords new possibilities for analysis, which we will illustrate in Chapter 3. We should also note that this flexibility exposes a problem that is not noticed when distances between labels are fixed: sometimes, it is not clear what the natural distance metric is. For example, there are different ways to measure dissimilarity between sets, and any of these measures can be justifiably used when the category labels are sets of items (as in the annotation of anaphoric relations). The different distance metrics yield different values of α for the same annotation data, making it difficult to interpret the resulting values. We will return to this problem in Section 3.4.1.

Cohen's κ_w

A weighted variant of Cohen's κ is presented in Cohen (1968). The implementation of weights is similar to that of Krippendorff's α—each pair of categories $k_a, k_b \in K$ is associated with a weight $d_{k_a k_b}$, where a larger weight indicates more disagreement. (Cohen uses the notation $\mathbf{v}$; he does not place any general constraints on the weights—not even a requirement that a pair of identical categories have a weight of zero, or that the weights be symmetric across the diagonal.) The coefficient is defined for two coders: the disagreement for a particular item i is the weight of the pair of categories assigned to it by the two coders, and the overall observed disagreement is the (normalized) mean disagreement of all the items. Let $k(c_n, i)$ denote the category assigned by coder c_n to item i; then the disagreement for item i is $\text{disagr}_i = d_{k(c_1,i)k(c_2,i)}$. The observed disagreement D_o is the mean of disagr_i for all items i, normalized to the interval $[0, 1]$ through division by the maximal weight $d_{\max}$.

$$D_o^{\kappa_w} = \frac{1}{d_{\max}} \frac{1}{i} \sum_{i \in I} \text{disagr}_i = \frac{1}{d_{\max}} \frac{1}{i} \sum_{i \in I} d_{k(c_1,i)k(c_2,i)}$$

If we take all disagreements to be of equal weight, that is $d_{k_a k_a} = 0$ for all categories k_a and $d_{k_a k_b} = 1$ for all $k_a \neq k_b$, then the observed disagreement is exactly the complement of the observed agreement as calculated in Section 2.2.4: $D_o^{\kappa_w} = 1 - A_o^\kappa$.

Like κ, the coefficient κ_w interprets expected disagreement as the amount expected by chance from a distinct probability distribution for each coder. These individual distributions are estimated by $\hat{P}(k|c)$, the proportion of items assigned by coder c to category k, that is the number of such assignments $\mathbf{n}_{ck}$ divided by the number of items $\mathbf{i}$.

$$\hat{P}(k|c) = \frac{1}{\mathbf{i}} \mathbf{n}_{ck}$$

The probability that coder c_1 assigns an item to category k_a and coder c_2 assigns it to category k_b is the joint probability of each coder making this assignment independently, namely $\hat{P}(k_a|c_1)\hat{P}(k_b|c_2)$. The expected disagreement is the mean of the weights for all (ordered) category pairs, weighted by the probabilities of the category pairs and normalized to the interval $[0, 1]$ through division by the maximal weight.

$$D_e^{\kappa_w} = \frac{1}{\mathbf{d}_{\max}} \sum_{j=1}^{k}\sum_{l=1}^{k} \hat{P}(k_j|c_1)\hat{P}(k_l|c_2)\mathbf{d}_{k_j k_l} = \frac{1}{\mathbf{d}_{\max}} \frac{1}{\mathbf{i}^2} \sum_{j=1}^{k}\sum_{l=1}^{k} \mathbf{n}_{c_1 k_j}\mathbf{n}_{c_2 k_l}\mathbf{d}_{k_j k_l}$$

If we take all disagreements to be of equal weight then the expected disagreement is exactly the complement of the expected agreement for κ as calculated in Section 2.2.4: $D_e^{\kappa_w} = 1 - A_e^{\kappa}$.

Finally, the coefficient κ_w itself is the ratio of observed disagreement to expected disagreement, subtracted from 1 in order to yield a final value in terms of agreement.

$$\kappa_w = 1 - \frac{D_o}{D_e}$$

As noted above, Cohen (1968) does not place any constraints on the weights; it gives an example with an asymmetric weight matrix based on subjective judgment of the severity of disagreement on nominal (unordered) categories. Cohen (1968) also demonstrates that κ_w with square difference weights $\mathbf{d}_{ab} = (a - b)^2$ is related to the product-moment correlation coefficient r, and Fleiss and Cohen (1973) show a similar relation to the intraclass correlation coefficient.

Subsequent work has explored the question of weights in more detail. Maclure and Willett (1987) note that the value of κ_w is highly dependent on the weight scheme, and recommend the square difference weight when category labels are numeric. Graham and Jackson (1993) assert that square difference weights are the most commonly used, while Brenner and Kliebsch (1996) note as the most common both absolute difference weights $\mathbf{d}_{ab} = |a - b|$ and square difference weights (in their terms, linear and quadratic). The latter work shows that on synthetic numeric data divided into equally populated categories, the absolute difference weights result in κ_w values that are less sensitive to the number of categories than square difference weights.

To our knowledge, weighted kappa has been used fairly infrequently in the NLP literature. One example of such use is in the 2012 competition on Automated Essay Scoring by The Hewlett Foundation.[8]

[8]https://www.kaggle.com/c/asap-aes/overview/evaluation

Table 2.6: Relations among coefficients

Category Distances	Nominal		Weighted	
Number of Coders	2	>2	2	>2
Shared distribution	π	multi-π	α	α
Individual distribution	κ	multi-κ	κ_w	?

2.2.7 RELATIONS AMONG COEFFICIENTS

The agreement coefficients we have seen can all be thought of as modifications of Scott's π along three different dimensions. One dimension is the calculation of expected agreement using separate probability distributions for the individual coders, as done by κ. Another dimension is a generalization of the original two-coder definitions to multiple coders, resulting in multi-π (Fleiss' κ) and multi-κ (Davies and Fleiss, 1982). A third dimension is the introduction of weighted agreement coefficients—α for multiple coders with a shared distribution, and κ_w for two coders with separate distributions. The relations between the various coefficients are depicted in Table 2.6.

What is missing from the picture is a coefficient that modifies π along all three dimensions—an agreement coefficient that is weighted, applies to multiple coders, and calculates expected agreement using a separate probability distribution for each coder. Such a coefficient can be thought of as a generalization of κ_w to multiple coders, or alternatively as a modification of α which uses individual coders' distributions for determining chance agreement. Developing such a coefficient is straightforward. However, since we argue in Section 2.5.1 that using a shared distribution for the calculation of expected agreement is more appropriate for assessing annotator reliability, we will not develop it here, but rather relegate it to the end of this chapter in Section 2.A.2, where we use it to demonstrate that the difference between shared- and individual-distribution coefficients grows smaller as the number of annotators increases.

2.2.8 AN INTEGRATED EXAMPLE

We end this section with an example illustrating how all of the agreement coefficients discussed above are computed. To facilitate comparisons, all computations will be based on the annotation statistics in Table 2.7. This confusion matrix reports the results of an experiment where two coders classify a set of utterances into three categories.

Th Unweighted Coefficien Observed agreement for all of the unweighted coefficients— S, κ, and π—is calculated by counting the items on which the coders agree (the figures on the diagonal of the confusion matrix in Table 2.7) and dividing by the total number of items.

$$A_o = \frac{46 + 32 + 10}{100} = 0.88$$

Table 2.7: An integrated coding example

		Coder A			
		Stat	IReq	Chck	Total
Coder B	Stat	46	6	0	52
	IReq	0	32	0	32
	Chck	0	6	10	16
	Total	46	44	10	100

Expected agreement for S is the reciprocal of the number of categories, or $\frac{1}{3}$; S is the observed agreement, discounted by this fraction.

$$A_e^S = \frac{1}{3}$$

$$S = \frac{A_o - A_e^S}{1 - A_e^S} = \frac{0.88 - \frac{1}{3}}{1 - \frac{1}{3}} = 0.82$$

Expected agreement for π is the sum over all categories of the square of the mean of the individual coders' proportions; π is the observed agreement, discounted by this value.

$$A_e^\pi = \left(\frac{46 + 52}{2 \times 100}\right)^2 + \left(\frac{44 + 32}{2 \times 100}\right)^2 + \left(\frac{10 + 16}{2 \times 100}\right)^2 = 0.49^2 + 0.38^2 + 0.13^2 = 0.4014$$

$$\pi = \frac{A_o - A_e^\pi}{1 - A_e^\pi} = \frac{0.88 - 0.4014}{1 - 0.4014} \approx 0.7995$$

Expected agreement for κ is the sum over all categories of the product of the individual coders' proportions; κ is the observed agreement, discounted by this value.

$$A_e^\kappa = \frac{46}{100} \times \frac{52}{100} + \frac{44}{100} \times \frac{32}{100} + \frac{10}{100} \times \frac{16}{100} = 0.396$$

$$\kappa = \frac{A_o - A_e^\kappa}{1 - A_e^\kappa} = \frac{0.88 - 0.396}{1 - 0.396} \approx 0.8013$$

We see that the values of π and κ are very similar, which is to be expected when agreement is high, since high agreement implies similar marginals. Notice that $A_e^\kappa < A_e^\pi$, hence $\kappa > \pi$; this reflects a general property of κ and π, already mentioned in Section 2.2.4, which will be elaborated in Section 2.5.1.

Weighted Coefficien   Suppose we notice that while statements and information requests are clearly distinct classifications; checks are somewhere between the two. We therefore opt to weigh the distances between the categories as follows. Recall that 1 denotes maximal disagreement, and identical categories are in full agreement and thus have a distance of 0; the choice of setting the intermediate distance at 0.5 is somewhat arbitrary.[9]

$$
\begin{array}{llll}
\text{STAT–STAT:} & 0 & \text{STAT–IREQ:} & 1 \\
\text{IREQ–IREQ:} & 0 & \text{STAT–CHCK:} & 0.5 \\
\text{CHCK–CHCK:} & 0 & \text{IREQ–CHCK:} & 0.5
\end{array}
$$

The observed disagreement is calculated by summing up *all* the cells in the contingency table, multiplying each cell by its respective weight, and dividing the total by the number of items (in the calculation below we ignore cells with zero items).

$$
D_o = \frac{46 \times 0 + 6 \times 1 + 32 \times 0 + 6 \times 0.5 + 10 \times 0}{100} = \frac{6+3}{100} = 0.09
$$

The only sources of disagreement in the coding example of Table 2.7 are the six utterances marked as IReq by coder A and Stat by coder B, which receive the maximal weight of 1, and the six utterances marked as IReq by coder A and Chck by coder B, which are given a weight of 0.5.

Expected disagreement for α is the sum over all category pairs of the product of the sum of the individual coders' judgments, weighted by the distance and by the total number of items 2×100 times the degrees of freedom $2 \times 100 - 1$; α is the observed disagreement, discounted by this value and subtracted from 1.

$$
\begin{aligned}
D_e^{\alpha} & = \frac{(46+52)\times(46+52)}{2\times100\times(2\times100-1)} \times 0 \quad + \frac{(44+32)\times(46+52)}{2\times100\times(2\times100-1)} \times 1 \quad + \frac{(10+16)\times(46+52)}{2\times100\times(2\times100-1)} \times 0.5 \\
& + \frac{(46+52)\times(44+32)}{2\times100\times(2\times100-1)} \times 1 \quad + \frac{(44+32)\times(44+32)}{2\times100\times(2\times100-1)} \times 0 \quad + \frac{(10+16)\times(44+32)}{2\times100\times(2\times100-1)} \times 0.5 \\
& + \frac{(46+52)\times(10+16)}{2\times100\times(2\times100-1)} \times 0.5 + \frac{(44+32)\times(10+16)}{2\times100\times(2\times100-1)} \times 0.5 + \frac{(10+16)\times(10+16)}{2\times100\times(2\times100-1)} \times 0 \\
& = \frac{1}{39800} \times (2 \times 98 \times 76 + 2 \times 98 \times 26 \times 0.5 + 2 \times 76 \times 26 \times 0.5) \approx 0.4879 \\
\alpha & = 1 - \frac{D_o}{D_e^{\alpha}} \approx 1 - \frac{0.09}{0.4879} \approx 0.8156
\end{aligned}
$$

Finally, expected disagreement for κ_w is the sum over all category pairs of the products of the individual coders' proportions, weighted by the distance; κ_w is the observed disagreement, dis-

---

[9]An anonymous reviewer suggests a data-driven approach to determine distances between labels, using something like the amount of confusion among annotators as a proxy for similarity. We, however, feel that such an approach is problematic. The fact that two labels are easily confused could indicate that they are similar, but it could also be the result of ill-written instructions or ill-conceived definitions. A reliability study is intended to identify such problems with an annotation scheme, but if we take confusability as an indication of similarity, then the problems are washed away. Put differently, annotator confusion is an instance of disagreement, so it doesn't seem right to incorporate it into the definition of a measure that's supposed to measure agreement.

counted by this value and subtracted from 1.

$$
\begin{aligned}
D_e^{\kappa_w} &= \frac{46}{100} \times \frac{52}{100} \times 0 \quad\quad + \frac{44}{100} \times \frac{52}{100} \times 1 \quad + \frac{10}{100} \times \frac{52}{100} \times 0.5 \\
&\quad + \frac{46}{100} \times \frac{32}{100} \times 1 \quad + \frac{44}{100} \times \frac{32}{100} \times 0 \quad + \frac{10}{100} \times \frac{32}{100} \times 0.5 \\
&\quad + \frac{46}{100} \times \frac{16}{100} \times 0.5 + \frac{44}{100} \times \frac{16}{100} \times 0.5 + \frac{10}{100} \times \frac{16}{100} \times 0 \\
&= 0.49 \\
\kappa_w &= 1 - \frac{D_o}{D_e^{\kappa_w}} = 1 - \frac{0.09}{0.49} \approx 0.8163
\end{aligned}
$$

2.3   MISSING DATA

An assumption that underlies all the coefficients that we have discussed is that all the coders classify all the items in the reliability sample. In practice, however, this is not always the case, either because of practical limitations on the experimental setup or because some of the coders fail to classify certain items, for whatever reason. When data points are missing, the coefficients need to be adjusted to minimize the loss.

If there are only two coders then missing data implies the existence of items with at most one judgment, and since such singular judgments cannot be compared with anything, the only remedy is to remove these items from the sample. We can thus only deal with missing data when the number of coders is three or greater.

We will not attempt to deal with missing data in coefficients that model chance using individual coder marginals (such as multi-κ). While this is possible in principle, the formulas become very complicated and their usefulness is quite dubious, because the values of shared- and individual-distribution coefficients converge with multiple coders (Section 2.5.1). We will therefore only deal with shared-distribution coefficients in this section (multi-π, α). Note also that no adjustment is needed if different items are classified by different coders, as long as the number of coders per item is constant, because these coefficients treat coders as interchangeable. If, however, the number of judgments per item is not constant, then the coefficients need to be adjusted.

One solution to the missing data problem is to eliminate certain data points in order to achieve a data set were all coders classify all items. This is probably the best practice when the total data loss would be small. For example, the annotation experiment of Poesio and Artstein (2005) had a total of 151 items, and data points were missing for 3 of them; eliminating these items from the analysis provided a quick solution to the missing data problem. Another example is Fleiss (1971), which reports a psychiatric study where each patient (item) was diagnosed by between 6 and 10 psychiatrists (coders), stating that "randomly selected diagnoses were dropped to bring the number of assignments per patient down to six". There is no indication of how much data were lost in this pruning. However, if the missing judgments are somewhat systematic, for example if they happen more commonly with certain categories, then dropping these items can result in biased reliability data.

An alternative to dropping additional data is to redefine the observed and expected agreement and disagreement so as to minimize the skewing of the coefficient values. We will present two ways of doing this, either giving equal weight to each *judgment* or to each *item*. The method which gives an equal weight to each judgment is advocated by Krippendorff (2004a, pages 230–232) for use with α; it is in line with the origins of α as a measure of variance, since the standard method of computing the F stastisic in an analysis of variance involves giving equal weight to each data point, not to each level. Krippendorff's justification for giving an equal weight to each judgment is that the total number of judgments is the best estimate of the actual distribution of items. Additional support comes from simulations by Mathet (2017), using a fully annotated dataset from which judgments were removed at random. The simulations compared giving equal weights to each judgment, each item, each pair of judgments, and removal of whole items; the method that resulted in coefficient values that were closest to those calculated on the full dataset was giving equal weights to each judgment. However, since Mathet's simulations drop judgments at random, they do not consider any skewing that may arise if judgements are missing for a systematic reason (for example, if judgments are missing for items of one particular category). For this reason we also provide a way to adjust the coefficients in order to give an equal weight to each item.

We start by calculating a normalized figure for observed agreement and disagreement per item. Let n_i stand for the number of judgments available for a particular item i; the total number of judgment pairs for item i is therefore $\binom{n_i}{2} = n_i(n_i - 1)/2$. Normalized agreement is the total number of agreeing judgment pairs and normalized disagreement is the total distance between the judgment pairs, both divided by the total number of judgment pairs.

$$\mathrm{agr}_i \quad = \quad \frac{1}{\binom{n_i}{2}} \sum_{k \in K} \binom{n_{ik}}{2} = \frac{1}{n_i(n_i - 1)} \sum_{k \in K} n_{ik}(n_{ik} - 1)$$

$$\mathrm{disagr}_i \quad = \quad \frac{1}{n_i(n_i - 1)} \sum_{j=1}^{k} \sum_{l=1}^{k} n_{ik_j} n_{ik_l} d_{k_j k_l}$$

If an item i receives only one judgment, then agr_i and disagr_i turn out to be $\frac{0}{0}$, or undefined; indeed in such a case one cannot talk of agreeing or disagreeing pairs at all. The overall observed (dis)agreement is calculated only on the items for which such a value exists. Let I' be the set of items for which there are two or more judgments available, let i' be the cardinality of this set, and let N' be the total number of judgments available for this set. Giving an equal weight to each judgment, observed (dis)agreement is the mean of the normalized (dis)agreement values of the individual items, weighted by the number of judgments per item.

$$A_o^\pi = \frac{1}{N'} \sum_{i \in I'} n_i \mathrm{agr}_i \qquad D_o^\alpha = \frac{1}{N'} \sum_{i \in I'} n_i \mathrm{disagr}_i$$

Giving an equal weight to each item, observed (dis)agreement is the unweighted mean of the (dis)agreement values of the individual items.

$$A_o^\pi = \frac{1}{\mathbf{i'}} \sum_{i \in I'} \mathrm{agr}_i \qquad D_o^\alpha = \frac{1}{\mathbf{i'}} \sum_{i \in I'} \mathrm{disagr}_i$$

The formulas for expected agreement and disagreement already give equal weight to each judgment, so the only modification necessary is to remove all singular judgments before computation. Let $\mathbf{n}'_k$ be the total number of judgments of category k that come from items for which there are at least two judgments in total. Expected agreement and disagreement then take the following shape.

$$A_e^\pi = \frac{1}{(N')^2} \sum_{k \in K} (\mathbf{n}'_k)^2 \qquad D_e^\alpha = \frac{1}{N'(N'-1)} \sum_{j=1}^{k} \sum_{l=1}^{k} \mathbf{n}'_{k_j} \mathbf{n}'_{k_l} \mathbf{d}_{k_j k_l}$$

If we want to give equal weight to each item, we have to weight each individual judgment by the inverse of the number of judgments in the item it comes from.

$$A_e^\pi = \frac{1}{(\mathbf{i'})^2} \sum_{k \in K} \left(\sum_{i \in I'} \frac{\mathbf{n}_{ik}}{\mathbf{n}_i} \right)^2 \qquad D_e^\alpha = \frac{N'}{N'-1} \frac{1}{(\mathbf{i'})^2} \sum_{j=1}^{k} \sum_{l=1}^{k} \left(\sum_{i \in I'} \frac{\mathbf{n}_{ik_j}}{\mathbf{n}_i} \right) \left(\sum_{i \in I'} \frac{\mathbf{n}_{ik_l}}{\mathbf{n}_i} \right) \mathbf{d}_{k_j k_l}$$

2.4   UNITIZING OR MARKABLE IDENTIFICATION

The coefficients described thus far all measure agreement on the **labelling** of items; the existence and identity of the labeled items is presupposed. Many tasks, however, require annotators to identify the units themselves, either as a task in its own right (such as various forms of segmentation), or as a preliminary step before labelling (for example, the identification of **markables** for named entity recognition or coreference resolution prior to their annotation). For these tasks we need to assess annotators' agreement on identifying the units (**unitizing**), labelling the identified units, or both. When discussing the task of unitizing, it is common to refer to the underlying data (from which units are identified) as a continuum. While the continuum is usually made of discrete units (words or characters for text annotation; frames for audio or video annotation), it is useful to abstract away from these units, since they are not at the level that annotators apply labels to.

The existing coefficients are applicable to a very limited set of applications, where annotators create new units for annotation, but the interest is not in the units as units, but only in the regions they occupy (for example, what parts of a text display a positive emotion, or what parts of a video show a smile). For the purpose of calculating agreement, it is possible to consider units much smaller than the ones created by the annotators (for example individual words in a text or frames in a video), and measure the reliability of labels on those smaller units. Such an operation is called **digitalization** (Krippendorff, 1995) or **discretization/atomization** (Mathet et al., 2015), and was applied, for example, in Kang et al. (2012) to the annotation of smiles and head nods in video, where it was noted that it does not measure agreement on the individuation of gestures, but only whether the annotators agree that at a certain time point a smile or head nod was present.

For most applications that require identification of units, it is considered important to both identify the extents (or spans) to which labels apply, and to identify individual, distinct units over these spans; therefore, suitable measures are needed for measuring agreement on these aspects. We are aware of two families of coefficients that address this need, which are based on different formulations of the problem. The $_u\alpha$ family (Krippendorff, 1995, 2013, 2019, Krippendorff et al., 2016) operates by comparing the units identified by each coder to the how the same spans are annotated by the other coders; the γ family (Mathet, 2017, Mathet et al., 2015) operates by defining an alignment between the units identified by different annotators, and calculating agreement between the aligned units on both their labels and their extents. The full proposals are too complicated to cover here, so we will just present the core ideas.

The various α-family coefficients for unitizing (to which we will refer as 'the $_u\alpha$ family') have been developed and improved since the initial introduction of α_U in Krippendorff (1995); the summary below is based on the discussion in Krippendorff et al. (2016). The concept behind the $_u\alpha$ family is that agreement is defined by the amount of overlap between identically labeled units. Thus, those portions of an annotator's units that overlap another annotator's unit with the same label count toward agreement, while portions that overlap either a unit with a different label or a part of the continuum where another annotator has not identified a label count toward disagreement. The calculation of disagreement differs between members of the family. For $_u\alpha$, overlap with either a differently labeled unit or with a non-unit counts as maximal disagreement. Another coefficient, $_{|u}\alpha$, only counts overlap with non-units as disagreement, and thus measures agreement on identifying *any* type of unit (this could be useful as a measure of agreement on markable identification, without regards to how annotators labeled these markables). The coefficient $_{cu}\alpha$ allows for differences in the amount of disagreement between labels, using the same distance metrics as α, but it can only measure agreement on those parts of units that overlap with other identified units. Finally, $_{(k)u}\alpha$ measures reliability of an individual label k. For each of the coefficients in the family, the specific method of counting agreement is used in the calculation of both observed and expected disagreement, and these values combine into the overall coefficient the same way as for α.

The γ coefficient (Mathet et al., 2015) works on the principle of alignment between units of different annotators: each unit identified by an annotator is aligned to (at most) one unit from every other annotator; it can also remain unaligned to some or all of the other annotators. Disagreement between aligned units is the sum of two factors: disagreement on the units' extent (or position), and disagreement on their label. When a unit is unaligned, it contributes a fixed amount of disagreement. Of the many alignments possible, the one which incurs the minimum overall disagreement is chosen. It follows that the maximal disagreement that can be incurred by a unit is that of an unaligned unit, because if the calculated disagreement between two units exceeds this value, then lower overall agreement is be obtained if they are considered unaligned. A variant γ_{cat} (Mathet, 2017) computes disagreement only on the labels (it still uses the units' positions to determine the alignment). Since alignment is not directly tied to overlap, the γ coefficients can deal with nested units, which is not possible with the $_u\alpha$ family. The γ coefficients use the same formula as α to discount observed agreement by the expected disagreement.

We have not seen coefficients for unitizing gain much acceptance in CL. We suspect that several factors conspire against their use. First, the coefficients are not very well known, and in their current formulations are fairly recent. Second, the coefficients are not simple to calculate, especially the expected agreement; we should note that both $_u\alpha$-family and γ-family coefficients are available as software packages,[10] which should make them accessible. But the most important barrier to acceptance is interpretability: the use of distance metrics means that very different coefficient values can be obtained. Choosing a natural distance metric is unclear for many CL tasks, and this makes these coefficients difficult to interpret.

2.5   BIAS AND PREVALENCE

Two issues with agreement coefficients, brought to light by Di Eugenio and Glass (2004), concern the behavior of the coefficients when the annotation data are severely skewed. One issue, which Di Eugenio and Glass call the **bias problem**, is that π and κ yield quite different numerical values when the annotators' marginal distributions are widely divergent; the other issue, the **prevalence problem**, is the exceeding difficulty in getting high agreement values when most of the items fall under one category. Looking at these two problems in detail is useful for understanding the differences between the coefficients.

2.5.1   ANNOTATOR BIAS

The difference between π and α, on the one hand, and κ, on the other hand, lies in the conception of chance agreement, whether it is the amount expected from the overall distribution of items among categories (π) or from individual coder priors (κ). As mentioned in Section 2.2.4, this difference has been the subject of much debate (Byrt et al., 1993, Craggs and McGee Wood, 2005, Di Eugenio and Glass, 2004, Fleiss, 1975, Hsu and Field, 2003, Krippendorff, 1978, 2004b, Zwick, 1988).

A claim often repeated in the literature is that shared-distribution coefficients like π and α are based on the assumption that different coders produce similar distributions of items among categories, with the implication that these coefficients are inapplicable when the annotators show substantially different distributions. Thus, Zwick (1988) suggests testing the individual coders' distributions using the modified χ^2 test of Stuart (1955), and discarding the annota-

---

[10]https://mathet.users.greyc.fr/agreement/

tion as unreliable if significant systematic discrepancies are observed. In response to this, Hsu and Field (2003, page 214) recommend reporting the value of κ even when the coders produce different distributions, because it is "the only [index] … that could legitimately be applied in the presence of marginal heterogeneity". Likewise, Di Eugenio and Glass (2004, page 96) recommend using κ in "the vast majority … of discourse- and dialogue-tagging efforts", where the individual coders' distributions tend to vary. However, these proposals are based on a misconception: that shared-distribution coefficients require similar distributions by the individual annotators in order to work properly. This is not the case. Both π-style and κ-style coefficients assume that the annotators code the data according to properties inherent to the data, and that variation arises from various sources, some systematic and some arbitrary. The difference is only in the understanding of the notion of "chance agreement". Therefore, regardless of how divergent the actual coders are, both kinds of coefficients are applicable; they just differ in meaning.

Another common claim is that individual-distribution coefficients like κ reward annotators for disagreeing on the marginal distributions. For example, Di Eugenio and Glass (2004, page 99) say that κ suffers from what they call the bias problem, described as "the paradox that κ_{Co} [our κ] increases as the coders become less similar". Similar reservations about the use of κ have been noted by Brennan and Prediger (1981) and Zwick (1988). We feel, however, that the bias problem is less paradoxical than it sounds. While it is true that for a fixed observed agreement, a higher difference in coder marginals implies a lower expected agreement and therefore a higher κ value, the conclusion that κ penalizes coders for having similar distributions is unwarranted. This is because observed agreement and expected agreement are not independent: both are drawn from the same set of observations. What κ does is discount some of the disagreement resulting from different coder marginals by incorporating it into the expected agreement. Whether this is desirable depends on the application for which the coefficient is used.

The most common application of agreement measures in CL is to infer the reliability of a large-scale annotation, where typically each piece of data will be marked by just one coder, by measuring agreement on a small subset of the data which is annotated by multiple coders. In order to make this generalization, the measure must reflect the reliability of the annotation *procedure*, which is independent of the actual annotators used. Reliability, or reproducibility of the coding, is reduced by all disagreements—both random and systematic. The most appropriate measures of reliability for this purpose are therefore shared-distribution coefficients like π and α, which generalize over the individual coders and exclude marginal disagreements from the expected agreement. This argument is presented in detail by Krippendorff (2004b) and reiterated by Craggs and McGee Wood (2005).

At the same time, individual-distribution coefficients like κ provide important information regarding the trustworthiness of those specific items on which the annotators agree. As an intuitive example, think of a person who consults two analysts when deciding whether to buy or sell certain stocks. If one analyst is an optimist and tends to recommend buying while the other is a pessimist and tends to recommend selling, they are likely to agree with each other less than two more neutral analysts, so overall their recommendations are likely to be less reliable—less reproducible—than those that come from a population of like-minded analysts. This repro-ducibility is measured by π. But whenever the optimistic and pessimistic analysts agree on a recommendation for a particular stock, whether it is "buy" or "sell", the confidence that this is indeed the right decision is higher than the same advice from two like-minded analysts. This is why κ rewards biased annotators, and it is not a matter of reproducibility (reliability) but rather of trustworthiness.

Having said this, we should point out that, first, in practice the difference between π and κ doesn't often amount to much. Moreover, the difference becomes smaller as agreement increases, because all the points of agreement contribute toward making the coder marginals similar (it took a lot of experimentation to create data for Table 2.7 so that the values of π and κ would straddle the conventional cutoff point of 0.80, and even so the difference is very small). Finally, one would expect the difference between π and κ to diminish as the number of coders grows; a formal proof is given by Artstein and Poesio (2005) and repeated below.[11]

We define B, the **overall annotator bias** in a particular set of coding data, as the difference between the expected agreement according to (multi)-π and the expected agreement according to (multi)-κ. Note that this is not related to sampling bias (the source of difference between π and α), nor is it the same as the Bias Index BI of Byrt et al. (1993). Overall annotator bias is a measure of variance: if we take c to be a random variable with equal probabilities for all coders, then the overall annotator bias B is the sum of the variances of $\hat{P}(k|c)$ for all categories $k \in K$, divided by the number of coders $\mathbf{c}$ minus one (for proof see Section 2.A.1).

$$B = A_e^\pi - A_e^\kappa = \frac{1}{\mathbf{c}-1} \sum_{k \in K} \sigma^2_{\hat{P}(k|c)}$$

Overall annotator bias can be used to express the difference between κ and π.

$$\kappa - \pi = \frac{A_o - (A_e^\pi - B)}{1 - (A_e^\pi - B)} - \frac{A_o - A_e^\pi}{1 - A_e^\pi} = B \cdot \frac{(1 - A_o)}{(1 - A_e^\kappa)(1 - A_e^\pi)}$$

This allows us to make the following observations about the relationship between π and κ.

1. For any particular coding data, $A_e^\pi \geq A_e^\kappa$, because B is the sum of non-negative numbers.

2. For any particular coding data, $\kappa \geq \pi$, because the difference between them is the product of non-negative numbers.

3. The difference between κ and π grows as the overall annotator bias grows: for a constant A_o and A_e^π, a greater B implies a greater value for $\kappa - \pi$.

---

[11]Craggs and McGee Wood (2005) also suggest increasing the number of coders in order to overcome individual annotator bias, but without proof.

4. The greater the number of coders, the lower the bias B, and hence the lower the difference between κ and π, because the variance of $\hat{P}(k|c)$ does not increase in proportion to the number of coders.

In other words, provided enough coders are used, it should not matter whether a shared-distribution or individual-distribution coefficient is used. This is not to imply that multiple coders increase reliability: the variance of the individual coders' distributions can be just as large with many coders as with few coders, but its effect on the value of κ decreases as the number of coders grows, and becomes more similar to random noise.

The same holds for weighted measures too; see Section 2.A.2 for definitions and proof. In an annotation study with 18 subjects (Poesio and Artstein, 2005), we calculated 3 variants of α: the original, a variant with a biased estimator for expected agreement, and variant which uses individual coder distributions to calculate expected agreement. We found that the values never differed beyond the third decimal point.

In summary, our views concerning the difference between π-style and κ-style coefficients are as follows: (i) Reporting two coefficients, as suggested by Di Eugenio and Glass (2004), is unlikely to help. Instead, the appropriate coefficient should be chosen based on the task (*not* on the observed differences between coder marginals). When the coefficient is used to assess reliability, a shared-distribution coefficient like π or α should be used; this is indeed common practice in CL, since Siegel and Castellan's K is identical to π. If the coefficient is used in order to assess the correctness of data points agreed upon by two coders (or more), then Cohen's κ or its weighted version κ_w may be more appropriate. (ii) However, the numerical difference between shared-distribution coefficients (π) and individual-distribution coefficients (κ) is often not very large, especially in cases of high agreement. (iii) Further, the numerical difference decreases as the number of annotators grows.

2.5.2   PREVALENCE

We touched upon the matter of skewed data in Section 2.2.3 when we motivated the need for chance correction: if a disproportionate amount of the data falls under one category, then the expected agreement is very high, so in order to demonstrate high reliability an even higher observed agreement is needed. This leads to the so-called "paradox" that observed agreement is very high, yet chance-corrcted agreement is low (Cicchetti and Feinstein, 1990, Di Eugenio and Glass, 2004, Feinstein and Cicchetti, 1990). Moreover, when the data are highly skewed in favor of one category, the high agreement also corresponds to high accuracy: if, say, 95% of the data fall under one category label, then random coding would cause two coders to jointly assign this category label to 90.25% of the items, and on average 95% of these labels would be correct, for an overall accuracy of at least 85.7%. This leads to the surprising result that when data are highly skewed, coders may agree on a high proportion of items while producing annotations that are indeed correct to a high degree, yet the reliability coefficients remain low.

Table 2.8: A simple example of agreement on dialogue act tagging

		Coder A		
		Common	Rare	Total
	Common	$1 - (\delta + 2\epsilon)$	ϵ	$1 - (\delta + \epsilon)$
Coder B	Rare	ϵ	δ	$\delta + \epsilon$
	Total	$1 - (\delta + \epsilon)$	$\delta + \epsilon$	1

This surprising result is, however, correct and justified. Reliability implies the ability to distinguish between categories, but when one category is very common, high accuracy and high agreement can also result from indiscriminate coding. The test for reliability in such cases is the ability to agree on the rare categories (regardless of whether these are the categories of interest). Indeed, chance-corrected coefficients are sensitive to agreement on rare categories. This is easiest to see with a simple example of two coders and two categories—one common and the other one rare; to further simplify the calculation we also assume that the coder marginals are identical, so that π and κ yield the same values. We can thus represent the judgments in a contingency table with just two parameters: ϵ is half the proportion of items on which there is disagreement, and δ is the proportion of agreement on the **Rare** category. Both of these proportions are assumed to be small, so the bulk of the items (a proportion of $1 - (\delta + 2\epsilon)$) are labeled with the **Common** category by both coders (Table 2.8). From this table we can calculate the observed agreement $A_o = 1 - 2\epsilon$ and the expected agreement $A_e = 1 - 2(\delta + \epsilon) + 2(\delta + \epsilon)^2$, as well as π and κ.

$$\pi, \kappa = \frac{1 - 2\epsilon - (1 - 2(\delta + \epsilon) + 2(\delta + \epsilon)^2)}{1 - (1 - 2(\delta + \epsilon) + 2(\delta + \epsilon)^2)} = \frac{\delta}{\delta + \epsilon} - \frac{\epsilon}{1 - (\delta + \epsilon)}$$

When ϵ and δ are both small, the fraction after the minus sign is small as well, so π and κ are approximately $\delta/(\delta + \epsilon)$, that is the value we get if we take all the items marked by one particular coder as **Rare**, and calculate what proportion of those items were labeled **Rare** by the other coder. This is indeed a measure of the ability to agree on the rare category, so it is a good measure of reliability.

We therefore do not agree with the recommendation of Di Eugenio and Glass (2004) to report an additional coefficient when one of the categories is very common (Di Eugenio and Glass recommend reporting $2A_o - 1$, which is the value of S when there are exactly two categories). If reliability is a concern, then the appropriate reliability coefficient should be reported, and S does not reflect reliability precisely because it is insensitive to the difference between common and rare categories. If reliability turns out to be low but it is still of interest to note that overall agreement was high, then it is best to report the raw observed agreement A_o, since this value is easier to interpret than S. The reporting of raw agreement figures should be accompanied by a note explaining that these figures are not corrected for chance and therefore do not reflect reliability.

2.A   APPENDIX: PROOFS FOR THEOREMS PRESENTED IN THIS CHAPTER

2.A.1   ANNOTATOR BIAS AND VARIANCE WITH MULTIPLE CODERS

In Section 2.5.1 we briefly noted that the difference between π and κ drops as the number of coders increases, because this difference is the overall variance of the different categories divided by the number of annotators. Here we give the formal proof. We start by taking the formulas for expected agreement from Section 2.2.5 and putting them into a form that is more useful for comparison with one another.

$$
\begin{aligned}
A_e^\pi &= \sum_{k \in K} \hat{P}(k)^2 = \sum_{k \in K} \left(\frac{1}{c} \sum_{m=1}^{c} \hat{P}(k|c_m) \right)^2 \\
&= \sum_{k \in K} \frac{1}{c^2} \sum_{m=1}^{c} \sum_{n=1}^{c} \hat{P}(k|c_m)\hat{P}(k|c_n) \\
A_e^\kappa &= \sum_{k \in K} \frac{1}{\binom{c}{2}} \sum_{m=1}^{c-1} \sum_{n=m+1}^{c} \hat{P}(k|c_m)\hat{P}(k|c_n) \\
&= \sum_{k \in K} \frac{1}{c(c-1)} \left(\sum_{m=1}^{c} \sum_{n=1}^{c} \hat{P}(k|c_m)\hat{P}(k|c_n) - \sum_{m=1}^{c} \hat{P}(k|c_m)^2 \right)
\end{aligned}
$$

The overall annotator bias B is the difference between the expected agreement according to π and the expected agreement according to κ.

$$
\begin{aligned}
B &= A_e^\pi - A_e^\kappa \\
&= \frac{1}{c-1} \sum_{k \in K} \frac{1}{c^2} \left(c \sum_{m=1}^{c} \hat{P}(k|c_m)^2 - \sum_{m=1}^{c} \sum_{n=1}^{c} \hat{P}(k|c_m)\hat{P}(k|c_n) \right)
\end{aligned}
$$

We now calculate the mean μ and variance σ^2 of $\hat{P}(k|c)$, taking c to be a random variable with equal probabilities for all of the coders: $\hat{P}(c) = \frac{1}{c}$ for all coders $c \in C$.

$$\mu_{\hat{P}(k|c)} = \frac{1}{c} \sum_{m=1}^{c} \hat{P}(k|c_m)$$

$$\sigma^2_{\hat{P}(k|c)} = \frac{1}{c} \sum_{m=1}^{c} (\hat{P}(k|c_m) - \mu_{\hat{P}(k|c)})^2$$

$$= \frac{1}{c} \sum_{m=1}^{c} \hat{P}(k|c_m)^2 - 2\mu_{\hat{P}(k|c)} \frac{1}{c} \sum_{m=1}^{c} \hat{P}(k|c_m) + \mu^2_{\hat{P}(k|c)} \frac{1}{c} \sum_{m=1}^{c} 1$$

$$= \left(\frac{1}{c} \sum_{m=1}^{c} \hat{P}(k|c_m)^2 \right) - \mu^2_{\hat{P}(k|c)}$$

$$= \frac{1}{c^2} \left(c \sum_{m=1}^{c} \hat{P}(k|c_m)^2 - \sum_{m=1}^{c} \sum_{n=1}^{c} \hat{P}(k|c_m)\hat{P}(k|c_n) \right)$$

The annotator bias B is thus the sum of the variances of $\hat{P}(k|c)$ for all categories $k \in K$, divided by the number of coders minus one.

$$B = \frac{1}{c-1} \sum_{k \in K} \sigma^2_{\hat{P}(k|c)}$$

Since the variance does not increase in proportion to the number of coders, we find that the more coders we have, the lower the annotator bias; at the limit, κ approaches π as the number of coders approaches infinity.

2.A.2   ANNOTATOR BIAS FOR WEIGHTED MEASURES

We have shown in Section 2.A.1 that the variance of the individual coders' distributions of items to categories is a useful measure for the annotator bias in a set of coding data, and that it correlates with the difference between π and κ. This measure of variance is less useful when the coding data are judged according to a weighted measure, because the discrepancies between the individual coders also have varying magnitudes. A measure of annotator bias for such coding data should therefore take the weights into account. Since the expected disagreement already considers the weights, we define the annotator bias B in an analogous way to our definition in Section 2.A.1. But first we need to define appropriate variants of α with the required properties.

We start with a variant of α which uses individual coder distributions for the calculation of expected agreement (this is the missing cell in Table 2.6, Section 2.2.7). We call this variant α_κ, which should serve as a reminder that it is shares properties of both κ and α. Like the other weighted coefficients, α_κ measures the observed and expected disagreement, whose ratio is subtracted from one.

$$\alpha_\kappa = 1 - \frac{D_o}{D_e}$$

The observed disagreement is the same as for the other weighted measures, that is the mean disagreement per item, where the disagreement per item is the mean distance between all the judgment pairs pertaining to it (Section 2.2.6).

The expected disagreement is the expected distance for an arbitrary judgment pair, which is the arithmetic mean of all possible distances between category pairs weighted by the probabilities for choosing particular pairs. We estimate the probability that coder c assigns an item to category k as the total number of such assignments $\mathbf{n}_{ck}$ divided by the overall number of assignments for this coder, which is the number of items $\mathbf{i}$.

$$\hat{P}(k|c) = \frac{1}{\mathbf{i}} \mathbf{n}_{ck}$$

The probability that two particular coders c_m and c_n assign an item to two distinct categories k_a and k_b is $\hat{P}(k_a|c_m)\hat{P}(k_b|c_n) + \hat{P}(k_b|c_m)\hat{P}(k_a|c_n)$. Since all coders judge all items, the probability that an arbitrary pair of coders assign an item to k_a and k_b is the arithmetic mean of $\hat{P}(k_a|c_m)\hat{P}(k_b|c_n) + \hat{P}(k_b|c_m)\hat{P}(k_a|c_n)$ over all coder pairs.

$$
\begin{aligned}
\hat{P}(k_a, k_b) &= \frac{1}{\binom{c}{2}} \sum_{m=1}^{c-1} \sum_{n=m+1}^{c} \hat{P}(k_a|c_m)\hat{P}(k_b|c_n) + \hat{P}(k_b|c_m)\hat{P}(k_a|c_n) \\
&= \frac{1}{\mathbf{i}^2 \binom{c}{2}} \sum_{m=1}^{c-1} \sum_{n=m+1}^{c} \mathbf{n}_{c_m k_a}\mathbf{n}_{c_n k_b} + \mathbf{n}_{c_m k_b}\mathbf{n}_{c_n k_a}
\end{aligned}
$$

The expected disagreement is the mean of the distances for all distinct category pairs, weighted by the above probabilities (recall that identical category pairs contribute a distance of zero, so it does not matter if and how they are counted).

$$
\begin{aligned}
D_e^{\alpha_\kappa} &= \sum_{j=1}^{k-1} \sum_{l=j+1}^{k} \hat{P}(k_j, k_l)\mathbf{d}_{k_j k_l} \\
&= \frac{1}{\binom{c}{2}} \sum_{j=1}^{k-1} \sum_{l=j+1}^{k} \sum_{m=1}^{c-1} \sum_{n=m+1}^{c} \left(\hat{P}(k_j|c_m)\hat{P}(k_l|c_n) + \hat{P}(k_l|c_m)\hat{P}(k_j|c_n) \right)\mathbf{d}_{k_j k_l} \\
&= \frac{1}{\binom{c}{2}} \sum_{j=1}^{k} \sum_{l=1}^{k} \sum_{m=1}^{c-1} \sum_{n=m+1}^{c} \hat{P}(k_j|c_m)\hat{P}(k_l|c_n)\mathbf{d}_{k_j k_l} \\
&= \frac{1}{\mathbf{i}^2 \binom{c}{2}} \sum_{j=1}^{k} \sum_{l=1}^{k} \sum_{m=1}^{c-1} \sum_{n=m+1}^{c} \mathbf{n}_{c_m k_j}\mathbf{n}_{c_n k_l}\mathbf{d}_{k_j k_l}
\end{aligned}
$$

It is easy to see that $D_e^{\alpha_\kappa}$ is the mean of the $D_e^{\kappa_w}$ values (Section 2.2.6) over all coder pairs. If we take all disagreements to be of equal weight, that is $d_{k_a k_b} = 1$ for all $k_a \neq k_b$, then this measure of expected disagreement is exactly the complement of the expected agreement for multi-κ as calculated in Section 2.2.5: $D_e^{\alpha_\kappa} = 1 - A_e^\kappa$.

We also define a coefficient α_b, which is just like α except that it uses a biased estimator for expected disagreement, like Scott's π.

$$D_e^{\alpha_b} = (\mathbf{ic} - 1)D_e^\alpha / \mathbf{ic}$$

The only purpose of this coefficient is to facilitate the proof below. It is easy to see that α and α_b approach each other as either the number of items or the number of coders grows.

Annotator bias is now defined as the difference between the expected disagreement according to the shared-distribution measure α_b and the expected disagreement according to the individual-distribution measure α_κ.

$$B = D_e^{\alpha_b} - D_e^{\alpha_\kappa}$$

We first put the expected disagreements according to α_b and α_κ into forms that are more useful for the comparison.

$$D_e^{\alpha_b} = \sum_{j=1}^{k}\sum_{l=1}^{k}\hat{P}(k_j)\hat{P}(k_l)d_{k_j k_l} = \sum_{j=1}^{k}\sum_{l=1}^{k}\frac{1}{c^2}\sum_{m=1}^{c}\sum_{n=1}^{c}\hat{P}(k_j|c_m)\hat{P}(k_l|c_n)d_{k_j k_l}$$

$$D_e^{\alpha_\kappa} = \frac{1}{\binom{c}{2}}\sum_{j=1}^{k}\sum_{l=1}^{k}\sum_{m=1}^{c-1}\sum_{n=m+1}^{c}\hat{P}(k_j|c_m)\hat{P}(k_l|c_n)d_{k_j k_l}$$

$$= \sum_{j=1}^{k}\sum_{l=1}^{k}\frac{1}{c(c-1)}\left(\sum_{m=1}^{c}\sum_{n=1}^{c}\hat{P}(k_j|c_m)\hat{P}(k_l|c_n) - \sum_{m=1}^{c}\hat{P}(k_j|c_m)\hat{P}(k_l|c_m)\right)d_{k_j k_l}$$

Now we calculate the annotator bias as the difference between the above measures.

$$B = D_e^{\alpha_b} - D_e^{\alpha_\kappa}$$

$$= \sum_{j=1}^{k}\sum_{l=1}^{k}\left((\frac{1}{c^2} - \frac{1}{c(c-1)})\sum_{m=1}^{c}\sum_{n=1}^{c}\hat{P}(k_j|c_m)\hat{P}(k_l|c_n)\right.$$
$$\left. + \frac{1}{c(c-1)}\sum_{m=1}^{c}\hat{P}(k_j|c_m)\hat{P}(k_l|c_m)\right)d_{k_j k_l}$$

$$= \frac{1}{c-1}\sum_{j=1}^{k}\sum_{l=1}^{k}\frac{1}{c^2}\left(c\sum_{m=1}^{c}\hat{P}(k_j|c_m)\hat{P}(k_l|c_m) - \sum_{m=1}^{c}\sum_{n=1}^{c}\hat{P}(k_j|c_m)\hat{P}(k_l|c_n)\right)d_{k_j k_l}$$

Unlike the case for unweighted measures, this measure of annotator bias does not correspond to the sum of the variances of a single random variable. But the bias still drops in proportion to an increase in the number of coders: the sums inside the parentheses grow in proportion to $\mathbf{c}^2$, and therefore the overall annotator bias B grows in proportion to $1/(\mathbf{c}-1)$.

Now, for any particular coding data, $D_e^{\alpha_\kappa} \geq D_e^{\alpha_b}$, and consequently $\alpha_\kappa \geq \alpha_b$; the greater the number of coders, the lower the difference between α_κ and α_b. We have already seen that α and α_b approach each other as either the number of items or the number of coders grows, and therefore α and α_κ also converge with more coders.

CHAPTER 3

Using Agreement Measures for CL Annotation Tasks

We will now review the use of intercoder agreement measures in CL since Carletta's original paper in the light of the discussion in the previous sections. We begin with a summary of Krippendorff's recommendations about measuring reliability (Krippendorff, 2004a, Chapter 11), then discuss how coefficients of agreement have been used in CL to measure the reliability of annotation, focusing in particular on the types of annotation where there has been some debate concerning the most appropriate measures of agreement.

We will also try to highlight examples of good practice. Krippendorff (2004a, Chapter 11) bemoans the fact that reliability is discussed in only around 69% of studies in content analysis; in CL as well, not all annotation projects include a formal test of intercoder agreement. In a meta-analysis of reports of annotator agreement in CL, Bayerl and Paul (2011) note that out of 587 publications that report linguistic annotation, only 326 reported measures of annotator agreement; these measures were mostly percent agreement and kappa, with fewer that 5% other measures. Some of the best known annotation efforts in CL, such as the creation of the Penn Treebank (Marcus et al., 1993) and the British National Corpus (Leech et al., 1994), do not report reliability results as they predate the Carletta paper; but even among the more recent efforts, many only report percentage agreement, as for the creation of the PropBank (Palmer et al., 2007) or the ongoing OntoNotes annotation (Hovy et al., 2006). We are not aware of any annotation effort in CL that applies a methodology as rigorous as that envisaged by Krippendorff and discusses it next to a study of the reliability of their coding scheme, but we will highlight a few studies that are particularly sound, focusing on the methodology and the coefficients used rather than on the scores.

3.1 GENERAL METHODOLOGICAL RECOMMENDATIONS

We summarize here some general recommendations about carrying out a reliability study emerging from content analysis (Krippendorff, 2004a, 2013, 2019) as well as some from CL practice.

3.1.1   GENERATING DATA TO MEASURE REPRODUCIBILITY

Krippendorff's recommendations are intended to apply to the field of Content Analysis, where the coding of texts is a preliminary step used to draw conclusions from the texts. A coded corpus is thus akin to the result of a scientific experiment, and it can only be considered valid if it is reproducible—that is, if the same coded results can be replicated in an independent coding exercise. Krippendorff therefore argues that any study using observed agreement as a measure of reproducibility must satisfy the following requirements.

- It must employ an exhaustively formulated, clear, and usable coding scheme together with step-by-step instructions on how to use it.

- It must use clearly specified criteria concerning the choice of coders (so that others may use such criteria to reproduce the data).

- It must ensure that the coders that generate the data used to measure reproducibility work independently of each other.

Some practices that are common in CL do not satisfy the above requirements. The first requirement is violated by the practice of expanding the written coding instructions and including new rules as the data get generated. The second requirement is often violated by using experts as coders, particularly long-term collaborators, as such coders may agree not because they are carefully following written instructions, but because they know the purpose of the research very well—which makes it virtually impossible for others to reproduce the results on the basis of the same coding scheme (the problems arising when using experts were already discussed at length in Carletta (1996)). Practices which violate the third requirement (independence) include asking coders to discuss their judgments with each other and reach their decisions by majority vote, or to consult with each other when problems not foreseen in the coding instructions arise. Any of these practices make the resulting data unusable for measuring reproducibility.

Krippendorff's own summary of his recommendations is that to obtain usable reproducibility data a researcher must use data generated by three or more coders, chosen according to some clearly specified criteria, and working independently according to a written coding scheme and coding instructions fixed in advance. Krippendorff also discusses the criteria to be used in the selection of the sample, including: the minimum number of units, obtained using a formula from Bloch and Kraemer (1989) and reported in Krippendorff (2004a, page 239); how to make the sample representative of the data population, namely each category should occur in the sample often enough to yield at least five chance agreements; how to ensure the reliability of the instructions, that is the sample should contain examples of all the values for the categories. These recommendations are particularly relevant in light of the comments of Craggs and McGee Wood (2005, page 290), which discourage researchers from testing their coding instructions on data from more than one domain. Given that the reliability of the coding instructions depends to a great extent on how complications are dealt with, and that every domain displays different complications, the sample should contain sufficient examples from all domains which have to be annotated according to the instructions.

3.1.2   ESTABLISHING SIGNIFICANCE

In hypothesis testing, it is common to test for the significance of a result against a null hypothesis of chance behavior; for an agreement coefficient this would mean rejecting the possibility that a positive value of agreement is nevertheless due to random coding. We can rely on the statement by Siegel and Castellan (1988, Section 9.8.2) that when sample sizes are large, the sampling distribution of K (Fleiss's multi-π) is approximately normal and centered around zero—this allows testing the obtained value of K against the null hypothesis of chance agreement by using the z statistic. It is also easy to test Krippendorff's α with the interval distance metric against the null hypothesis of chance agreement, because the hypothesis $\alpha = 0$ is identical to the hypothesis $F = 1$ in an analysis of variance.

However, a null hypothesis of chance agreement is not very interesting, and demonstrating that agreement is significantly better than chance is not enough to establish reliability. This has already been pointed out by Cohen:

> ...to know merely that κ is beyond chance is trivial since one usually expects much more than this in the way of reliability in psychological measurement. (Cohen, 1960, page 44)

The same point has been repeated and stressed in many subsequent works (e.g., Di Eugenio, 2000, Krippendorff, 2004a, Posner et al., 1990): The reason for measuring the reliability is to ensure that the coders do not deviate too much from perfect agreement (Krippendorff, 2004a, page 237).

The relevant notion of significance for agreement coefficients is therefore a confidence interval. Cohen (1960, pages 43-44) implies that when sample sizes are large, the sampling distribution of κ is approximately normal for any true population value of κ, and therefore confidence intervals for the observed value of κ can be determined using the usual multiples of the standard error. Donner and Eliasziw (1987) propose a more general form of significance test for arbitrary levels of agreement. In contrast, Krippendorff (2004a, Section 11.4.2) states that the distribution of α is unknown, so confidence intervals must be obtained by bootstrapping; a software package for doing this is described in Hayes and Krippendorff (2007).

3.1.3   INTERPRETING THE VALUE OF KAPPA-LIKE COEFFICIENTS

Even after testing significance and establishing confidence intervals, we are still faced with the problem of interpreting the meaning of agreement coefficients. Suppose, for example, we establish that for a particular task, K = 0.78 ± 0.05. Is this good or bad? Unfortunately, deciding what counts as an adequate level of agreement for a specific purpose is still little more than a

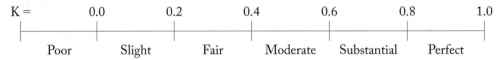

Figure 3.1: **Kappa values and strength of agreement according to** Landis and Koch (1977). Note that Landis and Koch's proposed interpretation of the value is only one among many in the literature; see discussion below.

black art: as we will see, different levels of agreement may be appropriate for resource building and for more linguistic purposes.

The problem is not unlike that of interpreting the values of correlation coefficients, and in the area of medical diagnosis, the best known conventions concerning the value of kappa-like coefficients, those proposed by Landis and Koch (1977) and reported in Figure 3.1, are indeed similar to those used for correlation coefficients, where values above 0.4 are also generally considered adequate (Marion, 2000–2012). Many medical researchers feel that these conventions are appropriate, and in language studies, a similar interpretation of the values has been proposed by Rietveld and van Hout (1993). In CL, however, most researchers follow the more stringent conventions from Content Analysis proposed by Krippendorff (1980, page 147), as reported by Carletta (1996, page 252): "content analysis researchers generally think of K > .8 as good reliability, with .67 < K < .8 allowing tentative conclusions to be drawn" (Krippendorff was discussing values of α rather than K, but the coefficients are nearly equivalent for categorical labels). As a result, ever since Carletta's enormously influential paper, CL researchers have attempted to achieve a value of K (more seldom, of α) above the magical 0.8 threshold, or, failing that, the 0.67 level allowing for "tentative conclusions". However, we should point out that the description of the 0.67 boundary in Krippendorff (1980) was actually "highly tentative and cautious", and in later work Krippendorff clearly considers 0.8 the absolute minimum value of α to accept for any serious purpose: "Even a cutoff point of $\alpha = .800$ ... is a pretty low standard..." (Krippendorff, 2004a, page 242). Later Content Analysis practice seems to have settled for even more stringent requirements: a textbook, Neuendorf (2002), analyzing several proposals concerning 'acceptable' reliability, concludes that "reliability coefficients of .9 or greater would be acceptable to all, .8 or greater would be acceptable in most situations, and below that, there exists great disagreement".

This is clearly a fundamental issue. Ideally, we would want to establish thresholds which are appropriate for the field of CL, but as we will see in the rest of this section, practical experience with using these coefficients in CL hasn't helped in settling the matter. In fact, weighted coefficients, while arguably more appropriate for many annotation tasks, make the issue of deciding when the value of a coefficient indicates sufficient agreement even more complicated because of the problem of determining appropriate weights (see Section 3.4.1). We will return to the issue of interpreting the value of the coefficients at the end of this chapter.

3.1.4   AGREEMENT AND MACHINE LEARNING

One important difference between the fields of CL and Content Analysis is the goals of annotation. Reidsma and Carletta (2008) point out that a common use of an annotated corpus in CL is not to confirm or reject a hypothesis, but to generalize the patterns using machine-learning algorithms. Through a series of simulations, Reidsma and Carletta demonstrate that agreement coefficients are poor predictors of machine-learning success: even highly reproducible annotations are difficult to generalize when the disagreements contain patterns that can be learned, whereas highly noisy and unreliable data can be generalized successfully when the disagreements do not contain learnable patterns. These results show that agreement coefficients should not be used as indicators of the suitability of annotated data for machine learning.

However, the purpose of reliability studies is not to find out whether annotations can be generalized, but whether they capture some kind of observable reality. Even if the pattern of disagreement allows generalization, we need evidence that this generalization would be meaningful. The decision whether a set of annotation guidelines are appropriate or meaningful is ultimately a qualitative one, but a baseline requirement is an acceptable level of agreement among the annotators, who serve as the instruments of measurement. Reliability studies test the soundness of an annotation scheme and guidelines, which is not to be equated with the machine-learnability of data produced by such guidelines.

3.2   LABELLING UNITS WITH A COMMON AND PREDEFINED SET OF CATEGORIES

The most basic and most common form of coding in CL is labelling segments of text with a limited number of linguistic categories: examples include part of speech tagging, dialogue act tagging, and named entity tagging. The practices used to test reliability for this type of annotation tend to be based on the assumption that the categories used in the annotation are mutually exclusive and equidistant; this assumption seems to have worked out well in practice, but we will also consider studies that question it.

3.2.1   PART-OF-SPEECH TAGGING

The simplest type of linguistic annotation is the annotation of parts of speech. Historically, this was also the first type of annotation to be carried out over a 1-million-word corpus, the Brown corpus (Francis and Kucera, 1982), and then over a 100-million-word corpus, the British National Corpus (Leech et al., 1994).[1] None of these early efforts involved systematic tests of the reliability of the annotation. Such studies were, however, carried out for later efforts, such as the annotation of the TIGER corpus of German (Brants and Plaehn, 2000), in which, however, only percentage agreement was computed. Agreement studies using chance-corrected measures were carried out for the annotation of the GENIA corpus (Tateisi and Tsuji, 2004)

---

[1]http://www.natcorp.ox.ac.uk/docs/gramtag.html

and by Mieskes and Strube (2006), among others. In both these studies an unweighted, shared-distribution measure was used, K. These studies generally report very high levels of agreement, particularly for so-called 'interactive' mode of annotation where annotators correct the output of an automatic POS tagger, pioneered by the BNC annotation and which is at the moment the standard method for this type of annotation (for example, Mieskes and Strube report K = 0.96 for this mode).

This considerable experience with POS annotation gives the field confidence that current tagsets are adequate for the purpose of creating large-scale POS-annotated corpora, at least for English. It is worth noting, however, that it is not clear from the literature whether any of these agreement studies satisfies the three requirements laid out by Krippendorff. It is equally clear that from a linguistic perspective, treating all distinctions between POS tags as having the same weight is a considerable simplification. For instance, even a coarse-grained tagset like the Penn Treebank POS tagset makes a distinction between singular and plural nouns; yet intuitively, disagreeing on whether, say, a particular instance of the word *deer* should be tagged as a plural noun (tag NNS) or a singular one (tag NN) is less of a disagreement than disagreeing on whether, say, a particular word should be classified as a determiner or a noun. This intuition is supported by the analysis carried out in the one detailed study of human performance at POS tagging we are aware of, by Babarczy et al. (2006). In analyzing the disagreements between two (highly experienced) annotators using the SUSANNE part of speech tagset, the authors examined disagreement at three levels of categories: **fin** labels, **coarse** labels, and **major parts of speech**. Fine labels are the actual POS tags of the SUSANNE tagset (which contains around 300 tags). Coarse labels are those of the simplified tagset that has been used for automatic annotation, obtained by removing the final character of the tag label (for example, replacing NN1c—the SUSANNE tag for singular count nouns—with NN1; this left around 180 categories). Finally, major parts of speech are labels such as N (noun), V (verb), etc. (only 18 labels). Babarczy et al. found, naturally, that percentage agreement was greater over major parts of speech (98.5%), slightly lower (98.0%) on coarse labels, and lower still on fine labels (97.4%). No chance-corrected agreement results were reported. Moreover, Babarczy et al. observed that many of the disagreements were among close categories: for example, 32% of the disagreements involved classification of proper names (the fine-grained version of the SUSANNE scheme requires making distinctions between surnames and organizations, for instance), and 15.8% of the disagreements were caused by the coders disagreeing on whether words like *training* should be tagged as nouns or participles in contexts like noun-noun compounds (e.g., *training centre*). This idea of identifying and separating levels of annotation requiring progressively more complex decisions has been proposed for many types of annotation tasks, such as dialogue acts (Section 3.2.2) and word senses (Section 3.5). This is justified especially when the different levels reflect separate and distinct decisions by the annotators (Artstein, 2017).

3.2.2   DIALOGUE ACT TAGGING

Dialogue act tagging is another type of linguistic annotation with which by now the CL community has had extensive experience. Dialogue-act-annotated spoken language corpora include MapTask (Carletta et al., 1997), Switchboard (Stolcke et al., 1997), Verbmobil (Jekat et al., 1995) and Communicator (e.g., Doran et al., 2001), among others. Historically, dialogue act annotation was also one of the types of annotation that motivated the introduction in CL of chance-corrected coefficients of agreement (Carletta et al., 1997) and, as we will see in this section, it has been the type of annotation that has originated the most discussion concerning annotation methodology and measuring agreement.

A number of coding schemes for dialogue acts have achieved values of K over 0.8 and have therefore been assumed to be reliable: for example, K = 0.83 for the 13-tag MapTask coding scheme (Carletta et al., 1997), K = 0.8 for the 42-tag Switchboard-DAMSL scheme (Stolcke et al., 1997), K = 0.90 for the smaller 20-tag subset of the CSTAR scheme used by Doran et al. (2001). All of these tests were based on the same two assumptions that underlay the tests of agreement on part of speech tagging discussed earlier: that every unit (utterance) is assigned to exactly one category (dialogue act), and that these categories are distinct. Therefore, again, unweighted measures, and in particular K, tend to be used to measure inter-coder agreement.[2]

However, a rather more serious challenge to these assumptions has arisen in the case of dialogue act tagging, from theories of dialogue acts based on the observation that utterances tend to have more than one function at the dialogue act level (Allen and Core, 1997, Bunt, 2000, 2009, Bunt et al., 2012, Traum and Hinkelman, 1992); for a useful survey, see Popescu-Belis (2005). An assertion performed in answer to a question, for instance, typically performs at least two functions at different levels: asserting some information—the dialogue act that we called Statement in Section 2.2.3, operating at what Traum and Hinkelman called the 'core speech act' level—and confirming that the question has been understood, a dialogue act operating at the 'grounding' level and usually known as Acknowledgment, Ack. In some systems, the fact that an utterance is performed to 'answer' a particular question is also marked—for example, by tagging it as a reply-XX in the MapTask coding scheme, as expressing a 'backward communicative function' in DAMSL (Allen and Core, 1997), or by using an 'answerhood' rhetorical relation in the system of Traum and Hinkelman. In older dialogue act tagsets, acknowledgments and statements were treated as alternative labels at the same 'level', forcing coders to choose one or the other when an utterance performed a dual function, according to a well-specified set of instructions (see for example the explain and acknowledge tags in the MapTask coding scheme). By contrast, in the annotation schemes inspired from these newer theories such as DAMSL (Allen and Core, 1997), coders are allowed to assign tags at different levels, e.g., they could tag a clarification question—an utterance that simultaneously addresses a question while introduc-

---

[2]To our knowledge, Carletta et al. (1997) were the only group among those carrying out these early studies who considered using α for measuring agreement on dialogue act annotation.

ing another question—as having a function both at the **backward-looking** level (Answer) and at the **forward-looking** level (IReq).[3]

This solution also addresses another problem with the older schemes: for in addition to performing dialogue acts at different levels, utterances can also perform multiple functions at the very same level—for example, the core level (in DAMSL parlance, they can perform more than one 'forward communication function'). Utterances such as (1), for instance, perform both what in DAMSL would be called a info-request dialogue act and some sort of suggestion (called open-option in DAMSL), or perhaps even a directive.

(1)   Could we meet at the Wigmore Hall at 11 am?

So-called 'checks' might be viewed as another example of utterances performing multiple core functions: For example, utterances 5.4–5.6 below might be viewed as expressing both a statement and an info-request: M is at the same time stating his or her belief that one boxcar of oranges is sufficient to make a tanker, and requesting S to confirm this belief (TRAINS 1991 (Gross et al., 1993), dialogue d91-2.2).[3]

(2)   5.4   M: I assume one
        5.5   one boxcar
        5.6   of oranges is enough to make a tanker
        6.1   S: yeah

In the MapTask scheme, checks are treated as a separate class of dialogue acts, which may be one of the reasons why the number one source of confusion found by Carletta et al. was that between the tags check and query-yn; collapsing all question-type tags into one resulted in an increase of the agreement from K = 0.83 to K = 0.89.[4] In DAMSL, by contrast, coders are allowed to annotate more than one forward communicative function.

Two annotation experiments with the DAMSL scheme were reported in Core and Allen (1997) and Di Eugenio et al. (1998). In both studies, coders were allowed to mark each (Forward and Backward) communicative function independently—that is, they were allowed to choose for each utterance one of the Statement tags (or possibly none), one of the Influencing-Addressee-Future-Action tags, and so forth—and agreement was evaluated separately for each dimension using (unweighted) K. Core and Allen (1997) found values of K ranging from 0.76 for answer to 0.42 for agreement to 0.15 for Committing-Speaker-Future-Action. Using different coding instructions and on a different corpus, Di Eugenio et al. (1998) observed higher agreement, ranging from K = 0.93 (for other-forward-function) to 0.54 (for the backward function agreement).

---

[3]http://hdl.handle.net/1802/1132

[4]Specifically, checks are defined as "[Questions asking] for confirmation of material which the speaker believes might be inferred, given the dialogue context"—Carletta et al. (1997, Figure 1). Carletta et al. point out that in practice the coders used the check tag to mark utterances querying information that the speaker believed had been told, as in: G: *Ehm, curve round slightly to your right.* F: *to my right?*

Core and Allen found that many disagreements resulted from some of the coders choosing different subsets of communicative functions: for example, one of the main sources of disagreement was the difficulty for coders to tell whether an utterance is an acceptance or simply an acknowledgment, two types of Backward Communicative Function treated as separate dimensions. They also observed a problem with checks: some coders would mark an utterance like 5.4–5.6 in (2) as having both a `statement` and an `info-request` function, whereas others would mark it as expressing only a `statement`, or only an `info-request`. Because agreement was measured for each communicative function independently, partial agreement on the overall 'label' (the entire set of labels assigned to an utterance in all dimensions) could not be taken into account in such cases. In cases in which annotations overlapped (as in the case of an utterance which one of the coders marked both a `statement` and an `info-request`, whereas the other coder only marked an `info-request`), Core and Allen would get perfect agreement along one dimension (`statement`), but no agreement at all along the `Influencing-Addressee-Future-Action` dimension. It might be argued that in such cases, using a weighted coefficient measuring agreement over the entire set of labels assigned to an utterance in all dimensions might provide a better indication of the actual agreement on the interpretation of that utterance.

Many researchers find that the value of agreement obtained with DAMSL was not adequate for their purposes. In addition, multi-dimensional schemes have been criticized with regards to their suitability to be used to create a training corpus for statistical classifiers (Popescu-Belis, 2005). If the corpus is used to train a single classifier simultaneously attempting to identify all communicative functions performed by an utterance—that is, if the tags for the separate dimensions are conflated for the purposes of classification into multi-dimensional tags in the sense discussed in Popescu-Belis (2005), then obviously the resulting search space for the classifier may be huge. For instance, Popescu-Belis (2005) claims that the DAMSL multi-dimensional tagset consists of 4 million potential combinations, even if in practice only a fraction of these tags are actually used (see discussion of the experiments by Stolcke et al. below). One objection to this criticism is that normally separate classifiers would be trained for each dimension, instead of attempting to train a single classifier making what many consider to be distinct inferences. A second objection regards allowing multiple tags at the same level for an item, as there is increasing evidence that this ability is required in a number of NLP tasks, and a number of methods for developing classifiers able to train in this situation exist, as discussed in more detail in Chapter 6.

These problems led many researchers to return to 'flat' tagsets for dialogue acts after experimenting with multidimensional ones, incorporating however in their schemes some of the insights motivating the work on schemes such as DAMSL. The best known example of this type of approach is the development of SWITCHBOARD-DAMSL by Jurafsky et al. (1997), who annotated the Switchboard corpus in order to study the interaction of dialogue acts and speech recognition (Stolcke et al., 1997). Jurafsky et al. started by running an annotation pilot using the DAMSL scheme. They found that only 220 of the possible combinations of tags occurred in the corpus, but also that agreement was not very high. A new tagset called SWITCHBOARD-

DAMSL was then developed consisting of only 42 tags, on which good agreement was found. This new tagset incorporates many ideas from the 'multi-dimensional' theories of dialogue acts, but does not allow marking an utterance as both an acknowledgment and a statement; a choice has to be made. Similarly, Doran et al. (2001) decided not to adopt the DAMSL scheme on grounds of complexity (without running a pilot), adopting instead a simplified version of the tagset developed by the CSTAR consortium, in part because it seemed more appropriate for the task.

Interestingly, subsequent developments of SWITCHBOARD-DAMSL backtracked on some of these decisions. The ICSI-MRDA tagset developed for the annotation of the ICSI Meeting Recorder corpus reintroduces some of the DAMSL ideas, in that annotators are allowed to assign multiple SWITCHBOARD-DAMSL labels to utterances (Shriberg et al., 2004). Shriberg et al. only achieved a comparable reliability to that obtained with SWITCHBOARD-DAMSL when using a tagset of only five 'class-maps'. This aspect of the ICSI-MRDA was further developed in the MALTUS scheme proposed by Popescu-Belis (2005), in which further constraints are introduced in the composition of class maps so as to greatly reduce the number of theoretically possible multi-labels from around 7 million to around 200.

In addition, Shriberg et al. (2004) also introduced a hierarchical organization of tags to improve reliability. The dimensions of the DAMSL scheme can be viewed as 'super-classes' of dialogue acts which share some aspect of their meaning. For instance, the dimension of `Influencing-Addressee-Future-Action` (IAFA) includes the two dialogue acts `Open-option` (used to mark suggestions) and `Directive` mentioned earlier, both of which bring into consideration a future action to be performed by the addressee. At least in principle, an organization of this type opens up the possibility for coders to mark an utterance such as (1) with the superclass (IAFA) in case they do not feel confident that the utterance satisfies the additional requirements for `Open-option` or `Directive`. This, in turn, would do away with the need to make a choice between these two options. This possibility wasn't pursued in the studies using the original DAMSL that we are aware of (Core and Allen, 1997, Di Eugenio, 2000, Stent, 2001), but was tested by Shriberg et al. (2004) and subsequent work, in particular Geertzen and Bunt (2006), who were specifically interested in the idea of using hierarchical schemes to measure partial agreement and in addition experimented with weighted measures of agreement—specifically, κ_w—for measuring agreement over their hierarchical tagging scheme. There are a number of problems with the Geertzen and Bunt proposal, ranging from the hierarchy they propose to the equations given in the paper for computing the distance metric **d**, but we feel nevertheless that the work is worth discussing as one of the few examples of use of weighted measures of agreement in CL.

Geertzen and Bunt were testing intercoder agreement with Bunt's DIT++ (Bunt, 2005), a scheme with 11 dimensions that builds on ideas from DAMSL and from Dynamic Interpretation Theory (Bunt, 2000). In DIT++, tags can be hierarchically related: for example, the class `information-seeking` is viewed as consisting of two classes, yes-no question (ynq) and

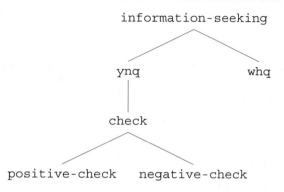

Figure 3.2: Hierarchical tags from Geertzen and Bunt (2006).

wh-question (whq). The hierarchy is explicitly introduced to allow coders to leave some aspects of the coding undecided. For example, the difficult case repeatedly mentioned in this section, check, is treated as a subclass of ynq in which, in addition, the speaker has a weak belief that the proposition that forms the belief is true. A coder who is not certain about the dialogue act performed using an utterance may simply choose to tag it as ynq. This organization is shown in Figure 3.2.

The distance metric **d** proposed by Geertzen and Bunt is based on the criterion that two communicative functions are related—disagreement is less than maximal ($\mathbf{d}(c_1, c_2) < 1$)—if they stand in an ancestor-offspring relation within a hierarchy. Furthermore, they argue, the magnitude of $\mathbf{d}(c_1, c_2)$ should be proportional to the distance between the functions in the hierarchy. A level-dependent correction factor is also proposed so as to leave open the option to make disagreements at higher levels of the hierarchy matter more than disagreements at the deeper level (for example, the distance between information-seeking and ynq might be considered greater than the distance between check and positive-check). The result is the following distance metric.[5]

$$\mathbf{d}(c_i, c_j) = 1 - h(c_i, c_j) \times a^{\Delta(c_i, c_j)} \times b^{\Gamma(c_i, c_j)}$$

Here, $h(c_i, c_j)$ is 1 if c_i and c_j are identical or stand in an ancestor relation in the hierarchy, and 0 if they don't; $0 < a < 1$ is a constant expressing the amount of disagreement associated with a certain distance between levels in the hierarchy and $\Delta(c_i, c_j)$ is the difference in depth between the levels of c_i and c_j; and $0 < b \leq 1$ is the depth-dependent correction factor and $\Gamma(c_i, c_j)$ is the minimal depth of c_i and c_j.[6] For example, assuming the tree in Figure 3.2, and given the

---

[5]Geertzen and Bunt define a measure of *closeness*, $\delta(c_1, c_2) = a^{\Delta(c_i, c_j)} \dot{b}^{\Gamma(c_i, c_j)}$, and then modify the equation for κ_w. We changed things slightly to relate the proposal more closely to the equations seen in Section 2.2.6.

[6]$h(c_i, c_j)$ was omitted by mistake from the version of this equation in the paper in the SIGDIAL proceedings (Harry Bunt, personal communication). Also, as far as we can see, identical categories have a distance of 0 only when $b = 1$.

Table 3.1: A comparison of κ and κ_w agreement values for the DIT++ annotation (excerpt from Geertzen and Bunt, 2006, Table 2)

Dimension	κ	κ_w	#pairs	AP Ratio
Contact management	1.00	1.00	8	0.17
Own comm. management	1.00	1.00	2	0.08
Social obl. management	1.00	1.00	61	0.80
Turn management	0.82	0.82	115	0.18
Dialog str. management	0.74	0.74	15	0.31
Time management	0.58	0.58	68	0.72
Allo feedback	0.42	0.58	17	0.14
Auto feedback	0.21	0.57	127	0.34

values $a = 0.75$ and $b = 1$ as in Geertzen and Bunt (2006), we get the following values for **d**.

$$
\begin{aligned}
\mathbf{d}(\text{ynq}, \text{whq}) &= 1 - 0 \times 0.75^0 \times 1 = 1 \\
\mathbf{d}(\text{ynq}, \text{ynq}) &= 1 - 1 \times 0.75^0 \times 1 = 0 \\
\mathbf{d}(\text{ynq}, \text{check}) &= 1 - 1 \times 0.75^1 \times 1 = 0.75
\end{aligned}
$$

The results of an agreement test with two annotators run by Geertzen and Bunt are shown in Table 3.1. The first two columns give the values for κ and κ_w; the third column is the number of pairs on which the coefficients were computed; the fourth column is the AP ratio for each dimension—the proportion of cases which were marked on that dimension by both annotators out of the number of cases which were marked by at least one annotator. As the table shows, taking into account partial agreement leads to values of κ_w that are higher than the values of κ for the same categories, particularly for feedback, a class for which Core and Allen (1997) got low agreement. Of course, even assuming that the values of κ_w and κ were directly comparable—we remark elsewhere on the difficulty of interpreting the values of weighted coefficients of agreement—it remains to be seen whether these higher values are a better indication of the extent of agreement between coders than the values of unweighted κ.

This discussion of coding schemes for dialogue acts and the best way of measuring agreement on this type of annotation was quite long, but it introduced issues that we will see discussed in the case of other CL annotation tasks as well. There are by now a number of well-established schemes for large-scale dialogue act annotation based on the assumption of mutual exclusivity between dialogue act tags, whose reliability is also well known; if one of these schemes is appropriate for modelling the communicative intentions found in a task, the most prudent recommendation at this point would be to use it. The readers should, however, be aware that the mutual exclusivity assumption is very dubious, and that multi-dimensional or hierarchical dialogue act tagsets need not automatically result in lower reliability or in an explosion in the number of labels. If a hierarchical tagset is used, readers should be aware that weighted coefficients do capture partial agreement. But none of these decisions would be unproblematic. A hierarchical scheme designed on the basis of our intuitions about intentions may not reflect genuine annotation difficulties: for example, in the case of DIT++, one might argue that it is more difficult to confuse yes-no questions with wh-questions than with statements. And once we start using weighted coefficients, interpreting the value we obtain becomes even more of a dark art. We will return to both of these problems in what follows.

3.2.3   NAMED ENTITIES

Named entity recognition is the task of identifying mentions of individuals and assigning them a type—e.g., finding and labelling all mentions of people or proteins in a text. This aspect of semantic interpretation has grown in importance thanks to its inclusion among the information extraction subtasks first in the Message Understanding Conference (MUC) and then in the Automatic Content Extraction (ACE) initiatives. Named entity identification is a matter of *unitizing* (Section 2.4), since it involves both locating the mentions and assigning them labels. However, the original formulations of the task did not directly address the unitizing aspects. While candidate mentions were not explicitly marked in the text, it was implicitly assumed that they are already available (perhaps it was thought they are easy to identify), and the task was conceived as a matter of *retrieval*—picking out the correct mentions that belong to each category. Thus, the MUC evaluation was scored using the F-measure, treating all the mentions in the key and the mentions identified by a system as potential candidate mentions (Chinchor, 1997b).[7]

The MUC guidelines for named entity tagging (Chinchor, 1997a) identified five types of named entities as being particularly relevant, and annotated: person, location, organization, temporal expression, and numerical expressions (e.g., "15 dollars"). We are not aware of a reliability study being carried out for the MUC annotation. With ACE (Doddington et al., 2004), the definition of the task was extended by allowing for seven types of entities instead of five (person, organization, geo-political, location, facility, vehicle, and weapon) and by introducing subtypes (such as 'building' or 'bridge' for the type 'facility').

This view of general-purpose named entity tagging as a simplified form of ontological labelling is quite natural, and efforts following ACE have tended to pursue this direction. Sekine et al. (2002) developed an Extended Named Entity Hierarchy, a taxonomy of types currently consisting of around 200 types. In named entity annotation for the biomedical domain, arguably the most common version of named entity tagging at the moment, named entity annotation according to an ontology was already the method adopted for the annotation of the GENIA corpus (Tateisi et al., 2000). Ontology-based annotation is becoming more common in connection with

---

[7]The F-measure does not concern itself with true negatives, so there is no need to consider candidate mentions which are not in the key and not identified by a system.

work on the Semantic Web (Cimiano and Handschuh, 2003, Handschuh, 2005) but we are not aware of any studies of agreement.

We are not aware of any study from the original MUC and ACE efforts which reports chance-corrected measures, though later efforts of named entity tagging do report them (e.g., Fleiss' κ in Madge et al., 2019). The ACE 2003 annotation of the English named entity labelling task reported 88% intercoder agreement, whereas in the case of biomedical annotation, Tateisi et al. (2000) reported an F-measure[8] of 75.85% on a set of 4 tags (protein, dna, rna, source), and Vlachos et al. (2006) reported 91% agreement on gene names. What makes named entity tagging interesting from our perspective is that it is a simplified version of the much more complex problem of wordsense tagging discussed later. On the one hand, the categories are usually clearly distinct, which suggests that the disjointness assumption behind unweighted measures such as K may be appropriate, except perhaps in the case of metonymy (for example in *Vietnam was the source of much soul-searching in the USA*, where 'Vietnam' could refer to the country or the war). On the other hand, even more than in the case of wordsense tagging, it is natural to view the set of labels as having a taxonomic organization (e.g., depending on the annotator's knowledge, an `organization` may be classified as a `company` or as a `governmental organization` or as a `non-profit`), hence different levels of precision may be reached, which suggests that weighed coefficients of agreement may be more appropriate.

3.2.4   OTHER LABELLING TASKS

Modern CL research is more and more concerned with extracting information that is less clearly 'linguistic' (in the traditional sense), thus overlapping more and more with the concerns of content analysis. One example of this trend is the work by Craggs and McGee Wood (2004) on annotating emotions and the work by Bruce, Wiebe, and collaborators on detecting subjective judgments.

The work by Craggs and McGee Wood (2004) on developing an annotation scheme for emotions and testing its reliability has several aspects worth mentioning. First of all, there is the problem of the units to which to apply the labels. As Craggs and McGee Wood point out, 'emotional episodes' are not associated with any specific linguistic event, but persist for a certain amount of time, fading after a while. We'll return later to the issue of unitizing, but we are not aware of any clear solution to this problem. The second interesting point about this work is that it is one of the few pieces of work in which Krippendorff's α is used with a weighted distance metric, in this case, to measure distance between emotions in 'Activation-Evaluation space'. Third, this is one of the few early studies in which coders were allowed to mark multiple labels (e.g., when a person is conveying both fear and sadness in one utterance).

The work by Bruce and Wiebe (1999) in detecting subjective judgments is an interesting, indeed a particularly sophisticated, example of analysis of the results of the annotation to

---

[8]This study used the F1 measure, which balances precision and recall, so the it gives the same results whichever annotator is taken as reference.

Coder A

		1	2	3	4	5	6	7	8	
	1	$n_{1,1}$	$n_{1,2}$	$n_{1,3}$	$n_{1,4}$	$n_{1,5}$	$n_{1,6}$	$n_{1,7}$	$n_{1,8}$	subjective
	2	$n_{2,1}$	$n_{2,2}$	$n_{2,3}$	$n_{2,4}$	$n_{2,5}$	$n_{2,6}$	$n_{2,7}$	$n_{2,8}$	$\vdots$
	3	$n_{3,1}$	$n_{3,2}$	$n_{3,3}$	$n_{3,4}$	$n_{3,5}$	$n_{3,6}$	$n_{3,7}$	$n_{3,8}$	$\vdots$
Coder B	4	$n_{4,1}$	$n_{4,2}$	$n_{4,3}$	$n_{4,4}$	$n_{4,5}$	$n_{4,6}$	$n_{4,7}$	$n_{4,8}$	$\vdots$
	5	$n_{5,1}$	$n_{5,2}$	$n_{5,3}$	$n_{5,4}$	$n_{5,5}$	$n_{5,6}$	$n_{5,7}$	$n_{5,8}$	$\vdots$
	6	$n_{6,1}$	$n_{6,2}$	$n_{6,3}$	$n_{6,4}$	$n_{6,5}$	$n_{6,6}$	$n_{6,7}$	$n_{6,8}$	$\vdots$
	7	$n_{7,1}$	$n_{7,2}$	$n_{7,3}$	$n_{7,4}$	$n_{7,5}$	$n_{7,6}$	$n_{7,7}$	$n_{7,8}$	$\vdots$
	8	$n_{8,1}$	$n_{8,2}$	$n_{8,3}$	$n_{8,4}$	$n_{8,5}$	$n_{8,6}$	$n_{8,7}$	$n_{8,8}$	objective

Figure 3.3: The profile of "subjective" for coder A is the vector of corresponding judgments by coder B.

identify the reasons for the disagreement. Bruce and Wiebe had 4 subjects (including 2 participants in the project) assign the tags subjective or objective, together with a certainty value, to 504 clauses from the Penn Treebank, observing a κ value of 0.599 (using the definition of Davies and Fleiss (1982), our multi-κ). Bruce and Wiebe then applied **correspondence analysis** to the pairwise confusion matrices between the four coders. First, they used the objective/subjective tagging together with the four-point certainty rank to create an eight-point scale ranging from "highly certain subjective" to "highly certain objective". Then, for each coder in a given pair they defined the **profil** for each point on the scale as the vector of the other coder's corresponding judgments. For example, the profile of "subjective" for coder A is an eight-point vector whose value at each point is the number of items labeled as such by coder B (see Figure 3.3). Finally, Bruce and Wiebe compared the coders' profiles in order to determine which points on the scale resulted in similar judgment patterns.

Already this allowed Bruce and Wiebe to observe, for instance, that there was much more agreement among their coders on highly certain values than on the highly uncertain ones, and more agreement on marking a clause as "subjective" than "objective". They then applied a combination of techniques for testing the significance of these differences. These techniques allowed them to conclude that although the judges disagreed, strong patterns of 'quasi-simmetry' could be detected, which in turn led them to explore the use of latent class models (Dempster et al., 1977, Goodman, 1974a) to identify what Bruce and Wiebe call the "bias-corrected versions of the judges' original classifications". Bruce and Wiebe apply these techniques to identify the 'latent categories' ('Latent Subjective' and 'Latent Objective') for each item, and propose to use these latent categories as the final classification of the items. Latent class models are one of the key topics of Chapter 4, in which we also discuss (Bruce and Wiebe, 1999) further.

3.3   MARKING BOUNDARIES AND UNITIZING

Many annotation tasks involve not only assigning labels to units, but also the identification of units ("markables") that bear labels—a process of **unitizing** (Section 2.4). The practice in CL for the forms of annotation discussed in the previous section is to assume that the units are linguistic constituents which can be easily identified, such as words, utterances, or noun phrases, and therefore there is no need to check the reliability of unit identification. We are only aware of few exceptions to this assumption, such as Carletta et al. (1997) on unitization for move coding and our own work on the GNOME corpus (Poesio, 2004b). In other cases, however, such as text segmentation and prosodic annotation, the identification of units is as important as their labelling, if not more important, and therefore checking agreement on unit identification is essential. In this section we discuss current CL practice with reliability testing of these two types of annotation.

3.3.1   SEGMENTATION AND TOPIC MARKING

The analysis of discourse structure—and especially the identification of discourse segments—is a very important area of research in discourse analysis and computational linguistics, and the type of annotation that more than any other led CL researchers to look for ways of measuring reliability and agreement, as it made them aware of the extent of disagreement on even quite simple judgments (Carletta et al., 1997, Hearst, 1997, Kowtko et al., 1992, Passonneau and Litman, 1993). Subsequent research identified a number of issues with discourse structure annotation, above all the fact that segmentation, though problematic, is still much easier than identifying more complex aspects of discourse structure, such as identifying the most important segments or the 'rhetorical' relations between segments of different granularity. As a result, many efforts to annotate discourse structure concentrate only on segmentation. We focus on segmentation in this section.

Discourse segments are portions of text that constitute a unit either because they are about the same 'topic' or because they have to do with achieving the the same intention (Grosz and Sidner, 1986) or performing the same 'dialogue game' (Carletta et al., 1997).[9] The annotation of texts into segments related to the same topic (Hearst, 1997, Reynar, 1998) is by now a common form of annotation, carried out on a fairly large scale, for example as part of the Text REtrieval Conference (TREC) and then Topic Detection and Tracking (TDT) initiatives (Voorhees and Harman, 1998, Wayne, 2000). These annotation efforts tend to focus on broader analyses such

---

[9]The notion of 'topic' is notoriously difficult to define and many competing theoretical proposals exist (Reinhart, 1981, Vallduví, 1993). As it is often the case with annotation, fairly simple definitions tend to be used in discourse annotation work: For example, in TDT, topic is defined for annotation purposes as 'an event of activity together with all related events and activities'.

as the division of streams of broadcast news into items about different events, but more fine-grained analyses have also been attempted. For example, Carlson et al. (2003) annotated so-called **discourse units** as the first step of their annotation of discourse structure. An interesting cross between topic-based and rhetorical structure-based analysis is the identification of **argumentative zones** carried out by Teufel et al. (1999), who segment scientific text according to its role (background, own claims, other people's claims, etc). Carletta et al. (1997) carried out a form of segmentation based on the version of conversational games theory proposed by Sinclair and Coulthard (1975), identifying the boundaries of games and transactions. Intention-based annotations in the Grosz and Sidner sense have also been attempted, althought typically on a smaller scale, for example by Passonneau and Litman (1993) and Nakatani et al. (1995), as well as as a part of RDA-style annotations (Moser and Moore, 1996, Moser et al., 1996).

The agreement results in these efforts tend to be on the lower end of the scale proposed by Krippendorff and adopted by Carletta, even for topic-based segmentation. Hearst (1997), for instance, found K = 0.647 for the task of annotating each paragraph junction as to whether or not it constitutes a topic boundary (binary decision); Reynar (1998), measuring agreement between his own annotation and the TREC segmentation of broadcast news, reports K = 0.764 for the same task; Ries (2001) reports even lower agreement of K = 0.36. Teufel et al. (1999) found higher reliability (K = 0.81) for their three main zones (own, other, background) although lower for the whole scheme (K = 0.71). For intention-based segmentation, Passonneau and Litman (1993) in the pre-K days reported an overall percentage agreement with majority opinion of 89%, but the agreement on boundaries was only 70%. For conversational games segmentation, Carletta et al. (1997) reported "promising but not entirely reassuring agreement on where games began (70%) ...," whereas the agreement on transaction boundaries was K = 0.59. Exceptions are two segmentation efforts carried out as part of annotations of rhetorical structure. Moser et al. achieved an agreement of K = 0.9 for the highest level of segmentation of their RDA annotation (Poesio et al., 2006). Carlson et al. (2003) managed to achieve very high agreement over unit boundaries (agreement was measured at several times; the initial results were already of K = 0.87, and the final result K = 0.97). This, however, was achieved by employing experienced annotators, and with considerable training.

One important reason why most agreement results on segmentation are on the lower end of the reliability scale is the fact, known to researchers in discourse analysis from as early as Levin and Moore (1978), that while analysts generally agree on the 'bulk' of segments, they tend to disagree on their exact boundaries. This phenomenon was also observed in more recent studies: see for example the discussion in Passonneau and Litman (1997), the comparison of the annotations produced by seven coders of the same text in Figure 5 of Hearst (1997, page 55), or the discussion by Carlson et al. (2003), who point out that the boundaries between elementary discourse units tend to be 'very blurry'. See also Pevzner and Hearst (2002) for similar comments made in the context of topic segmentation algorithms.

Table 3.2: Fewer boundaries, higher expected agreement

Case 1: Text Divided Into Broad Segments
$A_o = 0.96$, $A_e = 0.89$, $K = 0.65$

		Coder A		
		Boundary	No Boundary	Total
Coder B	Boundary	2	1	3
	No Boundary	1	46	47
	Total	3	47	50

Case 2: Text Divided Into Fine Discourse Units
$A_o = 0.88$, $A_e = 0.53$, $K = 0.75$

		Coder A		
		Boundary	No Boundary	Total
Coder B	Boundary	16	3	19
	No Boundary	3	28	31
	Total	19	31	50

This 'blurriness' of boundaries, combined with the prevalence effects discussed in Section 2.5.2, also explains the fact that topic annotation efforts which were only concerned with roughly dividing a text into segments (Carletta et al., 1997, Hearst, 1997, Passonneau and Litman, 1993, Reynar, 1998, Ries, 2002) generally report lower agreement than the studies whose goal is to identify smaller discourse units. When disagreement is mostly concentrated in one class ('boundary' in this case), if the total number of units to annotate remains the same then expected agreement on this class is lower when a greater proportion of the units to annotate belongs to this class. When in addition this class is much less numerous than the other classes, overall agreement tends to depend mostly on agreement on this class.

For instance, suppose we are testing the reliability of two different segmentation schemes—into broad 'discourse segments' and into finer 'discourse units'—on a text of 50 utterances, and that we obtain the results in Table 3.2. Case 1 would be a situation in which Coder A and Coder B agree that the text consists of two segments, obviously agree on its initial and final boundaries, but disagree by 1 position on the intermediate boundary—say, one of them places it at utterance 25, the other at utterance 26. Nevertheless, because expected agreement is so high—the coders agree on the classification of 98% of the utterances—the value of K is fairly low. In case 2, the coders disagree on three times as many utterances, but K is higher than in the first case because expected agreement is substantially lower ($A_e = 0.53$).

The fact that coders mostly agree on the 'bulk' of discourse segments, but tend to disagree on their boundaries, makes it likely that an all-or-nothing coefficient like K calculated on individual boundaries would underestimate the degree of agreement, suggesting low agreement even among coders whose segmentations are mostly similar. A weighted coefficient of agreement like α might produce values more in keeping with intuition, but we are not aware of any attempts at measuring agreement on segmentation using weighted coefficients. We see two main options. We suspect that the methods for measuring agreement on unitizing (see Section 2.4 above) may be appropriate for the purpose of measuring agreement on discourse segmentation. A second option would be to measure agreement not on individual boundaries but on windows spanning several units, as done in the methods proposed to evaluate the performance of topic detection algorithms such as P_k (Beeferman et al., 1999) or WINDOWDIFF (Pevzner and Hearst, 2002). Both of these methods aim at assigning partial credit to near misses, and both also specify a metric of disagreement which is additive—that is, the overall disagreement is obtained by adding disagreement over all 'categories' assigned to 'units'. They differ from the methods discussed so far in that the goal of assigning partial credit is achieved by computing pairwise disagreements over the number of boundaries present in a window sliding through the segment; if we allow for these windows to be our 'units', then the way disagreements are computed can be reinterpreted in terms of agreement coefficients. For instance, we can view P_k as assigning one of two category labels to a window: `same` if both ends of the window are in the same segment, `different` otherwise. The measure P_k now becomes the percentage of windows on which two or more coders agree—that is, observed agreement A_o. Similarly, WINDOWDIFF can be viewed as observed agreement when the category label assigned to each window is the number of boundaries in the window. This highlights the fact that P_k and WINDOWDIFF are simple percentage measures which are not corrected for chance; this can be remedied by reporting K or α instead of observed agreement.

Yet another possiblity might be to develop a measure based on the methods used in our own studies of agreement on the antecedents of discourse deixis, which are discourse segments (Section 3.4.2).

3.3.2   PROSODY

Prosodic annotation, like topic marking, crucially involves a step of (prosodic) boundary identification in addition to a step of labelling the units, and measuring agreement on boundaries is as crucial as measuring agreement on the labels. The most important difference from text segmentation is that different types of boundaries exist (Pierrehumbert and Hirschberg, 1990). Systematic studies of reliability on both boundary marking and prosodic phrases labelling have been conducted by, among others, Buhmann et al. (2002), Pitrelli et al. (1994), and Syrdal and McGorg (2000). An important difference between these studies is that whereas Syrdal and Mc-Gorg (2000) used coders with lots of training, Buhmann et al. (2002) set out to make sure that the annotation could be done reliably by students working at different sites. As in the case of text segmentation, agreement on prosodic segmentation is measured by comparing whether coders classify a word as a boundary or not, and the type of boundary assigned. Syrdal and McGorg (2000) measured agreement between their four expert coders separately on male and female voices, reporting 74% agreement on boundaries, for a value of κ of 0.65 for females and 0.62 for males. Buhmann et al. (2002), who tested eight students, do not provide percent agreement, but report κ 'in the range from 0.70 to 0.88' (presumably measured pairwise).

3.4   SET-BASED LABELS

The annotation tasks discussed so far involve assigning a specific label to each category, which allows the various agreement measures to be applied in a straightforward way. When the annotations are not taken from a fixed repository of labels, it may not be clear how to apply the agreement coefficients. Here we discuss several annotation tasks where labels can be approximated as sets of other objects, for the purpose of calculating reliability coefficients.

3.4.1   ANAPHORA

Annotators of anaphoric relations do not assign labels, but rather create links between anaphors and their antecedents. It is therefore not clear what the 'labels' should be for the purpose of calculating agreement. One possibility would be to consider the intended referent (real-world object) as the label, as in named entity tagging, but it wouldn't make sense to predefine a set of 'labels' applicable to all texts, since different objects are mentioned in different texts. An alternative is to use the marked antecedents as 'labels'. However, we do not want to count as a disagreement every time two coders agree on the discourse entity realized by a particular noun phrase but just happen to mark different words as antecedents. Consider the reference of the underlined pronoun *it* in the following dialogue excerpt (TRAINS 1991, dialogue d91-3.2).

(3)   1.1   M: ....
      1.4   first thing I'd like you to do
      1.5   is send engine E2 off with a boxcar to Corning to
                  pick up oranges
      1.6   as soon as possible
      2.1   S: okay
      3.1   M: and while it's there <u>it</u> should pick up the tanker

Some of the coders in a study we carried out (Poesio and Artstein, 2005) indicated *engine E2* as antecedent for the second *it* in utterance 3.1, whereas others indicated the immediately preceding pronoun, which they had previously marked as having *engine E2* as antecedent. Clearly, we do not want to consider these coders to be in disagreement.

A solution to this dilemma has been proposed by Passonneau (2004): use the emerging coreference sets as the 'labels' for the purpose of calculating agreement. This requires using weighted measures for calculating agreement on such sets, and consequently it raises serious questions about weighted measures—in particular, about the interpretability of the results, as we will see shortly.

Passonneau's Proposal

Passonneau (2004) recommends measuring agreement on anaphoric annotation by using *sets* of mentions of discourse entities as labels, that is, the emerging anaphoric/coreference chains. Treating anaphoric chains as sets, or equivalence classes of mentions, is a simplification which ignores possibly complex structures of anaphoric chains or the type of relation expressed by different anaphoric links. However, this proposal is in line with the conceptualization of entities as sets of mentions, commonly used in the evaluation of anaphora resolution systems (Vilain et al., 1995). But using anaphoric chains as labels would not make unweighted measures such as K a good measure for agreement. Practical experience suggests that except when a text is very short, few annotators will catch all mentions of a discourse entity: most will forget to mark a few, with the result that the chains (that is, category labels) differ from coder to coder and agreement as measured with K is always very low. What is needed is a coefficient that also allows for partial disagreement between judgments, when two annotators agree on part of the coreference chain but not on all of it.

Passonneau (2004) suggests solving the problem by using α with a distance metric that allows for partial agreement among anaphoric chains. Passonneau proposes a distance metric based on the following rationale: two sets are minimally distant when they are identical and maximally distant when they are disjoint; between these extremes, sets that stand in a subset relation are closer (less distant) than ones that merely intersect. This leads to the following distance metric between two sets A and B.

$$\mathbf{d}_P = \begin{cases} 0 & \text{if } A = B \\ \frac{1}{3} & \text{if } A \subset B \text{ or } B \subset A \\ \frac{2}{3} & \text{if } A \cap B \neq \emptyset, \text{ but } A \not\subset B \text{ and } B \not\subset A \\ 1 & \text{if } A \cap B = \emptyset \end{cases}$$

Alternative distance metrics take the size of the anaphoric chain into account, based on measures used to compare sets in Information Retrieval such as the coefficient of community of Jaccard (1912) and the coincidence index of Dice (1945) (Manning and Schuetze, 1999; both measures evaluate to 1 when the sets are disjoint, and to 0 when the sets are identical).

$$\mathbf{d}_J = 1 - \frac{|A \cap B|}{|A \cup B|} \qquad \text{(Jaccard)}$$

$$\mathbf{d}_D = 1 - \frac{2|A \cap B|}{|A| + |B|} \qquad \text{(Dice)}$$

In later work, Passonneau (2006) offers a refined distance metric which she called MASI (Measuring Agreement on Set-valued Items), obtained by multiplying Passonneau's original met-

Chain	K	α
None	0.628	0.656
Partial	0.563	0.677
Full	0.480	0.691

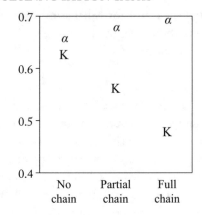

Figure 3.4: A comparison of the values of α and K for anaphoric annotation.

ric $\mathbf{d}_P$ by the metric derived from Jaccard $\mathbf{d}_J$.

$$\mathbf{d}_M = \mathbf{d}_P \times \mathbf{d}_J$$

Experience with α for Anaphoric Annotation
In the experiment mentioned above (Poesio and Artstein, 2005) we used 18 coders to test α and K under a variety of conditions. We found that even though our coders by and large agreed on the interpretation of anaphoric expressions, virtually no coder ever identified all the mentions of a discourse entity. As a result, even though the values of α and K obtained by using the ID of the antecedent as label were pretty similar, the values obtained when using anaphoric chains as labels were drastically different. The value of α increased, because examples like (3) would no longer be considered as full disagreements. However, the value of K was drastically reduced, because hardly any coder identified all the mentions of discourse entities (Figure 3.4).

The study also looked at the matter of individual annotator bias, and as mentioned in Section 2.5.1, we did not find differences between α and α_κ beyond the third decimal point. This similarity is what one would expect, given the result about annotator bias from Section 2.5.1 and given that in this experiment we used 18 annotators. These very small differences should be contrasted with the differences resulting from the choice of distance metrics, where values for the full-chain condition ranged from $\alpha = 0.642$ using Jaccard as distance metric, to $\alpha = 0.654$ using Passonneau's metric, to the value for Dice reported in Figure 3.4, $\alpha = 0.691$. These differences raise an important issue concerning the application of α-like measures for CL tasks: using α is going to make it even more difficult to compare the results of different annotation experiments, in that a 'poor' value or a 'high' value might result from 'too strict' or 'too generous' distance metrics, making it even more important to develop a methodology to identify appropriate values for these coefficients. This issue was further emphasized by the study reported next.

3.4.2   DISCOURSE DEIXIS

A second annotation study we carried out (Artstein and Poesio, 2006) shows even more clearly the possible side effects of using weighted coefficients. This study was concerned with the annotation of the antecedents of references to abstract objects, such as the example of the pronoun *that* in utterance 7.6 (TRAINS 1991, dialogue d91-2.2).

```
7.3   : so we ship one
7.4   : boxcar
7.5   : of oranges to Elmira
7.6   : and that takes another 2 hours
```

Previous studies of discourse deixis annotation showed that these are extremely difficult judgments to make (Byron, 2002, Eckert and Strube, 2000, Navarretta, 2000), except perhaps for identifying the type of object (Poesio and Modjeska, 2005), so we simplified the task by only requiring our participants to identify the boundaries of the area of text in which the antecedent was introduced. Even so, we found a great variety in how these boundaries were marked: exactly as in the case of discourse segmentation discussed earlier, our participants broadly agreed on the area of text, but disagreed on its exact boundary. For instance, in the example above, 9 out of 10 annotators marked the antecedent of *that* as a text segment ending with the word *Elmira*, but some started with the word *so*, some started with *we*, some with *ship*, and some with *one*.

We tested a number of ways to measure partial agreement on this task, and obtained widely different results. First of all, we tested three set-based distance metrics inspired by the Passonneau proposals that we just discussed: we considered discourse segments to be sets of words, and computed the distance between them using Passonneau's metric, Jaccard, and Dice. Using these three metrics, we obtained α values of 0.55 (with Passonneau's metric), 0.45 (with Jaccard), and 0.55 (with Dice). We should note that since antecedents of different expressions rarely overlapped, the expected disagreement was close to 1 (maximal), so the value of α turned out to be very close to the complement of the observed disagreement as calculated by the different distance metrics.

Next, we considered methods based on the position of words in the text. The first method computed differences between absolute boundary positions: each antecedent was associated with the position of its first or last word in the dialogue, and agreement was calculated using α with the interval distance metric. This gave us α values of 0.998 for the beginnings of the antecedent-evoking area and 0.999 for the ends. This is because expected disagreement is exceptionally high: coders tend to mark discourse antecedents close to the referring expression, so the average distance between antecedents of the same expression is smaller than the size of the dialogue by a few orders of magnitude. The second method associated each antecedent with the position of its first or last word *relative to the beginning of the anaphoric expression*. This time we found extremely low values of $\alpha = 0.167$ for beginnings of antecedents and 0.122 for ends—barely in the positive side. This shows that agreement among coders is not dramatically better than what would be expected if they just marked discourse antecedents at a fixed distance from the referring expression.

The three ranges of α that we observed—middle, high, and low—show agreement on the identity of discourse antecedents, their position in the dialogue, and their position relative to referring expressions, respectively. The middle range shows variability of up to 10 percentage points depending on the distance metric chosen. The lesson is that once we start using weighted measures we cannot anymore interpret the value of α using traditional rules of thumb such as those proposed by Krippendorff or Landis and Koch. This is because depending on the way we measure agreement, we can report α values ranging from 0.122 to 0.998 for the very same experiment! New interpretation methods have to be developed, which will be task- and distance-metric specific. We'll return to this issue in Section 3.6.

3.4.3   SUMMARIZATION

Evaluating content selection in summarization is a difficult problem (Radev et al., 2003), for which no single 'gold standard' can exist. Even if we only consider the simpler task of comparing summaries obtained by extracting sentences from the original document without any rephrasing, it is extremely unlikely that any two summaries will include exactly the same sentences—indeed, Lin and Hovy (2003) report that human summarizers agree with their own previous summaries in only about 82% of the cases. Current evaluation practice is to compare machine output to a set of reference summaries using word-based metrics such as ROUGE (Lin, 2004), similar to solutions for machine translation and other tasks involving generation. Earlier evaluation metrics for summarization involved identifying the most important 'factoids' contained in reference summaries, and scoring system-produced summaries against these factoids. As one might expect, the coders identifying these common factoids are likely to miss some, just as in the case of anaphoric annotation coders are likely to miss some anaphoric link (Passonneau, 2006). Clearly, a measure taking into account partial agreement such as α is needed to measure the agreement between coders producing such a summary.

Indeed, α has been used to measure agreement between coders producing factoid-like evaluation sets out of reference summaries for the Document Understanding Conference (DUC) competition (Nenkova and Passonneau, 2004, Passonneau, 2006). Nenkova and Passonneau developed the so-called **pyramid** method for evaluating system-produced summaries, which is based on comparing them with a list of hand-annotated and weighted **summarization content units** (SCU), which are the 'minimal propositions' contained in the text. After expert summarizers have produced reference summaries for each document, coders divide these summaries into SCUs: an SCU is a set of text portions—at most one portion from each reference summary—which express the same factoid. The **weight** of an SCU is the number of summaries which express this factoid. Each SCU is also given a mnemonic **label** which reflects the SCU's content in plain language. Table 3.3 gives examples of SCUs produced by two coders, expressing related factoids.

Table 3.3: Summarization content units produced by two annotators (adapted from Passonneau, 2006)

SCU Produced by Coder 1
Label: Americans asked Saudi officials for help
Weight: 4

Source	Span	
Sum1	1	*Saudi Arabian officials, under American pressure*
Sum2	2	*sought help from Saudi officials*
Sum3	3	*Through the Saudis, the United States asked*
Sum4	4	*U.S. and Saudi Arabian requests*

SCU Produced by Coder 2
Label: Through the Saudis, the U.S. tried to get cooperation
             from the Taliban
Weight: 5

Source	Span	
Sum1	1	*Saudi Arabian officials, under American pressure,*
	5	*asked Afghan leaders*
Sum3	2	*sought help from Saudi officials,*
	7	*who tried to convince Taliban leaders*
Sum4	3	*Through the Saudis, the United States asked*
Sum5	4	*U.S. and Saudi Arabian requests*
Sum2	6	*U.S. and Saudi officials then attempted*

The second column in the table is an indexing of spans of words which allows us to conveniently compare the words associated with each SCU. We see that from some summaries the coders chose identical spans for the SCUs in Table 3.3 (spans 3 and 4), from others they chose overlapping but non-identical spans (span 1 by coder 1 and spans 1 and 5 by coder 2), and from some summaries only one coder chose a contributing span for this SCU (span 7 by coder 2). We can think of each SCU as a set of spans: coder 2's SCU is the set $\{1, 2, 3, 4, 5, 6, 7\}$, while coder 1's SCU is the set $\{1, 2, 3, 4\}$ (coder 1 included spans 5 and 7 in a separate SCU, and span 6 in yet another SCU).

SCU identification can now be seen as dividing a text into sets of spans; this is similar to anaphoric annotation, where markables are divided into sets which form coreference chains. To measure the reliability of SCU identification, Nenkova and Passonneau (2004) use Krippendorff's α with the distance metric of Passonneau (2004), while Passonneau (2006) uses the newer MASI distance metric (Section 3.4.1).

3.5   WORD SENSES

Wordsense tagging is one of the hardest annotation tasks. Whereas in the case of part-of-speech and dialogue act tagging the same categories are used to classify all units, in the case of word-sense tagging different categories must be used for each word, which makes writing a single coding manual specifying examples for all categories impossible: the only option is to rely on a dictionary. Unfortunately, different dictionaries make different distinctions, and often coders can't make the fine-grained distinctions that trained lexicographers can make. The problem is particularly serious for verbs, which tend to be polysemous rather than homonymous (Palmer et al., 2007).

These difficulties, and in particular the difficulty of tagging senses with a fine-grained repertoire of senses such as that provided by dictionaries or by WordNet (Fellbaum, 1998), have been highlighted by the first three SENSEVAL initiatives. Already during the first SENSE-VAL, Véronis (1998) carried out two studies of intercoder agreement on wordsense tagging in the so-called ROMANSEVAL task. One study was concerned with agreement on polysemy—that is, the extent to which coders agreed that a word was polysemous in a given context. Six naive coders were asked to make this judgment about 600 French words (200 nouns, 200 verbs, 200 adjectives) using the repertoire of senses in the *Petit Larousse*. On this task, a (pairwise) percentage agreement of 0.68 for nouns, 0.74 for verbs, and 0.78 for adjectives was observed, corresponding to K values of 0.36, 0.37, and 0.67, respectively. The 20 words from each category perceived by the subjects in this first experiment to be most polysemous were then used in a second study, of intercoder agreement on the sense tagging task, which involved six different naive subjects. Interestingly, the coders in this second experiment were allowed to assign multiple tags to words, although they did not make much use of this possibility; so κ_w was used to measure agreement, using the Dice coefficient for overlap between sets (cf. Section 3.4.1). In this experiment, Véronis observed (weighted) pairwise agreement of 0.63 for verbs, 0.71 for adjectives, and 0.73 for nouns, corresponding to κ_w values of 0.41, 0.41, and 0.46, but with wide variety of values when measured per word—ranging from 0.007 for adjective *correct* to 0.92 for noun *détention*. Similarly mediocre results for intercoder agreement between naive coders were reported in the subsequent editions of SENSEVAL. Agreement studies for SENSEVAL-2, where WordNet senses were used as tags, reported a percentage agreement for verb senses of around 70%, whereas for SENSEVAL-3 (English Lexical Sample Task), Mihalcea et al. (2004) report a percentage agreement of 67.3% and average K of 0.58.

Two types of solutions have been proposed for the problem of low agreement on sense tagging. The solution proposed by Kilgarriff (1999) is to use professional lexicographers and arbitration. The study carried out by Kilgarriff does not therefore qualify as a true study of repli-cability in the sense of the terms used by Krippendorff, but it did show that this approach makes

Table 3.4: Group 1 of senses of *call* in Palmer et al. (2007, page 149)

Sense	Description	Example	Hypernym
WN1	name, call	"They named[a] their son David"	LABEL
WN3	call, give a quality	"She called her children lazy and ungrateful"	LABEL
WN19	call, consider	"I would not call her beautiful"	SEE
WN22	address, call	"Call me mister"	ADDRESS

[a]The verb *named* appears in the original WordNet example for the verb *call*.

it possible to achieve percentage agreement of around 95.5%. An alternative approach has been to address the problem of the inability of naive coders to make fine-grained distinctions by introducing coarser-grained classification schemes which group together dictionary senses (Bruce and Wiebe, 1998, Buitelaar, 1998, Palmer et al., 2007, Véronis, 1998). Hierarchical tagsets were also developed, such as HECTOR (Atkins, 1993) or, indeed, WordNet itself (where senses are related by hyponymy links). In the case of Buitelaar (1998) and Palmer et al. (2007), the 'supersenses' were identified by hand, whereas Bruce and Wiebe (1998) and Véronis (1998) used clustering methods such as those from Bruce and Wiebe (1999) to collapse some of the initial sense distinctions. Palmer et al. (2007) illustrate this practice with the example of the verb *call*, which has 28 fine-grained senses in WordNet 1.7: they conflate these senses into a small number of groups using various criteria—for example, four senses can be grouped in a group they call Group 1 on the basis of subcategorization frame similarities (Table 3.4).

For the English Verb Lexical Sense task of SENSEVAL-2, Palmer et al. achieved a percentage agreement among coders of 82% with grouped senses, as opposed to 71% with the original WordNet senses. Bruce and Wiebe (1998) found that collapsing the senses of their test word (*interest*) on the basis of their use by coders and merging the two classes found to be harder to distinguish resulted in an increase of the value of K from 0.874 to 0.898. Using a related technique, Véronis (1998) found that agreement on noun wordsense tagging went up from a K of around 0.45 to a K of 0.86. We should note, however, that the post hoc merging of categories is not equivalent to running a study with fewer categories to begin with; as mentioned above in Section 3.2.1, such merging of categories is generally justified when there is reason to believe that the categories form a multi-level structure requiring separate and distinct decisions by the annotators (Artstein, 2017).[10]

Attempts were also made to develop techniques to measure partial agreement with hierarchical tagsets. A first proposal in this direction was advanced by Melamed and Resnik (2000), who developed a method for computing K with hierarchical tagsets that could be used in SENSEVAL for measuring agreement with tagsets such as HECTOR. Melamed and Resnik pro-

[10]We are not aware of any annotation effort attempting to use a tagset based on Buitelaar's CORELEX, a reconstruction of the WordNet repertoire of noun wordsenses according to Pustejovsky's Generative Lexicon theory (Buitelaar, 1998).

posed to 'normalize' the computation of observed and expected agreement by taking each label which is not a leaf in the tag hierarchy and distributing it down to the leaves in a uniform way, and then only computing agreement on the leaves. For example, with a tagset like the one in Table 3.4, the cases in which the coders used the label 'Group 1' would be uniformly 'distributed down' and added in equal measure to the number of cases in which the coders assigned each of the four WordNet labels. The method proposed in the paper has, however, problematic properties when used to measure intercoder agreement. For example, suppose tag A dominates two sub-tags A1 and A2, and that two coders mark a particular item as A. Intuitively, we would want to consider this a case of perfect agreement, but this is not what the method proposed by Melamed and Resnik yields. The annotators' marks are distributed over the two sub-tags, each with probability 0.5, and then the agreement is computed by summing the joint probabilities over the two subtags (equation 4 of Melamed and Resnik, 2000), with the result that the agreement over the item turns out to be $0.5^2 + 0.5^2 = 0.5$ instead of 1. To correct this, Dan Melamed (personal communication) suggested replacing the product in equation 4 with a minimum operator. However, the calculation of expected agreement (equation 5 of Melamed and Resnik, 2000) still gives the amount of agreement which is expected if coders are forced to choose among leaf nodes, which makes this method inappropriate for coding schemes that do not force coders to do this.

One way to use Melamed and Resnik's proposal while avoiding the discrepancy between observed and expected agreement is to treat the proposal not as a new coefficient, but rather as a distance metric to be plugged into a weighted coefficient like α. Let A and B be two nodes in a hierarchical tagset, let L be the set of all leaf nodes in the tagset, and let $P(l|T)$ be the probability of selecting a leaf node l given an arbitrary node T when the probability mass of T is distributed uniformly to all the nodes dominated by T. We can reinterpret Dan Melamed's modification of equation 4 in Melamed and Resnik (2000) as a metric measuring the distance between nodes A and B.

$$\mathbf{d}_{M+R} = 1 - \sum_{l \in L} \min(P(l|A), P(l|B))$$

This metric has the desirable properties—it is 0 when tags A ad B are identical, 1 when the tags do not overlap, and somewhere inbetween in all other cases. If we use this metric for Krippendorff's α we find that observed agreement is exactly the same as in Melamed and Resnik (2000) with the product operator replaced by minimum (Dan Melamed's modification).

We can also use other distance metrics with α. For example, we could associate with each sense an **extended sense**—a set $\mathbf{es}(s)$ including the sense itself and its grouped sense—and then use set-based distance metrics from Section 3.4.1, for example Passonneau's $\mathbf{d}_P$. To illustrate how this approach could be used to measure (dis)agreement on wordsense annotation, suppose that two coders have to annotate the use of *call* in the following sentence (from the WSJ part of the Penn Treebank, section 02, text w0209):

(4)   This gene, **called** "gametocide", is carried into the plant by a virus that remains active for a few days.

The standard guidelines (in SENSEVAL, say) require coders to assign a WN sense to words. Under such guidelines, if coder A classifies the use of *called* in (4) as an instance of WN1, whereas coder B annotates it as an instance of WN3, we would find total disagreement ($d_{k_a k_b} = 1$) which seems excessively harsh as the two senses are clearly related. However, by using the broader senses proposed by Palmer et al. (2007) in combination with a distance metric such as the one just proposed, it is possible to get more flexible and, we believe, more realistic assessments of the degree of agreement in situations such as this. For instance, in case the reliability study had already been carried out under the standard SENSEVAL guidelines, the distance metric proposed above could be used to identify *post-hoc* cases of partial agreement by adding to each WN sense its hypernyms according to the groupings proposed by Palmer et al. For example, A's annotation could be turned into a new set label {WN1,**LABEL**} and B's mark into the set {WN3,**LABEL**}, which would give in a distance $d = 2/3$, indicating a degree of overlap. The method for computing agreement proposed here could could also be used to allow coders to choose either a more specific label or one of Palmer et al.'s superlabels. For example, suppose A sticks to WN1, but B decides to mark the use above using Palmer et al.'s **LABEL** category, then we would still find a distance $d = 1/3$.

An alternative way of using α for wordsense annotation was developed and tested by Passonneau et al. (2006). The approach of Passonneau et al. is to allow coders to assign multiple labels (WordNet synsets) for wordsenses, as done by Véronis (1998) and more recently by Rosenberg and Binkowski (2004) for text classification labels and by Poesio and Artstein (2005) for anaphora. These multi-label sets can then be compared using the MASI distance metric for α (Passonneau, 2006). The problem with this approach is that in practice, coders very seldom assign more than one label to units (Poesio and Artstein, 2005, Véronis, 1998).

3.6   SUMMARY

We conclude with what in our view are the main points emerging from CL's experience with chance-corrected coefficients of agreement. These points can be grouped under three main headings: methodology, choice of coefficients, and interpretation of coefficients.

3.6.1   METHODOLOGY

One clear result of our survey has already been announced at the beginning of this chapter: still too few studies of the reliability of a coding scheme in CL apply a methodology as rigorous as that envisaged by Krippendorff. All too often, agreement studies are just a race to get a high score. It is true that the methodology adopted for large annotation efforts has greatly improved: one need only compare the central role played by reliability testing in the case of the Penn Discourse Treebank (Miltsakaki et al., 2004) or OntoNotes (Hovy et al., 2006) with the absence of any tests in the case of the Penn Treebank (Marcus et al., 1993) or the British National Corpus (Leech et al., 1994). But even in the case of such large annotation efforts, only percent agreement gets measured. There are a number of reasons for this. One is that annotation efforts tend to be carried out by engineers (which often do not have the time or the inclination for a rigorous test) or by linguists (many of whom believe that trying to get untrained subjects to make linguistic judgments is hopeless). But the difficulty in interpreting the results also plays a role: many researchers do not see the point in carrying out a reliability study if then they can't interpret its results. Still, we find this status of affairs rather unsatisfactory, as in our experience coefficients of agreement, together with the other information discussed below, do provide a better indication of the quality of the resulting annotation than simple percent agreement.

One area in which a motivated difference may be emerging between Content Analysis practice and CL methodology is in the role of experts. The main concern in Content Analysis is to ensure that the results of a given study are reproducible; to guarantee this, one must make sure that the coding on which these results are based can be reliably reproduced by individuals whose only training is provided by the coding scheme. One of the main purposes of reliability testing in CL, on the other hand, is to test schemes used for resource creation—that is, the 'result' will be an annotated corpus, not some scientific claim. Now, most annotation tasks of interest to CL require judgments which are too complex to be drawn by naive coders, so in practice professionals rather than naive coders are employed for serious resource creation efforts whenever financial resources allow. This can be achieved either by using professionals, as advocated by Kilgarriff (1999), or through an intensive training, as done in OntoNotes or the RST Discourse Treebank (Carlson et al., 2003). Of course, even experts disagree with one another; for example, Ratnaparkhi (1996) identifies systematic disagreements between annotators of the Penn Treebank, and Manning (2011) notices gaps in the annotation guidelines; both suggest that these inconsistencies place an artificial ceiling on the performance of part-of-speech taggers trained and tested on this corpus. We therefore consider it important, even when annotators are drawn from a population of experts, to conduct formal reliability tests in order to ensure that the annotations are consistent. This practice may not offer the same cast-iron guarantee as using naive coders who only follow written instructions, and the resulting corpora cannot be used to make claims about spontaneous linguistic judgments. However, in practice the only alternative would be to limit corpus annotation in CL to the kind of "oversimplified or superficial but reliable text analyses" that quite rightly Krippendorff finds to be of as limited usefulness as "fascinating interpretations that nobody can replicate" (Krippendorff, 2004a, pages 213–214).

3.6.2   CHOOSING A COEFFICIENT

Up until the papers by Passonneau (2004) and Di Eugenio and Glass (2004), K was viewed for all intents and purposes as the only available option for measuring reliability. By now, however, a number of alternative options have become available.

As far as we know, the debate between shared-distribution and individual-distribution coefficients (Section 2.5.1) has not featured prominently in the CL literature; it has been limited to the exchange between Di Eugenio and Glass (2004), in favor of Cohen's κ, and Craggs and McGee Wood (2005) (and Krippendorff), in favor of K and α. There is an overwhelming consensus in CL practice: K and α are used in the vast majority of the studies we reported. We agree with the view that K and α are more appropriate, as their interpretation of chance does not include the bias of specific coders. But we also believe that ultimately this issue is of little consequence as the differences between shared- and individual-distribution coefficients get smaller and smaller as the number of annotators grows (Artstein and Poesio, 2005), and we believe that increasing the number of annotators is the best strategy, also to increase the variability of data.

One of the goals of Artstein and Poesio (2008) was to bring to the attention of the CL community the fact that in many cases an argument can be made for using weighted coefficients, and that the choice between weighted and unweighted measures is of great importance. We think there are at least two types of coding schemes in which partial agreement measures may be considered:

- coding schemes with hierarchical tagsets and

- coding schemes with set-valued interpretations (anaphora, summarization).

We discussed various examples of both, and argued that at least in the second case, weighted coefficients are almost unavoidable. The problem is that the results obtained with these measures are not easy to interpret. Our suggestion would therefore be as follows.

- Use clearly disjoint labels and a binary distance function when possible (that is, K).

- Use weighted measures when the task demands it, but then do not expect to be able to interpret the value thus obtained using scales such as those proposed by Krippendorff or Landis and Koch.

3.6.3 INTERPRETING THE VALUES

We perceive the lack of consensus on how to interpret the value of the coefficient of agreement as the most serious problem with current practice in reliability testing, and one of the main reasons for the reluctance of many in CL to embark in reliability studies.

We already said that Krippendorff's position is quite clearly that a value of 0.8 is the absolute minimum for any serious claims to be supported by the data. As far as resource creation is concerned, our own experience is more consistent with Krippendorff and Neuendorf's than with that of Landis and Koch: both in our earlier work (Poesio, 2004a, Poesio and Vieira, 1998) and in the more recent efforts (Poesio and Artstein, 2005) we found that only values above 0.8 ensured an annotation of reasonable quality (Poesio, 2004a).

However, it is doubtful that a single cutoff point is appropriate for all purposes. Even the lower 0.67 level has often proved impossible to achieve in CL research, particularly on discourse, except via substantial training (see, e.g., Hearst, 1997, Poesio and Vieira, 1998); often, substantial agreement among coders results in values of K or α around the 0.7 level replicated across studies. Provided that significance is reached, we feel that this level of agreement may be all that one may hope to achieve for certain types of judgments, and we agree therefore with Craggs and McGee Wood (2005) that insisting that the magic 0.8 threshold be reached is unhealthy; on this, see also Krippendorff's remarks about losing validity to reach reliability. (We especially hope this book won't result in readers viewing weighted coefficients as a particularly nifty trick to raise their K score!)

Unfortunately, weighted coefficients, while arguably more appropriate for many annotation tasks, as we have seen, make the issue of deciding when the value of a coefficient indicate sufficient agreement even more complicated. With weighted measures, the value of the coefficient greatly depends on the distance metric chosen, as we saw at the end of Section 3.4.1.

This being the situation, however, we feel that simply reporting the value of a chance-corrected coefficient of agreement is not informative enough. Given that coefficients such as K or α do not have a clear interpretation, and given also the distorting effects of skewed distributions, simply reporting the value of K is not enough in order to understand what the results actually mean. On this point we agree with Di Eugenio and Glass (2004), but we feel that their solution of reporting two coefficients (or three in case of high prevalence) rather than one is not sufficient. Researchers should clearly report the methodology that was followed to collect the reliability data (number of coders, whether they coded independently, whether they relied exclusively on an annotation manual). The study should also indicate whether agreement was statistically significant, and provide the confusion matrix or agreement table so that readers can find out whether overall figures of agreement hide disagreements on less common categories. For an example of good practice in this respect, see Teufel and Moens (2002).

CHAPTER 4

Probabilistic Models of Agreement

4.1 INTRODUCTION

The chance-corrected coefficients of agreement discussed in Chapters 2 and 3 have been extensively used in NLP, AI, and every other scientific field requiring coders to label data to assess the reliability of an annotation scheme, under the assumption that a sufficiently high level of agreement indicates the coders have developed a similar understanding of the coding instructions and can so produce consistent results. This extensive use has also, however, unveiled a number of issues which subsequent research has attempted to address, as also discussed in Chapter 2. For instance, we saw there that there has been much debate in the literature regarding how to measure agreement beyond chance, and how to interpret the values reported by particular coefficients.

One of the key theoretical advances to emerge from this period of debate is the connection between agreement and the distinction between **easy** and **difficu** items, where easy items are defined by, e.g., Aickin (1990) and Gwet (2014) as those on which we can observe deliberate consensus among coders, whereas difficult items are those whose annotations contain disagreement or where the agreement happens due to chance.[1] As we will see, this distinction lies at the heart of many of the analysis methods discussed in this chapter, and/or of their theoretical formulation; and also plays an important role in many of the probabilistic annotation models discussed in the second part of this book.

One respect in which this distinction has been claimed to affect measures of agreement concerns the selection of the set of annotations used to estimate agreement. While different coefficients of agreement assume different models for chance, all of them end up estimating this quantity from the entire set of annotations. According to these researchers, this raises the issue that the estimate of agreement due to chance is influenced by both deliberate agreement (on easy items) and random agreement (on hard items). A second issue with coefficients of agreement is that one cannot test which model of chance is more appropriate for a set of annotations. This motivated researchers to put forward **probabilistic models of agreement** (1) which can

---

[1]The terms easy and difficult (or hard) items are also used in Beigman Klebanov and Beigman (2009) and Gwet (2014). Other researchers talk about conclusive and inconclusive items (Guggenmoos-Holzmann, 1996), systematic vs. fortuitous agreement (Guggenmoos-Holzmann and Vonk, 1998), or agreement for cause vs. by chance (Aickin, 1990). Other definitions and conceptualizations of 'easy' and 'difficult' have also been proposed—in particular, ones according to which these are not black and white notions, as we will see.

separate between the two aforementioned types of agreement, and (2) whose assumptions can be assessed using fitness tests. To achieve (1), the concept of agreement was redefined in terms of the distinction between easy and difficult items introduced above. In the first part of this chapter we discuss different probabilistic models of agreement designed to measure the reliability of a coding scheme for reproducibility (inter-coder agreement) and coder stability (intra-coder agreement) *after* estimating easy and difficult items, focusing with practical examples on the advances these approaches bring over agreement statistics.

As seen in Chapter 2, the reason for aiming to achieve a reliable scheme is that such a scheme is necessary to collect good quality annotations, i.e., annotations that are not noisy and contain correct judgments. But although reliability is a prerequisite for good quality, several studies have demonstrated it is not sufficient, at least when measured using coefficients of agreement; this is because agreement indices are not entirely dependable indicators of data quality (Passonneau and Carpenter, 2014, Reidsma and Carletta, 2008).[2] Probabilistic models identifying easy and hard items such as those discussed in Section 4.2 of this chapter offer some advantages in this direction, but only limited; in particular it has been shown that training with difficult items can affect the performance of machine learning models when testing on the easy cases (Beigman and Klebanov, 2009, Beigman Klebanov and Beigman, 2009, Klebanov and Beigman, 2014). Knowing the difficulty status of the items can thus help to some extent, but does not address the deeper issue of dealing with the noise in the form of bias often found in annotated data (Bruce and Wiebe, 1998, 1999, Reidsma and op den Akker, 2008, Wiebe et al., 1999). Systematic biases, e.g., annotator biases toward one category, can be picked up by machine learning models and misguide them; this also has a negative effect on their evaluation, inflating performance reports (Reidsma and Carletta, 2008).

One line of research aiming to capture and correct for the bias found in annotated data is work on so called **latent class models of agreement** (Dawid and Skene, 1979, Formann, 1994, Goodman, 1974b, Uebersax et al., 1989, Uebersax, 1988, Uebersax and Grove, 1990). Latent class models of agreement model the observed agreement patterns of the coders as manifestations of some unobserved (latent) classes. In these models the annotators are associated with a coding behaviour that is dependent on the latent class of the items they are presented with. It is this design choice that allows bias to be captured and corrected for at inference time. Conceptually, the latent classes assigned to the items can be thought of as noise-refined adjudicated labels. In the second part of this chapter we discuss a couple of such models, for fixed and varying panels of coders, focusing with practical examples on the interplay between reliability and validity. This will set the scene for the following chapter, focused on annotation adjudication—

---

[2]Another point that cannot be overstated is that coefficients of agreement measure the reliability of a coding scheme, which cannot be equated with its validity (see Section 2.2). A high agreement between coders does not necessarily mean they are capturing the 'truth' of the phenomenon they were asked to annotate; it might simply be that the coders share similar biases and agree on the wrong categories. We can see a particularly clear example of this in the annotation of highly subjective judgments that depend, say, on the coder's aesthetic, political, or religious views: two coders with, say, the same political view may reach perfect agreement, without this meaning that whatever judgments they agree on are 'the truth' (Basile, 2020).

latent class models of agreement being the precursors of what we nowadays call **probabilistic models of annotation**.

4.2   EASY ITEMS, DIFFICULT ITEMS, AND AGREEMENT

"With many judgments that characterize natural language, one would expect that there are clear cases as well as borderline cases that are more difficult to judge" (Wiebe et al., 2005)

We saw in Chapter 2 that chance-corrected coefficients of agreement are based on the idea of discounting agreement due to chance from observed agreement. Let ϕ be one of these agreement indices, and let A_o and A_e be the observed and chance agreement probabilities; we then have:

$$\phi = \frac{A_o - A_e}{1 - A_e}$$

Rearranging the terms in the formula above, we see that observed agreement can in turn be defined as a linear combination of perfect and chance agreement, with weights given by the agreement index:

$$A_o = \phi + (1 - \phi)A_e$$

This reformulation suggests two populations of items in the observed agreements: those on which consensus was reached deliberately—the 'easy' items—and those on which agreement only occurred by chance—the 'difficult' ones. This relationship between agreement and item difficulty is spelled out in the diagram below:

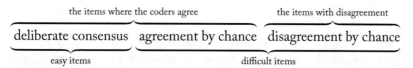

A classic example of easy and difficulty cases is introduced by Grove et al. (1981), and also discussed by Gwet (2014). Diagnosticians in the medical field find the textbook cases easy to solve and generally agree on, while non-textbook cases cause them difficulty and lead to either disagreement or random agreement. The easy vs. difficult dichotomy in this example is based on the distinction between textbook and non-textbook cases. Anybody who has been involved in an annotation project in NLP has observed this very same phenomenon of having clear-cut ('textbook') examples of a particular category as well as complex cases on which annotators disagreed. Under this reformulation, the agreement index ϕ is an indicator of the prevalence of easy items in the corpus.[3]

As seen in Chapter 2, much of the debate and disaccord about coefficients of agreement is centered around the issue of estimating the probability of chance agreement. Scott's π (Scott,

---

[3]Difficulty is a matter of degree, of course. We will discuss models that incorporate a more gradual notion of item difficulty in Chapter 5.

1955) assumes that coders share the same distribution when annotating by chance, while Cohen's κ (Cohen, 1960) assumes separate distributions for each coder. But all coefficients of agreement discussed in Chapter 2 assume that coders' judgments are independent. Furthermore, they estimate chance agreement from the entire set of items to annotate; consequently, this estimate will be based both on random agreement and on deliberate agreement. The position of, e.g., Aickin (1990) and Gwet (2014) is that this approach is likely to overestimate chance agreement. According to these authors, judgments on 'easy' items are not genuinely independent; only judgments on the hard cases are, and thus, only a subset of all items should be used to compute chance agreement. They argue that issues with coefficients of agreement such as the 'prevalence paradox' discussed in Chapter 2 can only be overcome, therefore, by adopting probabilistic models of agreement that estimate which items in a corpus are easy and difficult through probabilistic inference, and then measuring chance agreement using these estimates of the hard items. They also argue that these methods offer additional benefits, such as the tools to assess whether a model is suitable for a particular dataset.

In the rest of this section we present two key probabilistic agreement models: Aickin's α (Aickin, 1990), proposed as a method for measuring inter-coder agreement—which can therefore be used as a test for reproduciblity—and the model proposed by Guggenmoos-Holzmann (1996) for assessing intra-coder agreement—appropriate for measuring stability. In both cases we illustrate with practical examples how these estimates relate to those offered by a standard coefficient of agreement like those discussed in Chapter 2. We also discuss variants of these models, and in particular Gwet's AC_1 model (Gwet, 2008), widely adopted in the medical and social science literature and in some NLP research.

4.2.1   AICKIN'S α

Th Model   The approach proposed in Aickin (1990) to specify his measure α of agreement above chance would, on the surface, appear to be radically different from the approach followed to define the coefficients of agreement discussed in Chapter 2:

> The α parameter is defined as the fraction of the entire subject population made up of subjects that the two raters A and B classified identically for cause, rather than by chance (Aickin, 1990, p. 294)

This definition is based on the assumption that the set of N items to annotate consists of two subpopulations: the set E of easy-to-annotate items, and the set H of hard-to-annotate items. The distribution of items into easy and hard underlying Aickin's theory, and the notion of agreement, is illustrated for the case of two coders a and b, and two categories 1 and 2 in Table 4.1, borrowed from Gwet (2014, p. 109).

In the table, N_H and N_E are the number of hard and easy items, respectively. By definition, there is no disagreement on easy items, hence there is perfect agreement on their classification. Also by definition, the same items are considered to be easy by both a and b, so there are no items classified as hard by a and easy by b, or vice versa. However, in the case of hard items, there

Table 4.1: Distribution of hard and easy items in Aickin's model

Coder a		Coder b					
		Hard Items		Easy Items		Total	
		1	2	1	2		
Hard Items	1	N_{11}^H	N_{12}^H			N_{1+}^H	N_H
	2	N_{21}^H	N_{22}^H			N_{2+}^H	
Easy Items	1			N_1^E	0	N_1^E	N_E
	2			0	N_2^E	N_2^E	
Total		N_{+1}^H	N_{+2}^H	N_1^E	N_2^E	N	
		N_H		N_E			

can be both disagreement and agreement by chance—hence, for instance, N_{11}^H is the number of hard items of which a and b agree by chance on category 1.

Aickin's α is then defined as:

$$\alpha = \frac{N_E}{N}, N_E = N_1^E + N_2^E$$

where N_E is the total number of easy items. The (obvious) problem is that a direct calculation of α is not possible, because N_E is not known. Hence, Aickin specified a probabilistic model for estimating such quantities, one of whose parameters is α.

Aickin (1990) formulated his model for two coders and K categories. Each of the two coders—let us refer to them again as coder a and coder b—has their own annotation probability over the categories, parameterized by π; for example, annotator a produces annotation k with probability $\pi_{a,k}$. The observed agreement of the two coders on an item is specified by the following function:

$$d(k, k') = \begin{cases} 1 & \text{if } k \text{ and } k' \text{ are considered to be in agreement} \\ 0 & \text{otherwise} \end{cases}$$

Probability distributions used in this chapter

Bernoulli: the probability distribution of an event with two outcomes, e.g., positive or negative.
Binomial: the probability distribution for the number of successes (e.g., the number of positive outcomes) in a sequence of independent Bernoulli distributed events.
Categorical: the generalization of Bernoulli to categorical variables.

- -

More about these distributions in Kruschke (2015) and Bishop (2016).

The agreement function allows having an agreement not only between identical annotations but also between other category pairs. The items are assumed to be of two types, easy and difficult, and we shall encode this information with the help of a binary indicator; let l_i be this indicator with positive value suggesting that item i is easy. As previously discussed, an item where the coders disagree is automatically assumed to be difficult, thus $l_i = 0$. On the other hand, the items with annotations in agreement have their difficulty status determined based on the prevalence α of the easy items in the corpus:

$$l_i \sim \text{Bernoulli}(\alpha)$$

If an item is deemed difficult, i.e., $l_i = 0$, the two annotations, $y_{i,a}, y_{i,b} \in \{1, 2, \ldots, K\}$, are assumed to be generated independently by the coders:

$$p(y_{i,a}, y_{i,b} | l_i = 0) = \pi_{a,y_{i,a}} \pi_{b,y_{i,b}}$$

In case the item is considered easy, however (i.e., $l_i = 1$), the annotations—which again, can only be matching categories, else the item would be considered difficult—have a joint probability equal to the likelihood of the coders producing the respective agreement pair relative to all other agreement pairs:

$$p(y_{i,a}, y_{i,b} | l_i = 1) = \frac{\pi_{a,y_{i,a}} \pi_{b,y_{i,b}}}{\sum_{k,k'} d(k, k') \pi_{a,k} \pi_{b,k'}}$$

Summing over the difficulty status of an item, the joint probability of the annotations produced by the two coders is as follows[4]:

$$\begin{aligned}
p(y_{i,a}, y_{i,b}) &= p(y_{i,a}, y_{i,b}, l_i = 0 | \alpha) + p(y_{i,a}, y_{i,b}, l_i = 1 | \alpha) \\
&= p(l_i = 0 | \alpha) \times p(y_{i,a}, y_{i,b} | l_i = 0) + p(l_i = 1 | \alpha) \times p(y_{i,a}, y_{i,b} | l_i = 1) \\
&= (1 - \alpha) \times \pi_{a,y_{i,a}} \pi_{b,y_{i,b}} + \alpha \times d(y_{i,a}, y_{i,b}) \times \frac{\pi_{a,y_{i,a}} \pi_{b,y_{i,b}}}{\sum_{k,k'} d(k, k') \pi_{a,k} \pi_{b,k'}}
\end{aligned}$$

The joint probability above was expressed for the annotations of a particular item, but it is the same for any two annotations produced by the coders. Dropping the item indices, we have:

$$p(y_a, y_b) = (1 - \alpha) \times p(y_a, y_b | l = 0) + \alpha \times p(y_a, y_b | l = 1)$$

It follows that under the model of Aickin (1990) the agreement between the coders has the following likelihood[5]:

---

[4]An extension of the model to three or more coders, intuitively, would simply require increasing the per-coder parameters to model for each of them their annotation probability.

[5]To simplify the presentation we assumed $d(k, k') = 1$ when $k = k'$ and 0 otherwise.

$$A_o = \sum_k p(y_a = k, y_b = k)$$

$$= \alpha + (1 - \alpha) \times \sum_k p(y_a = k, y_b = k | l = 0)$$

$$= \alpha + (1 - \alpha) \sum_k \pi_{a,k} \pi_{b,k}$$

$$= \alpha + (1 - \alpha) A_e, \text{ where } A_e = \sum_k \pi_{a,k} \pi_{b,k}$$

The result above relates back to the decomposition of the observed agreement we expressed before for chance-corrected coefficients of agreement. Rearranging the terms, we get the more familiar expression describing an agreement index:

$$\alpha = \frac{A_o - A_e}{1 - A_e}, \text{ where } A_e = \sum_k \pi_{a,k} \pi_{b,k}$$

This equation shows that Aickin's definition of agreement as the amount of deliberate agreement in the corpus—the prevalence of easy items—has in fact a form closely related to that of the coefficients of agreement discussed earlier. But unlike with κ and other coefficients of agreement, where agreement due to chance is computed using all the annotations, both deliberate and random, with α the agreement due to chance ultimately is based only on the portion of annotations considered random by the model (those from the hard items, where the two coders annotate independently).

Aickin (1990) proposed to estimate the parameters of his model using maximum likelihood estimation. Normally, we leave out the inference details, but this being the first probabilistic model in the book, we felt it would help build a stronger intuition of what the model actually learns. Following Aickin's original algorithm, the following equations are iterated through until convergence:

$$\alpha^{(t+1)} = \frac{A_o - A_e^{(t)}}{1 - A_e^{(t)}}, \text{ where } A_e^{(t)} = \sum_k \pi_{a,k}^{(t)} \pi_{b,k}^{(t)}$$

$$\pi_{a,k}^{(t+1)} = \frac{n_{a,k}/I}{1 - \alpha^{(t)} + \alpha^{(t)} \pi_{b,k}^{(t)}/A_e^{(t)}}, \forall k \in \{1, 2, \dots, K\}$$

$$\pi_{b,k}^{(t+1)} = \frac{n_{b,k}/I}{1 - \alpha^{(t)} + \alpha^{(t)} \pi_{a,k}^{(t)}/A_e^{(t)}}, \forall k \in \{1, 2, \dots, K\}$$

At the initial stage ($t = 0$), the annotation probability of the coders are initialized to the coder distributions used in Cohen's κ, i.e., $\pi_{a,k}^{(0)} = n_{a,k}/I$, and $\pi_{b,k}^{(t)} = n_{b,k}/I$, where $n_{a,k}$ is the number of items annotated by coder a with category k, and I is the total number of items. In this case, the initial estimate for Aickin's α is identical to Cohen's κ, i.e, $\alpha^{(1)} = \kappa$. Note, however, how the estimates for α (and for π_a, and π_b, used to compute chance agreement) continue to get refined.

A nice consequence of the way Aickin's α is formulated, also noted by Gwet (2014), is that it avoids the so-called paradox associated with Cohen's κ (Cohen, 1960) when low agreement values are reported even though the coders show high agreement (refer back to Section 2.5.2 for a discussion of this paradox). The paradox happens when the data is unbalanced leading to a high chance agreement in Cohen's κ. In Aickin's α the chance agreement will not be affected by the data being unbalanced because this gets computed following the annotation behaviour of the coders on the hard items only.

Using Aickin's α   We just discussed that although κ is not an estimator of α, the two concepts are theoretically related. Their relation is concretely illustrated by a simulation from Aickin (1990) which aims to show how his α estimate of agreement beyond chance relates to κ (Cohen, 1960) in various settings. For a range of α values and coder marginals (assumed for this simulation to be the same for both coders, i.e., $\pi_a = \pi_b$), data samples of different sizes are being generated and then used to recover α (using maximum likelihood) and to compute κ. The results are illustrated in Figure 4.1. The simulations show that under uniform coder marginals (and sufficient sample size) Cohen's κ provides similar agreement estimates to Aickin's α; when the coder distributions are more heterogeneous, however, the former deviates substantially from the latter.

Aickin also provides an example of application of his model to a real dataset and discusses the conclusions that can be drawn from this example for agreement among coders. This example also illustrates another useful advantage probabilistic models of agreement have: unlike agreement statistics, they offer us the means, i.e., using fitness tests, to assess whether a model's assumptions are appropriate for a dataset. (For a brief intro to the notion of fitness tests refer back to Section 1.2). Table 4.2 summarizes data about the occupational status of people diagnosed with cancer (Brownson et al., 1989). The classifications were first extracted from a registry (the rows) and then redone through a telephone interview (the columns). For this data the author chose only the cells from the main diagonal to be in agreement. The result of a chi-squared test showed the model did not fit well the data. The largest residuals were related to cells 5 and 6, so the author collapsed the two into a single category which then lead to an adequate fit. The estimated prevalence of the easy items was $\alpha = 0.868$. Based on the behaviour of κ w.r.t. α observed in the simulation presented above, given the estimated coder marginals for these annotations are heterogeneous, we can assume κ would have offered a biased estimate of agreement beyond chance if it was used instead.

Margins	α	Sample Size					
		20		60		100	
		ML α	Kappa	ML α	Kappa	ML α	Kappa
$\frac{1}{2}, \frac{1}{2}$	.3	−.010	−.026	.002	−.005	−.001	−.005
	.5	−.013	−.041	−.002	−.011	.002	−.004
	.7	−.023	−.052	−.006	−.017	−.001	−.007
	.8	−.021	−.048	−.007	−.017	−.003	−.009
$\frac{1}{3}, \frac{2}{3}$	.3	−.043	−.070	−.012	−.060	−.009	−.057
	.5	−.032	−.102	−.001	−.075	−.008	−.080
	.7	−.032	−.124	−.002	−.078	−.004	−.077
	.8	−.038	−.127	−.001	−.068	−.004	−.066
$\frac{1}{4}, \frac{3}{4}$	.3	−.081	−.108	−.020	−.101	−.023	−.112
	.5	−.080	−.182	−.011	−.152	−.010	−.155
	.7	−.055	−.214	−.016	−.180	−.011	−.170
	.8	−.049	−.217	−.006	−.152	−.008	−.154
$\frac{1}{3}, \frac{1}{3}, \frac{1}{3}$	.3	−.010	−.030	−.004	−.010	.000	−.004
	.5	−.013	−.038	−.001	−.011	−.003	−.008
	.7	−.021	−.048	−.006	−.017	−.003	−.009
	.8	−.026	−.050	−.006	−.015	−.001	−.007
$\frac{1}{4}, \frac{1}{4}, \frac{1}{2}$	.3	−.010	−.051	−.006	−.041	−.001	−.037
	.5	−.002	−.067	−.004	−.056	.005	−.046
	.7	−.023	−.094	−.009	−.064	−.002	−.051
	.8	−.024	−.091	−.008	−.055	−.004	−.046
$\frac{1}{5}, \frac{1}{5}, \frac{3}{5}$	.3	−.004	−.046	−.012	−.090	−.005	−.085
	.5	−.022	−.138	−.009	−.127	.001	−.116
	.7	−.029	−.165	−.007	−.134	−.007	−.130
	.8	−.034	−.166	−.006	−.120	−.008	−.119
$\frac{1}{5}, \frac{2}{5}, \frac{2}{5}$	.3	−.004	−.032	.000	−.019	−.001	−.017
	.5	−.007	−.048	−.004	−.030	−.002	−.024
	.7	−.016	−.060	−.006	−.031	−.002	−.023
	.8	−.024	−.062	−.009	−.031	−.002	−.020
$\frac{1}{4}, \frac{1}{4}, \frac{1}{4}, \frac{1}{4}$	.3	−.008	−.026	.000	−.007	−.001	−.006
	.5	−.007	−.033	−.002	−.011	.000	−.006
	.7	−.017	−.043	−.005	−.015	−.004	−.010
	.8	−.020	−.043	−.004	−.013	−.002	−.008

Figure 4.1: Simulation results (Aickin, 1990) that show how well a maximum likelihood estimator recovers a range of α values from data samples of various sizes and some predefined coder marginals. This is compared with κ (Cohen, 1960). (*Continues.*)

Margins	α	Sample Size					
		20		**60**		**100**	
		ML α	Kappa	ML α	Kappa	ML α	Kappa
$\frac{1}{5}, \frac{1}{5}, \frac{1}{5}, \frac{2}{5}$	.3	−.005	−.041	.000	−.029	.000	−.027
	.5	−.017	−.071	−.004	−.045	−.003	−.040
	.7	−.014	−.071	−.006	−.047	−.004	−.041
	.8	−.026	−.079	−.009	−.045	−.003	−.035
$\frac{1}{6}, \frac{1}{6}, \frac{1}{6}, \frac{1}{2}$	.3	−.018	−.080	.001	−.065	−.006	−.072
	.5	−.024	−.125	−.005	−.103	−.003	−.098
	.7	−.022	−.138	−.006	−.109	−.002	−.101
	.8	−.032	−.147	−.002	−.092	−.006	−.094
$\frac{1}{6}, \frac{1}{6}, \frac{1}{3}, \frac{1}{3}$	.3	−.004	−.034	−.003	−.023	.000	−.018
	.5	−.010	−.052	−.005	−.033	−.002	−.026
	.7	−.015	−.057	−.008	−.036	−.003	−.026
	.8	−.023	−.063	−.006	−.031	−.002	−.022

Figure 4.2: (*Continued.*) Simulation results (Aickin, 1990) that show how well a maximum likelihood estimator recovers a range of α values from data samples of various sizes and some predefined coder marginals. This is compared with κ (Cohen, 1960).

Table 4.2: Top: the occupational status of people diagnosed with cancer as extracted from a registry (the rows) and as classified through a telephone interview (the columns). Bottom: parameter estimates from the Aickin (1990) model.

Registry Class	Interview Class						
	1	2	3	4	5	6	7
1. Managerial/professional	60	5	1	0	3	1	0
2. Technical/sales/administrative support	2	67	0	1	1	2	0
3. Service occupations	7	2	67	1	3	6	0
4. Farming/forestry/fishing	0	0	0	27	1	1	0
5. Precision production/craft/repair	2	1	0	0	64	7	0
6. Operators/fabricators/laborers	0	2	2	1	5	82	0
7. Armed forces	1	0	0	0	0	2	13
Estimated registry distribution	.15	.14	.35	.09	.18		.10
Estimated interview distribution	.18	.20	.08	.11	.38		.05
Estimated prevalence of easy cases	.87						

Among all of these available probabilistic models of agreement we decided to present in more detail the model of Aickin (1990) as historically it was the first model of this type. But despite its advantages, Aickin's α has found relatively limited application, especially in NLP, possibly because of the much more limited practical experience with interpreting its results in comparison with other statistics (Hsu and Field, 2003).

Gwet's AC_1 The model proposed by Aickin (1990) is not the only model leveraging the distinction between easy and difficult items to better capture agreement beyond chance among coders. Possibly the best known model of this type is the AC_1 coefficient proposed by Gwet (2008). There are two main conceptual differences between the α and the AC_1 coefficients.[6] The first difference is that whereas in the case of the model proposed by Aickin (1990) the sets of easy and hard items are assumed to be the same for all coders, in AC_1 (Gwet, 2008) the easy and the hard items can differ from coder to coder. The second difference regards the pool of items used to specify the items with deliberate agreement when reporting agreement beyond chance. In Aickin's α, agreement beyond chance is specified as the prevalence of the easy items, defined as the percentage of items having deliberate agreement out of the *entire* item population. Gwet's AC_1 index also measures the agreement beyond chance using the items with deliberate agreement, but this value is only computed relative to those items that do not involve random agreement. This means that the model of Aickin (1990) reports perfect agreement beyond chance only if there are no hard items in the corpus. That is not the case for AC_1, which is 1 if there is perfect agreement between the coders, be that on easy or hard items. Gwet's model only report imperfect agreement scores if there are disagreements.

Gwet's AC_1 has become almost as widely used as κ, at least in the medical and social science literature, and is now beginning to be used in NLP (Jwalapuram et al., 2019) but not much practical experience has yet accumulated regarding how to interpret its results. We would certainly encourage NLP researchers obtaining unclear results with κ to experiment with the statistic so as such the field can acquire such practical experience.

Other Models: Beigman Klebanov and Beigman, Guggenmoos Other proposals aiming at the identification of easy and hard items to analyse agreement have been made in Guggenmoos-Holzmann and Vonk (1998) and Beigman Klebanov and Beigman (2009).

4.2.2 MODELLING STABILITY

An assessment of stability is a test for the reliability of a coding scheme that involves measuring the degree to which coders agree with themselves over a period of time. In this section we discuss another well-known agreement model based on a classification of items into easy/difficult, the model for stability of Guggenmoos-Holzmann (1996).

---

[6]It is unclear how well Gwet's model captures these assumptions considering that to compute the index he introduces a heuristic approximation, but we discuss them nevertheless.

As in the models seen above, the Guggenmoos-Holzmann model encodes the difficulty status of items with a binary indicator for each item. Let l_i be this indicator, for $i \in \{1, 2, \ldots, I\}$, with positive value indicating that item i is easy. As in Aickin's and Gwet's models, the items whose annotations are in disagreement are considered difficult *a priori*, and have $l_i = 0$; only those items with annotations that show consensus can be either easy or difficult, with probability modeled by κ, the prevalence of the easy items in the corpus:

$$l_i \sim \mathsf{Bernoulli}(\kappa)$$

(See diagram in the previous section.) Let us consider next the probability of the annotations. For difficult items, $l_i = 0$, the probabilities of the labels are binomially distributed: if w is the probability of a positive rating on a difficult item and there are m out of n such positive ratings, then we have:

$$p(y_{i,1:n}|l_i = 0) = \binom{n}{m} w^m (1 - w)^{n-m}$$

If an item is easy, i.e., $l_i = 1$, the probabilities of the labels $y_{i,1:n}$ are determined by whether agreement is in the positive or in the negative class. Let ν be the probability of an easy item receiving positive annotations only, and again let m be their number; then we have:

$$p(y_{i,1:n}|l_i = 1) = \begin{cases} \nu & \text{if } m = n \\ 1 - \nu & \text{if } m = 0 \end{cases}$$

Marginalizing over the difficulty status indicators, an item i with n annotations out of which m are positive has the following probability:

$$p(y_{i,1:n}|\kappa) = \begin{cases} \kappa \nu^{I(m=n)}(1 - \nu)^{I(m=0)} + (1 - \kappa)w^m(1 - w)^{n-m} & \text{if } m \in \{0, n\} \\ (1 - \kappa)\binom{n}{m}w^m(1 - w)^{n-m} & \text{otherwise} \end{cases}$$

In a later paper, Guggenmoos-Holzmann and Vonk (1998) discuss how to model coder stability when the data has been annotated twice and with labels coming from K categories. In this case we have ν_k model the probability of consensus on category k when the item is easy, and w_k the likelihood of a category k annotation on a difficult item. It follows then, that for some item i, its two annotations $y_{i,1}, y_{i,2}$ have the following probability:

$$p(y_{i,1}, y_{i,2}|\kappa) = \begin{cases} \kappa \nu_k + (1 - \kappa)w_k^2 & \text{if } y_{i,1} = y_{i,2} = k, \forall k \in \{1, 2, .., K\} \\ (1 - \kappa)w_{y_{i,1}} w_{y_{i,2}} & \text{otherwise} \end{cases}$$

4.2.3   CODER STABILITY: A DISCUSSION

The discussion in this section, based on notes from Guggenmoos-Holzmann (1996) and Guggenmoos-Holzmann and Vonk (1998), has the objective to provide further intuition about the relationship between the just introduced model by Guggenmoos-Holzmann (1996), the model proposed by Aickin (1990), and the κ coefficient of agreement proposed by Cohen (1960).

Equivalence Under Certain Conditions   In the discussion we show, first of all, that under certain parameter constraints, the model of Guggenmoos-Holzmann (1996) is equivalent to the models of Aickin (1990) and Cohen (1960). This is seen most easily when the stability of a coder is assessed on data items annotated twice with binary labels. Such data can be summarized using a 2×2 agreement table. We remind the reader that under the model of Guggenmoos-Holzmann (1996), the likelihood of the agreement patterns found in such a table takes the following form:

likelihoods   easy annotation   difficult annotation

$p(1,1)$	$p(1,0)$		ν			w^2	$w(1-w)$
----------	----------	=	-------	-------		-------	----------
$p(0,1)$	$p(0,0)$	$\kappa\times$		$1-\nu$	$+(1-\kappa)\times$	$(1-w)w$	$(1-w)^2$

The model of Aickin (1990) can be used to assess stability on dichotomous data by employing a single parameter π to stand for the coder's probability to produce a positive rating. The likelihood of the agreement patterns found in a 2×2 agreement table thus becomes:

likelihoods   easy annotation   difficult annotation

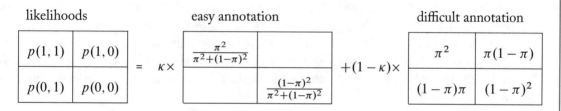

$p(1,1)$	$p(1,0)$		$\frac{\pi^2}{\pi^2+(1-\pi)^2}$			π^2	$\pi(1-\pi)$
----------	----------	=	-------	-------		-------	----------
$p(0,1)$	$p(0,0)$	$\kappa\times$		$\frac{(1-\pi)^2}{\pi^2+(1-\pi)^2}$	$+(1-\kappa)\times$	$(1-\pi)\pi$	$(1-\pi)^2$

A simple visual inspection of the likelihood of the agreement patterns under the two models indicates that the former (Guggenmoos-Holzmann, 1996) is equivalent to the latter (Aickin, 1990) when the following constraint is imposed to its parameters:

$$\nu = \frac{w^2}{w^2 + (1-w)^2}$$

A consequence of this constraint is that the odds of agreement on easy items $\frac{\nu}{1-\nu}$ are now the same as the odds of agreement on difficult items $\frac{w^2}{(1-w)^2}$. Another observation is that when the marginals of the agreement table are equal (but not necessarily uniform)—i.e., when $p(1,1) + p(1,0) = p(1,1) + p(0,1)$—the model of Guggenmoos-Holzmann (1996) becomes equivalent to the index of Cohen (1960) by constraining ν, the positive agreement probability on easy items, to be the same as w, the probability of a positive rating on difficult items:

$$\nu = w$$

The equivalence holds true w.r.t. the index of Scott (1955) as well. That is because, as seen back in Chapter 2 (Section 2.2.4), with equal coder marginals, the agreement statistics

Table 4.3: The distribution of a pathologist's ratings for the presence of prostate cancer after three rounds of annotation

Number of Positive Ratings	Number of Patients
3	29
2	2
1	9
0	30
Total	70

of Cohen (1960) and Scott (1955) give the same estimate. Finally, if the collected data indicates not only equal but also uniform marginals, then the equivalence extends to also include the statistic of Bennett et al. (1954).

An Example   We end this discussion with a practical example of application of Guggenmoos-Holzmann's model. The example is from Guggenmoos-Holzmann and Vonk (1998), and uses data collected from a pathologist asked to rate 3 times in random order 70 patients for the presence of cancer based on ultrasound prostate biopsies. The data is summarized in Table 4.3 and was used to fit two versions of the Guggenmoos-Holzmann's model: the model as it is, and a constrained version which makes it equivalent to (the multi-rater version of) the κ index of Cohen (1960).

Table 4.4 presents the estimates of the parameters. Notably, there is a 14 percentage points difference between the prevalence of the easy items as estimated by the full model and as estimated by the constrained version. A chi-squared test indicates the full model fits the data perfectly whereas for the constrained version it indicates a lack of fit. The fitness test demonstrates that for this particular dataset the index of Cohen (1960) provides a biased estimate of agreement beyond chance. We want to highlight here that without the theory that comes with probabilistic models we would not have been able to draw such a conclusion, the agreement statistics on their own providing no such diagnostic to judge their bias.

4.3   LATENT CLASS ANALYSIS OF AGREEMENT PATTERNS

The **latent class analysis** family of probabilistic methods for agreement analysis were developed to address two further issues emerging out of the experience with coefficients of agreement: **bias** and **interpretability**.

Bias   As often mentioned in this and previous chapters, agreement among coders (reliability) does not necessarily suggest that the coders are capturing the 'truth' about the specific phe-

Table 4.4: Parameter estimates for the full and a constrained version of the Guggenmoos-Holzmann (1996) model of coder stability. *The constraint makes the model equivalent to the multi-rater index of Cohen (1960).

Parameter	Guggenmoos-Holzmann (1996)	Constrained* Model ($v = w$)
κ	0.65	0.79
v	0.64	0.45
w	0.18	$= v$

nomenon under analysis (validity)—in fact, the notion of validity is explicitly rejected by many proponents of methods for measuring agreement, in particular those coming from content analysis and the social sciences (see, e.g., the discussion in Chapter 11 of Krippendorff (2004a)). (The situation is different from statisticians applying their methods to medical diagnosis, such as Uebersax and other researchers whose proposals we discuss in this chapter.)

One circumstance in which reliability clearly has no bearing on validity is the situation of similarly biased coders agreeing on the wrong labels. The presence of bias in annotated data is widespread and well-documented, especially in this era of crowdsourcing (Bruce and Wiebe, 1998, 1999, Hovy et al., 2013, Moreno et al., 2015, Passonneau and Carpenter, 2014, Paun et al., 2018a, Reidsma and op den Akker, 2008, Simpson et al., 2011, 2013, Venanzi et al., 2014). The issue is that the patterns caused by coder biases can be picked up by a classifier and misguide its judgments. The problem raised by bias for NLP practice was highlighted by Reidsma and Carletta (2008). Reidsma and Carletta investigate the effect of the noise which is inherently present in annotated data on the performance of a machine learning classifier. They consider two types of noise. **Random noise** is the source of disagreement caused by, e.g., attention slips (Klebanov et al., 2008). Although Reidsma and Carletta's results initially indicate the performance of the classifier increases with the reliability scores of the corpus, when the evaluation is performed on a dataset free of noise the performance is found to be more or less constant, irrespective of the reliability of the training set. In addition, Reidsma and Carletta also looked at the effect of noise produced by systematic biases, such as coders overusing one category. Reidsma and Carletta (2008) found that an evaluation on biased datasets, even on ones with higher reliability scores, does lead to an over-estimation of the performance of the classifier when checked against an unbiased ground truth.

Interpretability   A more fundamental limitation of agreement statistics discussed in previous chapters is that they only provide an overall measurement of reliability, a headline, summarizing into a single term all the information on agreement, with no indication about the quality of the individual labels. This information about the quality of the labels is critical for establishing whether or not a corpus is suitable, say, for training and testing models.

Latent Class Models of Agreement   One line of work that addresses these issues of bias and interpretability is latent class models of agreement (Dawid and Skene, 1979, Formann, 1994, Goodman, 1974b, Uebersax et al., 1989, Uebersax, 1988, Uebersax and Grove, 1990). These probabilistic approaches relate the observed agreement patterns of the coders to a set of un-observed (latent) classes. The annotation behavior of the coders is modeled w.r.t. these latent classes, a design choice which allows bias to be captured and corrected for at inference time when each instance is assigned with a latent class that best explains the collected judgments. These latent classes can conceptually be thought of as noise-refined adjudicated labels and come with a confidence score, straightaway addressing the interpretability limitation of agreement statistics. Equally important, they allow us to separate between the agreement of the coders on the correct judgments and their agreement in error, information that is conflated in agreement statistics.

Latent class models of agreement are the precursors of modern **probabilistic models of annotation** which are treated separately in the following chapter.[7] For this reason, this section only covers two classic models from the field; one designed for a *varying panel of coders* which assumes the coders share the same annotation behavior, and another formulated for a *fixed panel* which associates each coder with a separate behavior to model their individual accuracy and biases. To simplify presentation, the models assume dichotomous ratings and a constant number of annotations across all items. These constraints are relaxed in the following chapter. The section concludes with an NLP case study that shows how a latent agreement model can be used in an NLP annotation project.

4.3.1   VARYING PANEL OF CODERS

Th Model   A latent class model of agreement designed for a varying panel of coders (Uebersax et al., 1989) is an appropriate choice when the provenance of the annotations is unknown or when the items were annotated by different sets of coders such that the number of annotations done by each of them is too small to get a sense of their individual annotation behaviour. For this reason, the signature assumption of this model is to consider the annotations the result of a pooled (collective) coder behaviour. In Table 4.5 we have a dataset summarized by the agreement patterns produced by a varying panel of physicians: almost 15,000 radiographic films were rated 8 times each as either indicative of tuberculosis (coded as 1) or not (coded as 0). We shall kick-

---

[7]A characteristic of latent agreement models that distinguishes them from today's models of annotation is that the latent classes do not necessarily correspond to the class space of the annotations. This distinction is important as it highlights how people think about these models. In agreement models each item is assigned with the latent class that best explains the agreement pattern produced by the coders; thus, across the items, there may be the need for two or more latent classes to best accommodate all the agreement patterns found in the annotations. This was commonly encountered, e.g., in the medical field, where the annotations would be binary, like a positive or a negative diagnostic, and the latent classes would correspond to the status of the patients, which does not necessarily need to be binary, e.g., they could be interpreted as subtypes of a disorder, or as different symptomatic levels like 'not symptomatic', 'moderately symptomatic', and 'highly symptomatic'. In the field of models of annotation however the annotations received for an item are perceived as noisy labels of its true label; consequently, this implies a bijective relationship between the latent classes and the class space of the annotations.

Table 4.5: A summary of the data collected from a varying panel of physicians asked to rate radiographic films as indicative or not of tuberculosis (Uebersax et al., 1989)

Number of Positive Ratings	Observed Frequency
0	13,560
1	877
2	168
3	66
4	42
5	28
6	23
7	39
8	64
Total	14,867

start this section with the generative process assumed by a varying panel model for a dataset such as this.

The model assumes each item, a radiographic film in our dataset example, belongs to a latent class. The interpretation of the latent classes is done a posteriori to the estimation of the parameters and depends on their values (unless you use informative priors). For example, you may find the coders annotate items assigned to a particular latent class with positive annotations only. You can then interpret this class as positive for tuberculosis (see the discussion from 4.3.1 for a complete example). Now back to the generative process. Let I be the number of items, K be the number of latent classes, and π_k the probability of an item $i \in \{1, 2, \ldots, I\}$ being assigned some class $k \in \{1, 2, \ldots, K\}$ (the prevalence of this class in the corpus); this information is stored in a latent class indicator z_i:

$$p(z_i = k | \pi) = \pi_k$$

The coders are assumed to annotate based on a pooled behavior that depends on the class of the items they are presented with. (This assumption allows to capture their collective accuracy and biases.) Formally, the probability of any coder producing annotation $y_{i,n}$ for an item i with latent class z_i follows a Bernoulli distribution with parameter θ_{z_i}:

$$p(y_{i,n} | \theta, z_i) = \theta_{z_i}^{y_{i,n}} (1 - \theta_{z_i})^{1 - y_{i,n}}$$

Consequently, the set of annotations collected for an item, $y_{i,1:N}$, where N_i of them are positive, follows a Binomial distribution:

$$p(y_{i,1:N}|\theta, z_i) = \binom{N}{N_i} \theta_{z_i}^{N_i} (1 - \theta_{z_i})^{N-N_i}$$

Summing over the latent classes we get the probability of an item receiving a certain agreement pattern from a varying panel of coders. More generally, let x be a random variable representing the number of positive ratings in an agreement pattern; the probability of this pattern containing m positive ratings is:

$$p(x = m) = \binom{N}{m} \sum_{k=1}^{K} \pi_k \theta_k^m (1 - \theta_k)^{N-m}$$

We can also compute the probability of an item belonging to some latent class k when annotated with an agreement pattern which has m positive ratings:

$$p(z = k|x = m) = \frac{\pi_k \theta_k^m (1 - \theta_k)^{N-m}}{\sum_{h=1}^{K} \pi_h \theta_h^m (1 - \theta_h)^{N-m}}$$

As mentioned before, after the inference procedure, the parameter estimates can be inspected and we can assign meaningful interpretations to the latent classes. Say for example that K_{pos} is the subset of the latent classes we decided to interpret as 'positive', e.g., in our data example the patients classified so would be diagnosed with tuberculosis. We can then compute the probability of an item being labeled 'positive' given an agreement pattern with m out of N positive ratings as follows:

$$p(z = \text{'positive'}|x = m) = \sum_{k \in K_{pos}} p(z = k|x = m)$$

Application of the Model   Uebersax et al. (1989) apply the model just described to the data summarized back in Table 4.5. They fit three versions of the model, with two, three, and four latent classes and find the three-class version to provide a good fit to the data (fitness was assessed with a chi-squared test). The prevalence of the classes was found to be $\pi = (0.96, 0.03, 0.01)$. The pooled coder behaviour for the three classes, i.e., the likelihood of any coder to rate an item positive depending on the class it belongs to, was estimated to be $\theta = (0.01, 0.27, 0.90)$. Based on these estimates the authors interpret the latent classes as two negative classes ('unaffected cases' and 'cases with less serious conditions that have an elevated probability of being diagnosed positive') and one positive class with respect a tuberculosis diagnostic.

The estimated parameters can be used to compute various probabilities of interest. For example, suppose we want to classify a patient as positive for tuberculosis only when our confidence in this label is above 0.9. Using the formulas presented before we find that we would need

Table 4.6: The agreement patterns collected from a panel of 5 medical experts asked to judge 859 cases as indicative or not for performing a carotid endarterectomy procedure (Uebersax et al., 1989)

Coder$_1$	Coder$_2$	Coder$_3$	Coder$_4$	Coder$_5$	Pattern Frequency
1	1	1	1	1	69
1	1	1	1	0	2
1	1	1	0	1	4
1	1	1	0	0	1
1	1	0	1	1	2
1	1	0	1	0	1
1	0	1	1	1	82
1	0	1	1	0	4
1	0	1	0	1	23
1	0	1	0	0	8
1	0	0	1	1	67
1	0	0	1	0	24
1	0	0	0	1	42
1	0	0	0	0	41
0	0	1	1	1	5
0	0	1	0	1	8
0	0	1	0	0	8
0	0	0	1	1	5
0	0	0	1	0	28
0	0	0	0	1	49
0	0	0	0	0	386

a minimum number of 3 coders rating unanimously the item for this to happen (the positive predictive agreement in this case is 0.93).

4.3.2 FIXED PANEL OF CODERS

Th Model A latent agreement model designed for a fixed panel of coders (Uebersax et al., 1989) assumes each coder has their own annotation behavior. Table 4.6 shows the agreement patterns produced by a panel of 5 medical experts asked to judge 859 cases as indicative or not for performing a carotid endarterectomy procedure. Let us discuss how this type of data is modelled.

Table 4.7: Parameter estimates for a three latent-class model of agreement designed for a fixed panel of five coders

Latent Class	Prevalence	Coder Estimates				
κ	π_κ	$\theta_{1,\kappa}$	$\theta_{2,\kappa}$	$\theta_{3,\kappa}$	$\theta_{4,\kappa}$	$\theta_{5,\kappa}$
1	0.58	0.07	0.00	0.02	0.06	0.10
2	0.26	0.90	0.01	0.33	0.60	0.78
3	0.15	1.00	0.58	0.98	0.94	0.98

As with the model designed for a varying panel of coders, the first step in the generative process is to assign a latent class to each item. The difference is that now, instead of using a pooled behaviour to generate the annotations, a coder-specific annotation behaviour is used. Formally, the probability of coder n producing annotation $y_{i,n}$ on an item i whose latent class is z_i follows a Bernoulli distribution with parameter θ_{n,z_i}:

$$p(y_{i,n}|\theta_n, z_i) = \theta_{n,z_i}^{y_{i,n}}(1 - \theta_{n,z_i})^{1-y_{i,n}}$$

The likelihood of the annotations $y_{i,1:N}$ for an item i assigned to latent class z_i now becomes:

$$p(y_{i,1:N}|\theta_{1:N}, z_i) = \prod_{n=1}^{N} \theta_{n,z_i}^{y_{i,n}}(1 - \theta_{n,z_i})^{1-y_{i,n}}$$

Summing over the latent classes we get the probability of an item receiving a certain agreement pattern from the fixed panel of coders:

$$p(y_{i,1:N}|\theta_{1:N}) = \sum_{k=1}^{K} \pi_k \prod_{n=1}^{N} \theta_{n,z_i}^{y_{i,n}}(1 - \theta_{n,z_i})^{1-y_{i,n}}$$

We can also compute the probability of an item belonging to some latent class k when annotated with a certain agreement pattern $y_{1:N}$:

$$p(z = k|y_{1:N}) = \frac{\pi_k \prod_{n=1}^{N} \theta_{n,k}^{y_n}(1 - \theta_{n,k})^{1-y_n}}{\sum_{h=1}^{K} \pi_h \prod_{n=1}^{N} \theta_{n,h}^{y_n}(1 - \theta_{n,h})^{1-y_n}}$$

Example of Application of the Fixed Panel Model   Uebersax et al. (1989) apply the just described latent class agreement model to the data presented back in Table 4.6. They experiment with three versions of the model, with two, three, and four latent classes, and find the three class version to fit the data well. Table 4.7 shows the parameter estimates. Following these estimates, the authors interpret the latent classes as 'nonindications', 'equivocal indications', and 'valid indications' for performing a carotid endarterectomy.

Table 4.8: The agreement table of two coders asked to label sentences as either 'subjective' (Subj) or 'objective' (Obj) and supply confidence ratings ranging from 0 to 3. The table combines the data for the sentences with 0,1 and 2,3 ratings.

		Coder J				
		$Subj_{2,3}$	$Subj_{0,1}$	$Obj_{0,1}$	$Obj_{2,3}$	Total
	$Subj_{2,3}$	158	43	15	4	220
	$Subj_{0,1}$	0	0	0	0	0
Coder D	$Obj_{0,1}$	3	2	2	0	7
	$Obj_{2,3}$	38	48	49	142	277
	Total	199	93	66	146	504

Once estimated, the parameters can be used to compute various probabilities of interest. For example, the probability of a case being a valid indication for surgery given unanimous positive ratings by the panel is 0.995. If one of the members of the panel rates the case negative however, the probability of a valid indication will depend on the identity of the coder who made this annotation: if the fourth coder ($\theta_{4,3} = 0.94$) provides the negative annotation the probability is 0.943; if it was the second coder instead, who is more conservative ($\theta_{2,3} = 0.58$), the probability drops to 0.622. Note how in the varying panel model described earlier the (1,1,1,0,1) and (1,0,1,1,1) agreement patterns hold the same information about the probability of a positive case. This would not be in line though with how we really interpret multiple opinions and highlights an important advantage the fixed panel model has over the model designed for a varying panel of coders in drawing inferences from agreement patterns.

4.3.3   AN NLP CASE STUDY

As an example of NLP application of latent agreement models, in this section we discuss the case study from Wiebe et al. (1999), whose aim was to annotate a corpus for subjectivity classification.

Wiebe et al. (1999) asked 4 coders to label around 500 news-related sentences as to whether they contain 'subjective' or 'objective' information following the guidelines expressed in the coding manual. To allow the annotators to express their confidence in the labels, they also asked them to provide a rating ranging from 0 (least certain) to 3 (most certain). Table 4.8 shows the agreement between two of the coders involved in the study. The confusion matrix offers an indication of their relative preferences: coder D is biased more toward the 'objective' category, while coder J has a higher preference for the subjective category.

Next, the authors employed a two class latent agreement model to capture and correct for the bias of the coders. The latent classes inferred by the model can be interpreted as the "true" status of the sentences, subjective or objective, as adjudicated from the labels supplied by the

Table 4.9: The reliability scores, measured with κ (Cohen, 1960), for various coder pairs, across two annotation studies. The certainty values range from 0 (least certain) to 3 (most certain).

Coder Pairs	Certainty Values	First Study		Second Study	
		κ Score	% Corpus	κ Score	% Corpus
M & D		0.60	100	0.76	100
M & J		0.63	100	0.67	100
D & J	0, 1, 2 or 3	0.57	100	0.65	100
B & J		0.62	100	0.64	100
B & M		0.60	100	0.59	100
B & D		0.58	100	0.59	100
M & D		0.62	96	0.84	92
M & J	1, 2 or 3	0.78	81	0.81	81
D & J		0.67	84	0.72	82
M & D		0.67	89	0.89	81
M & J	2 or 3	0.88	64	0.87	67
D & J		0.76	68	0.88	62

fixed panel of four coders. Having done this, the coders were asked to participate in interactive discussions where they were presented with the sentences for which their classifications differed from the ones produced by the latent agreement model. The coders reviewed their decisions and provided feedback back to the authors. Based on their feedback, 22 of the labels produced by the latent agreement model were changed, and a second version of the coding manual produced.

Using the updated coding manual, the same coders were then asked to annotate a second corpus, similar in size to the first one. (The datasets used in this case study are subsets of the *Wall Street Journal* section of the Penn Treebank (Marcus et al., 1993).) Table 4.9 presents the reliability scores of the coders for the two annotated datasets. It can be seen from the table that the scores went up across the board in the second round of annotations. In some cases, e.g., for those sentences for which the coders are more certain in their labels, the improvements in reliability were substantial.

In summary, Wiebe et al. (1999) demonstrate in their case study how a latent class agreement model was used to guide the revision of a coding manual for a sentence subjectivity classification task, with results indicating substantial improvements in reliability. The authors then went to use the latent classes inferred by the model as gold standard labels for the corpus that resulted out of the annotation. They demonstrated the utility of this corpus by training and evaluating machine learning classifiers with good performance. We should also mention here the work of Bruce and Wiebe (1998) who also employ a latent class agreement model, but to help formulate a refined and more reliable set of categories for a wordsense disambiguation task.

4.4 SUMMARY

In this chapter we returned to the question of how to interpret the results of reliability studies by presenting models that address this question by rephrasing the problem of reliability as one of estimating the confidence we can have on a particular label given the behavior of the coders. Some of these models (Aickin, Guggenmoos-Holzmann, Gwet) are based on the distinction between easy and difficult items; other models (Uerbersax, Bruce and Wiebe) posit the existence of latent classes and model the likelihood of a coder assigning a given label to an item given that item's latent class. These latter models are the first examples of probabilistic models of annotation, which are discussed in detail in the following chapter. Throughout, we exemplify the use of goodness of fit tests to assess the quality of a model.

PART II

Analysing and Using Crowd Annotations

CHAPTER 5

Probabilistic Models of Annotation

5.1 INTRODUCTION

Traditionally, the task of annotating corpora was carried out by experts (Francis and Kucera, 1982, Hovy et al., 2006, Ide and Pustejovsky, 2017, Leech et al., 1994, Marcus et al., 1993). Increasingly, however, the amount of data required to train the state of the art has gone beyond what can be achieved with traditional expert annotation, so the field has started exploring alternative solutions, from unsupervised learning, to distant learning and other forms of automatic annotation (Mintz et al., 2009), to crowdsourcing (Poesio et al., 2017, Snow et al., 2008). Crowd labels can offer similar quality to those produced by expert annotators (Callison-Burch, 2009, Nowak and Rüger, 2010, Snow et al., 2008), but come at a lower cost and the collection process is easier to scale. Crowdsourcing comes in different forms, each relying on different incentives for the participants: microtask crowdsourcing via platforms such as Amazon Mechanical Turk remains the most prevalent (Sheng et al., 2008, Snow et al., 2008, Sorokin and Forsyth, 2008), but citizen science–based efforts (Cooper et al., 2010, Smith et al., 2011) and games with a purpose (Ahn, 2006, Fort et al., 2014, Lafourcade et al., 2015, Poesio et al., 2013, 2019, Venhuizen et al., 2013) have also been employed.

Both expert and crowdsourced annotations require adjudication to resolve the differences in judgement from the collected interpretations. Past practice relied on manual adjudication where feasible, on choosing the label proposed by most coders, or on other types of heuristics (e.g., including questions with known answers to weight the coders in a majority vote estimate). Such practices however, although appealing due to their ease of implementation, have limitations. For example, in adjudication, choosing the interpretation provided by the majority of the coders implicitly ignores their accuracy and biases, or the characteristics of the items they were asked to annotate. This led to the development from very early on (Dawid and Skene, 1979) of more advanced so-called (automatic) **aggregation methods** taking this information about coders and items into account. These aggregation methods are the topic of this chapter. The aggregation models discussed in this chapter have also been argued to provide a more complete understanding of the annotation task than provided by coefficients of agreement, which only offer a headline measurement of agreement beyond chance, itself the subject of repeated debates (Beigman and Klebanov, 2009, Passonneau and Carpenter, 2014, Reidsma and Carletta,

2008). Please consult Chapter 4 for a more in-depth discussion of how probabilistic models can address the limitations of agreement statistics.

Probabilistic models of annotation offer a formal specification framework for the annotation process: we can describe the coders, the items and their interactions; our assumptions are then considered when inferring the corpus labels. They have been widely adopted in many areas of science, from the medical domain (Albert and Dodd, 2004, Dawid and Skene, 1979, Formann, 1994, Raykar et al., 2010, Uebersax, 1988, Uebersax and Grove, 1990), to computer vision (Simpson et al., 2013, Smyth et al., 1994, Whitehill et al., 2009), and natural language processing (Bruce and Wiebe, 1998, 1999, Carpenter, 2008, Habernal and Gurevych, 2016, Hovy et al., 2013, Nguyen et al., 2017, Passonneau and Carpenter, 2014, Paun et al., 2018b, Plank et al., 2014a, Sabou et al., 2014, Simpson and Gurevych, 2019, Snow et al., 2008). This chapter introduces the concepts in the literature on models of annotation gradually, aiming to cover the most important work done across the years in this field. Each section includes, in addition to a literature review, a discussion of a practical example to better familiarize the reader with the theoretical implications of the work done or to present key results. We begin in Section 5.2 with a simple annotation model for a classification task introducing the terminology and some key assumptions often made about the annotation process. In Section 5.3, the basic model is extended to cover the annotation behaviour of the coders. In Section 5.4, we address the issue of item difficulty and how it affects the way the coders annotate. In Section 5.5, we discuss hierarchical priors for the annotators, useful to better estimate their behaviour when the data is scarce. In Section 5.6, we discuss how to model the characteristics of the items to discriminate better between the labels or to have a richer model of annotator ability. Section 5.7 presents models of annotation for sequential data as found in named entity recognition or information extraction tasks where the items have inter-dependent labels. In Section 5.8, we discuss modelling anaphoric annotations for coreference resolution tasks where the labels are not predefined classes but entity mentions. In Section 5.9, we discuss how the annotations can be aggregated with a variational autoencoder, turning to neural networks to learn the interactions between the items and the coders. We conclude the chapter with Section 5.10 with notes on modelling other types of annotation data than those covered previously with the help of a general-purpose framework that utilizes the distances between the annotations instead of the annotations themselves.

5.2   TERMINOLOGY AND A SIMPLE ANNOTATION MODEL

In a standard classification task the annotators (or coders—we will use the two terms interchangeably) are presented with a set of items and are asked to label them by choosing from a predefined set of classes. Take, for example, the task of recognizing textual entailment (Dagan et al., 2006). In this task the coders are presented with two sentences and are asked to judge whether the second sentence, called the **hypothesis**, can be inferred from the first, called the **premise** or **context** (Dagan et al., 2006, Snow et al., 2008). In this task the items are pairs of sentences and the set of classes consists of positive and negative labels that indicate entailment status. Here is an example of an item the coders should mark as a positive case of textual entailment:

(5)   Premise: "Crude Oil Prices Slump".
        Hypothesis: "Oil prices drop".

Whereas the following example, where the hypothesis is the same as before, but the premise has changed, is not a case of entailment:

(6)   Premise: "The government announced last week that it plans to raise oil prices".
        Hypothesis: "Oil prices drop".

In crowdsourcing, items such as those exemplified above are labelled by multiple coders and a corpus is built including all these annotations. In a well known example, Snow et al. (2008) used Amazon Mechanical Turk (AMT) to annotate 800 pairs of sentences with entailment judgements from 164 coders, collecting in total 8,000 annotations. Each sentence pair was annotated 10 times, and the workload of the coders varied from 20 items minimum to the entire dataset in some cases. The corpus, conveniently named RTE (Recognizing Textual Entailment), was made publicly available and has become a popular choice in the literature on annotation models (Hovy et al., 2013, Moreno et al., 2015, Paun et al., 2018a, Raykar et al., 2010). We will use this dataset in many of the practical sections in this chapter.

The annotations, once collected, need to be separated from noise. Table 5.1 presents a summary of the annotation patterns produced by the coders for the textual entailment task described above. It can be observed that the dataset contains a fair amount of disagreement and the labels proposed by the majority of coders are not always 'right', at least as judged a posteriori by a panel of experts. For example, there are 62 sentence pairs that 6 out of 10 coders judge as positive cases of textual entailment, but the experts reach the same conclusion only on 44 of them. But the correct labels can be found among the annotations; in this case we just need better tools than simple heuristics such as majority voting to identify them. The main drawback of a majority vote is that it assumes all coders have the same ability, which is really not a plausible assumption when analysing annotations. A long line of work spanning across many decades has resulted in probabilistic models of annotation to address this problem (Carpenter, 2008, Dawid and Skene, 1979, Hovy et al., 2013, Kim and Ghahramani, 2012, Moreno et al., 2015, Passonneau and Carpenter, 2014, Paun et al., 2018a, Raykar et al., 2010, Smyth et al., 1994, Snow et al., 2008, Uebersax et al., 1989, Venanzi et al., 2014, Whitehill et al., 2009, inter alia).

Simply put, a model of annotation is a probabilistic framework for identifying the most reliable interpretations out of the potentially noisy crowd annotations. This is done by encoding our assumptions about the annotation process, e.g., the interactions between the items and the coders. Our assumptions are then considered when inferring the probability of corpus labels. Standard models of annotation follow two core assumptions: (1) each item is assumed to have

Table 5.1: A summary of the annotation patterns from the Recognizing Textual Entailment (RTE) dataset (Snow et al., 2008)

Number of Positive Annotations	Number of Items	Number of Items per Gold Class	
		Negative Class	Positive Class
0	5	5	0
1	25	25	0
2	90	90	0
3	105	102	3
4	103	92	11
5	65	50	15
6	62	18	44
7	59	11	48
8	108	3	105
9	105	4	101
10	73	0	73
Total	800	400	400

one correct interpretation, often referred to in the literature as the true class of the item, a terminology we will henceforth use in our discussions; and (2) conditioned on the true class of an item, the coders are assumed to annotate independently. It should be noted that both of these assumptions are often merely convenient oversimplifications. The first assumption, in particular, ignores plenty of empirical evidence that ambiguity is widespread across many domains and tasks, such as in part of speech tagging (Plank et al., 2014b), wordsense disambiguation (Passonneau et al., 2012), coreference resolution (Poesio and Artstein, 2005, Poesio et al., 2019, Recasens et al., 2011, Versley, 2008), or image labelling (Peterson et al., 2019), to name a few. We will return to this point at greater length in Chapter 6. The second assumption also comes short, e.g., when the difficulty of the items affects the annotation ability of the coders; this is an aspect we will get back to later in the chapter.

For pedagogical reasons, we will begin our discussion of models of annotation with a simple example (Albert and Dodd, 2004, Carpenter, 2008, Paun et al., 2018a, Uebersax et al., 1989). We shall start with its generative process, which implements the set of assumptions the model makes about the way the annotations are produced. In this model, the items (the pairs of sentences in our recognizing textual entailment example), indexed by $i \in \{1, \dots, I\}$, are first assigned a true class c_i (the true entailment status of a pair of sentences) based on the prevalence π of the true classes in the corpus (the percentage of sentence pairs with positive and negative entailment):

$$c_i \sim \mathsf{Categorical}(\pi)$$

Probability distributions used in this chapter

Bernoulli: a probability distribution for a binary variable.
Categorical: the generalization of Bernoulli to categorical variables.
Beta: a distribution often used to model the probability of a binary variable as it is the conjugate prior of Bernoulli. (See next box.) An intuitive introduction to Beta can be found at: https://stats.stackexchange.com/questions/47771/what-is-the-intuition-behind-beta-distributionwiththebattingaveragesexample)
Dirichlet: often used to model categorical probability distributions, as it is the multivariate generalization of Beta and the conjugate prior of the Categorical distribution.
Normal: a probability distribution for continuous variables.
Multivariate Normal: a generalization of the Normal to multi-dimensional continuous variables.

- -

For a thorough introduction to these distributions, see Bishop (2016).

The true class of an item c_i is one of K classes (positive or negative entailment in our running example), and the prevalence π acts as a prior. For example, the prior probability of an item having class k (like a pair of sentences being a positive or a negative instance of textual entailment) would be:

$$p(c_i = k|\pi) = \pi_k$$

The simple model assumes that each annotation $y_{i,n}$, indexed by $n \in \{1, \ldots, N_i\}$, on an item i, is generated according to a population-wide/collective annotation behaviour associated with the true class of the item, parameterized below by ζ_{c_i}, the distribution characterizing coder behavior:

$$y_{i,n} \sim \mathsf{Categorical}(\zeta_{c_i})$$

This initial model does not distinguish between the different abilities the annotators may have and assumes instead they all follow a common behaviour. This is an example of what is often referred to as a (completely) **pooled model**: the population-wide/collective behaviour is formulated in terms of a confusion matrix (the ζ in the equation above), whose rows are probability distributions governing the annotation behaviour of the coders on items of a certain true class, e.g., the probability of labelling some pair of sentences as a negative or a positive instance of entailment when their true status is either positive or negative. Formally, the probability of an annotator choosing label k' for an item i whose true class is k is given by:

$$p(y_{i,n} = k'|c_i = k, \zeta) = \zeta_{k,k'}$$

The parameters $\zeta_{k,k'}$ on the main diagonal of the confusion matrix capture the class-specific accuracy of the coders while the off-diagonal parameters capture their bias. In a binary annotation task like the task from our running example, the parameters on the main diagonal stand for the overall true negative rate of the annotators ($\zeta_{0,0}$), called **specificity** in these frameworks, and the overall true positive rate ($\zeta_{1,1}$), called **sensitivity**.

Finally, the model can be completed by providing fixed **conjugate priors** for regularization. For example, using uniform priors, we would have:

$$\pi \sim \text{Dirichlet}(1)$$
$$\zeta_k \sim \text{Dirichlet}(1), \forall k \in \{1, ..., K\}$$

Conjugate priors

Conjugate priors allow for tractable posterior inferences. Using a prior that is conjugate to a likelihood function will result in a posterior part of the same probability family as the prior.

- -

Read more about conjugate priors in Cohen (2016).

Fitting the model just described on the dataset summarized in Table 5.1 results in an estimated prevalence of $\pi = (0.55, 0.45)$ and an overall coder specificity of $\zeta_{0,0} = 0.65$ and sensitivity $\zeta_{1,1} = 0.84$. These estimates inform us there is a relatively balanced number of positive and negative instances of entailment in the corpus and that the coders can identify the positive instances considerably better than the negative ones. The estimates derived from gold (expert) labels indicate an evenly balanced prevalence $\pi = (0.5, 0.5)$ and a coder specificity of $\zeta_{0,0} = 0.66$ and sensitivity $\zeta_{1,1} = 0.80$. Thus, the model does a decent but not a great job at recovering these estimates. The inferred textual entailment status of the sentence pairs matches the gold labels on 709 out of 800 cases, for an accuracy of about 0.89. Later on, we will be able to do considerably better when we will fit the coders with their own annotation behaviour instead of assuming a pooled behaviour.

5.3   MODELLING ANNOTATOR BEHAVIOUR

A limitation of the model presented above is its assumption that all coders share the same annotation behaviour. This makes the model unable to capture the coders' individual accuracy and biases. This limitation was addressed by Dawid and Skene (1979), a seminal work which introduced a model in that each annotator is characterized by their own response parameters. Arguably, this model, that dates back to the late seventies, remains the most widely known and used model of annotation out there (Bruce and Wiebe, 1999, Kim and Ghahramani, 2012, Passonneau and Carpenter, 2014, Raykar et al., 2010, Smyth et al., 1994, Snow et al., 2008, Uebersax et al., 1989).

Similar to the pooled model, in the model of Dawid and Skene (1979) each item i is first assigned a true class c_i based on the prevalence π of the true classes in the corpus. But unlike in the simple model, which assumes a collective behaviour to govern the generation of the annotations, the Dawid and Skene model uses annotator-specific distributions, indicated here as β. Models such as this one, with individual structures, are often referred to as **unpooled models**.

Formally, the generative process of this model assumes that each annotation $y_{i,n}$ for an item i is produced based on the behaviour of the annotator on items whose true class is the same as the true class assigned to this item[1]:

$$y_{i,n} \sim \mathsf{Categorical}(\beta_{jj[i,n],c_i})$$

Dawid and Skene (1979) fit maximum likelihood estimates using expectation maximization (EM) (Dempster et al., 1977)—interestingly, being one of the first applications of this algorithm—but the model can easily be extended to include fixed prior information for regularization. For example, given J coders and assuming (conjugate) uniform priors, we would have:

$$\pi \sim \mathsf{Dirichlet}(1)$$
$$\beta_{j,k} \sim \mathsf{Dirichlet}(1), \forall j \in \{1, \ldots, J\}, \forall k \in \{1, \ldots, K\}$$

Another unpooled model, widely-used as well, predominantly in NLP (e.g., Habernal and Gurevych, 2016, Plank et al., 2014a, Sabou et al., 2014), is the Multi-Annotator Competence Estimation (MACE) model proposed by Hovy et al. (2013). This model has a simpler parameterization of the accuracy and bias of the coders compared to the model proposed by Dawid and Skene (1979), formulated in terms of a credibility parameter θ_j and a spamming behaviour ϵ_j. When presented with an item, MACE assumes the annotator first makes a decision on whether they know the right answer or not:

$$z_{i,n} \sim \mathsf{Bernoulli}(\theta_{jj[i,n]})$$

Annotators with high credibility (θ_j close to 1) are more likely to correctly annotate the items. When an annotator knows the answer ($z_{i,n} = 1$) it is assumed their annotation matches the true class of the item:

$$y_{i,n} = c_i$$

But when they do not know the answer ($z_{i,n} = 0$), the annotators annotate following their spamming preference:

$$y_{i,n} \sim \mathsf{Categorical}(\epsilon_{jj[i,n]})$$

---

[1]Notation: $jj[i, n]$ specifies the index of the coder who produced the nth annotation on item i.

Convenient priors can be used to complete the specification of the model, e.g.:

$$c_i \sim \mathsf{Categorical}\left(\frac{1}{K}\right) \; {}^2$$
$$\theta_j \sim \mathsf{Beta}(1, 1), \forall j \in \{1, ..., J\}$$
$$\epsilon_j \sim \mathsf{Dirichlet}(1), \forall j \in \{1, ..., J\}$$

Paun et al. (2018a) compared the model from Dawid and Skene (1979) with MACE (Hovy et al., 2013) over four NLP datasets with different characteristics in terms of their size, the number of annotations per item, and the quality of the annotators. Their evaluation considered several measures of accuracy, for both the labels and the annotators. This evaluation found little difference between the two models regarding the models' accuracy at predicting the best label. In terms of the different assumptions these models make about the annotation behaviour of the coders, the simpler annotator parameterization of MACE could be advantageous in conditions of sparsity and appears to be sufficiently versatile, particularly for projects which do not have the objective of analysing the behavior of the coders in detail; in such cases, the modelling of annotators in Dawid and Skene (1979) is generally more appropriate. As a reminder, the main diagonal of the confusion matrices used to model the coders in Dawid and Skene (1979) captures their class-specific accuracy, whereas the credibility parameters in MACE only provide a cross-class estimate of accuracy. Likewise for the bias of the coders, which is class-specific for the model of Dawid and Skene (1979), and just a cross-class distribution in MACE. The bias estimates are given by the off-diagonal elements of the confusion matrices for the former model, and by the spamming preference distributions in case of the latter. In the practical section below we shall illustrate these distinctions by illustrating their use with the RTE dataset.

Practical Application

The models we introduced in this section are widely used and at the heart of many other advances in the literature. Having a good understanding of these models is therefore important. To offer the reader a better familiarity with these models, we fit them to the Recognizing Textual Entailment (RTE) dataset introduced in the previous section, and discuss how they perform. Both models were implemented using Stan (Carpenter et al., 2017), a tool for Bayesian inference based on Hamiltonian Monte Carlo.

Let us begin with an analysis of the estimated parameters. The model of Dawid and Skene (1979) estimated the prevalence of the true classes to be $\pi = (0.48, 0.52)$, a close estimate to the $(0.5, 0.5)$ prevalence present in the gold standard. The sensitivity and specificity of the annotators are shown in Figure 5.1: the left graphic presents the specificity of the coders against their

---

[2]Although Hovy et al. (2013) do not learn a distribution for the prevalence of the true classes, it would be straightforward to replace the uniform prior with the same categorical model of prevalence as found in Dawid and Skene (1979).

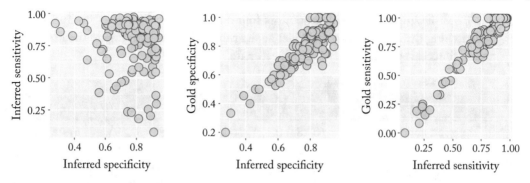

Figure 5.1: Annotator estimates from the model of Dawid and Skene (1979). The leftmost diagram maps inferred specificity and inferred sensitivity, whereas the other two diagrams show the correlation between inferred and gold values.

sensitivity, while the middle and the right graphics plot the inferred specificity and sensitivity against gold estimates, computed by comparing the annotations with labels produced by experts. The first graphic shows that coders have different abilities: some are better at recognising the positive cases of textual entailment (i.e., have high sensitivity), while others, those with high specificity, are better at correctly rejecting the hypothesis they were presented with. The last two graphics indicate that the model does well at recovering the 'true' confusion of the annotators: an analysis using Pearson's correlation evidences a strong correlation between the model-inferred and expert-estimated quantities, with 0.9 for specificity and 0.96 for sensitivity.

Table 5.2 complements the first graphic from Figure 5.1 with estimates of some typical categories of annotators found not only in the RTE dataset, but in crowdsourcing in general (Passonneau and Carpenter, 2014, Paun et al., 2018a, Simpson et al., 2011, 2013). We can see that in the model of Dawid and Skene (1979), good and highly accurate annotators have substantially more probability mass on the main diagonal of their confusion matrix β (these are the class-level estimates for their accuracy compared to the off-diagonal entries (these estimates indicate their bias). In the model of Hovy et al. (2013), coders of that type are found to have high credibility θ and (close to) random spamming behaviour (vector ϵ specifying the probability distribution of spamming w.r.t. the classes assigns nearly identical probabilities to both classes). These estimates are complementary, considering the relationship between the coder parameterizations assumed by the two models: a high sensitivity and specificity are indications of high credibility; and a low bias indicates a no particularly strong spamming preference. Moving on to biased coders, under the model of Dawid and Skene (1979), these have substantially more mass in the column of their confusion matrix that is associated with the class they are biased towards; while in MACE (Hovy et al., 2013), the biased coders receive a low credibility and a high spamming preference for the biased class. Again, the estimates of the two models complement each other. See Passonneau and Carpenter (2014) for a detailed discussion of the use of

Table 5.2: Example of typical annotators found in a dataset. The gold* confusion is computed by matching the annotations of a coder against the gold standard; due to the limited number of annotations this provides only a rough estimate.

Example of a Typically Found Annotator	Gold* Confusion	Dawid and Skene (1979)	Hovy et al. (2013)
The good annotator	$\begin{pmatrix} 0.88 & 0.12 \\ 0.25 & 0.75 \end{pmatrix}$	$\beta_{17} = \begin{pmatrix} 0.81 & 0.19 \\ 0.24 & 0.76 \end{pmatrix}$	$\theta_{17} = 0.65$ $\epsilon_{17} = (0.58, 0.42)$
The highly accurate annotator	$\begin{pmatrix} 0.80 & 0.20 \\ 0.00 & 1.00 \end{pmatrix}$	$\beta_{119} = \begin{pmatrix} 0.94 & 0.06 \\ 0.04 & 0.96 \end{pmatrix}$	$\theta_{119} = 0.95$ $\epsilon_{119} = (0.47, 0.53)$
The annotator biased towards the first class	$\begin{pmatrix} 1.00 & 0.00 \\ 1.00 & 0.00 \end{pmatrix}$	$\beta_{88} = \begin{pmatrix} 0.91 & 0.09 \\ 0.92 & 0.08 \end{pmatrix}$	$\theta_{88} = 0.08$ $\epsilon_{88} = (0.95, 0.05)$
The annotator biased towards the second class	$\begin{pmatrix} 0.20 & 0.80 \\ 0.00 & 1.00 \end{pmatrix}$	$\beta_{65} = \begin{pmatrix} 0.28 & 0.72 \\ 0.08 & 0.92 \end{pmatrix}$	$\theta_{65} = 0.25$ $\epsilon_{65} = (0.08, 0.92)$

the annotator models inferred by the Dawid and Skene (1979) approach to analyze the outcome of an annotation project.

Finally, let us have a look at the quality of the adjudicated labels. As it turns out, both the model of Dawid and Skene (1979) and that of Hovy et al. (2013) infer the same labels, resolving correctly—according to the gold standard—743 pairs of sentences for their entailment status, for an accuracy of about 0.93. The models overperform a simple majority vote baseline by three percentage points.

We conclude by reiterating the main drawback of the majority vote aggregation heuristic: this approach assumes that all coders have the same labelling ability, which, as the analysis done in this section showed once more, is not an appropriate assumption to make when working with coders.

Label Switching

Many models of annotation are at their core mixture models (see Gelman et al., 2013, for an introduction to mixture models). For example, in the case of the Dawid and Skene (1979) model, the mixture weights are given by the prevalence, and the mixture components are the rows of the confusion matrices of the annotators. But when estimating the parameters of a mixture, one needs to deal with the so-called **label switching** problem due to the likelihood's invariance under the permutation of the parameters' indices: for a mixture of K components, there are $K!$ ways of re-mapping the indices of its parameters (the components and the weights) and the likelihood will stay unchanged in all of these cases. In a Bayesian setting, assuming priors which do not distinguish between the components will result in a symmetric posterior, and the problem persists.

In the case of annotation models, the problem is that we would like to have an alignment between the indices of the mixture and those of the annotations provided by the coders, but this is not guaranteed. For example, in the RTE dataset there are $K = 2$ classes and therefore $K! = 2$ permutations possible and equally likely. The model estimated a prevalence $\pi = (0.48, 0.52)$, but it could have just as well estimated $\pi = (0.52, 0.48)$. And in this latter case, the annotator estimates would also be row-permuted, e.g., the estimates for the good annotator from Table 5.2 would be $\begin{pmatrix} 0.25 & 0.75 \\ 0.88 & 0.12 \end{pmatrix}$. Clearly, the first estimate is the desired solution for a natural interpretation where the class space of the annotations corresponds to that of the true class of the items.

One way to address the label switching problem is to use informative priors or custom initialization that 'direct' the mixture towards the permutation of interest, i.e., the one which offers the aforementioned alignment. Going back to our practical example, for the model of Dawid and Skene (1979), one can start the inference with or assume as prior uniform distributions with some small additional probability mass on the diagonal of the annotators' confusion matrices. In the Stan implementation discussed in this section we chose to use uniform priors and initialize the parameters of the model following the approach just described.

5.4   MODELLING ITEM DIFFICULTY

The models of annotation discussed in the previous section assume that the coders annotate independently given the true class of the items. For example, in the model of Dawid and Skene (1979), the coders produce labels based on their annotation behaviour (their per-class accuracy and biases) that is assumed general for all items, disregarding the specific characteristics of each item they were asked to annotate, such as their difficulty. Recognizing that some items are more challenging than others violates the aforementioned independence assumption. Take as an example the annotation patterns collected by Snow et al. (2008) for the task of recognizing textual entailment presented back in Table 5.1. When exploring the dataset, on some sentence pairs we can observe that consensus is easily reached, e.g.:

(7)   Text: "The three-day G8 summit will take place in Scotland".
      Hypothesis: "The G8 summit will last three days".

The example above was unanimously labeled as a positive case of entailment. Intuitively, this looks like an easy judgment to make. But there are cases more open to interpretation which create disagreement, e.g.:

(8)   Text: "EU membership is a strategic necessity for Turkey, as Ankara will inevitably suffer greater foreign policy problems in the future unless it makes it into the Union".
      Hypothesis: "Turkey to join the EU".

In the example above, half the coders found the hypothesis can be inferred from the text it is accompanied by, while the other half concluded differently. Although the text does not reference

Turkey actually joining the EU, it is known the country has been negotiating its entry into the union for many years, so one can understand why some coders might make this judgment. Additionally, timeline-wise, the hypothesis is open-ended, which may create further confusion.

As seen in Chapter 4, the fact that items to annotate have varying degrees of difficulty has long been recognized in the literature on statistical methods for annotation analysis. In fact, the distinction between easy and difficult items served as the foundation for many agreement models discussed in that chapter. However, such models generally modeled the difficulty of items as a dichotomy, distinguishing between 'easy' items where you could only have agreement and in particular, deliberate agreement between the coders, and 'hard' items where the coders would disagree or happen to agree by chance. This distinction allowed such researchers to better quantify the 'agreement beyond chance', a measurement used to assess the reliability of a coding scheme. This whole line of work came as a response to the measurements offered by coefficients of agreement, the standard metrics for reliability, long argued to give biased estimates. (See Chapter 4 for a discussion of some of these approaches.)

The empirical evidence from annotation practice, however, suggests a more **graded notion of difficu y** is needed. The annotation models we introduce in this section model the difficulty of the items on a continuum, and in relation to the ability of the coders: on **easy items** one expects there to be a larger probability for the coders to correctly annotate them, while the **hard items** should lower this probability.

Carpenter's Subtractive Model of Difficu y

Following previous work in item-response theory and ideal point models (Gelman and Hill, 2007, Rasch, 1993, Skrondal and Rabe-Hesketh, 2004), Carpenter (2008) developed a model of annotation which assumes that the probability of an annotator being correct on an item is based on a subtractive relationship between their ability and the difficulty of the item. The model is specified for binary data and parameterizes annotator ability on the log-odds scale in terms of their sensitivity (the true negative rate) and specificity (the true positive rate). The difficulty of an item is also expressed on the log-odds scale. Formally, for an item i whose true class is positive ($c_i = 1$), the model assumes an annotation is produced based on the sensitivity α_j of the annotator j that produced annotation n of the item and the difficulty of the item θ_i[3]:

$$y_{i,n} \sim \text{Bernoulli}(\text{logistic}(\alpha_{jj[i,n]} - \theta_i))$$

If the true class of the item is negative ($c_i = 0$), the specificity of the annotator β_j is involved instead:

$$y_{i,n} \sim \text{Bernoulli}(1 - \text{logistic}(\beta_{jj[i,n]} - \theta_i))$$

According to this model, an item is considered easy when the difficulty parameter is negative ($\theta_i < 0$). In this case, both the sensitivity and the specificity of the annotators increase, thus they have a greater probability to provide the correct answer (0 for negative items or 1 for

---

[3]Notation: the term logistic() indicates the standard logistic function.

positive ones). Conversely, an item is considered hard when the difficulty parameter is positive ($\theta_i > 0$); in this case, the parameter reduces the sensitivity and the specificity of the annotators, thus increasing their chance of incorrectly annotating an item (providing a 0 for a positive item or a 1 for a negative one). Notice also that when the difficulty of the items is $\theta_i = 0$ the model becomes equivalent to a log-odds reparameterization of the model from Dawid and Skene (1979). Finally, the model can be completed with appropriate priors:

$$\pi \sim \text{Beta}(1, 1)$$
$$\alpha_j \sim \text{Normal}(0, 5), \forall j \in \{1, ..., J\}$$
$$\beta_j \sim \text{Normal}(0, 5), \forall j \in \{1, ..., J\}$$
$$\theta_i \sim \text{Normal}(0, 1), \forall i \in \{1, ..., I\}$$

The model is not identified because a constant can be added to the annotator ability and item difficulty parameters and the annotation probabilities would not change. This can be addressed by constraining the difficulty parameters to sum to 0. Another solution is to use a hierarchical prior, e.g.:

$$\theta_i \sim \text{Normal}(0, \sigma), \forall i \in \{1, ..., I\}$$
$$\sigma \sim \text{Normal}(0, 4)$$

Item response theory

A common application of item response models is to analyze data associated with individuals and test items. A classic example is the Rasch model (Rasch, 1993) which, just like the model by Carpenter (2008), assumes that the probability of a person being correct on a test item is based on a subtractive relationship between their ability and the difficulty of the item. The model takes a supervised approach, however, and estimates the ability of the individuals and the difficulty of the test items using information about the correctness of their responses. Such information is not assumed to be available by the models discussed in this section whose approach to learning is unsupervised.

Read more about item response theory in Gelman and Hill (2007).

Whitehill et al.'s Multiplicative Model of Difficulty

In their Generative model of Labels, Abilities, and Difficulties (GLAD), Whitehill et al. (2009) proposed a different account of the effect of item difficulty on the ability of the coders to the one proposed by Carpenter.

Unlike the models of Dawid and Skene (1979) and Carpenter (2008) which allow the ability of the annotators to vary by class, GLAD assumes a single, cross-class behaviour α_j. This is parameterized on the log-odds scale and models an annotator's probability of correctness, i.e., the probability to annotate an item as positive when its true class is positive or to provide a negative label when the item is negative. Under this parameterization, a negative ability ($\alpha_j < 0$) indicates that the annotator is mostly adversarial (provides the wrong class), a borderline ability ($\alpha_j = 0$) implies the coder annotates randomly, whereas a positive ability ($\alpha_j > 0$) is assigned to annotators who label the items with their true class most of the time (the larger α_j is, the bigger their probability to provide the correct answer becomes).

In GLAD, the difficulty of the items stands in a multiplicative relationship with the ability of the coders. The difficulty of an item i is modelled by a parameter $\beta_i \geq 0$, constrained to the positive side of a log-odds scale. The annotations for an item i whose true class is c_i have the following probability of correctness:

$$p(y_{i,n} = c_i) = \mathsf{logistic}(\alpha_{jj[i,n]}\beta_i)$$

The role of the difficulty parameter β_i is perhaps more easily understood in terms of its inverse β_i^{-1}. On what are considered easy items (when $0 < \beta_i^{-1} < 1$) the annotators' accuracy is increased, reaching perfect accuracy as $\beta_i^{-1} \to 0$. On the more difficult items (characterized by $\beta_i^{-1} > 1$) the coders have a lower probability of correctness, reaching random chance as $\beta_i^{-1} \to \infty$. We conclude the specification of the model with an example of priors for the parameters:

$$\pi \sim \mathsf{Beta}(1, 1)$$
$$\alpha_j \sim \mathsf{Normal}(0, 1), \forall j \in \{1, ..., J\}$$
$$\beta_i \sim \mathsf{Normal}_+(0, 1), \forall i \in \{1, ..., I\}\,^4$$

Although Whitehill et al. (2009) use a single, cross-class, ability parameter per annotator, it would be easy to extend the model to consider distinguishing between their positive and negative class ability; simply assign annotators with specificity and sensitivity parameters as in the model from Carpenter (2008) presented before.

An Illustration of the Two Models of Difficu y

The models from Carpenter (2008) and Whitehill et al. (2009) show two different effects the difficulty of the items has on the ability of the annotators. In Figure 5.2 we plotted the logistic curve characterizing the correctness probability of an annotator on items with different levels of difficulty: the black curve is the response curve for items of no (borderline) difficulty, the green curves stand for a few examples of annotation behaviour on easy items, while the red curves correspond to the response curves on a couple of items deemed hard by the two models under analysis.

In the model of Carpenter (2008) (see Figure 5.2), the difficulty parameter translates the logistic curve along the x-axis. A nice property of this effect is that the difficulty of an item and the ability of an annotator lie on the same continuum, in the sense that for an item of a

---

[4]Notation: Normal$_+$ stands for the positive half-normal distribution. In this particular case it represents the positive side of a standard normal distribution.

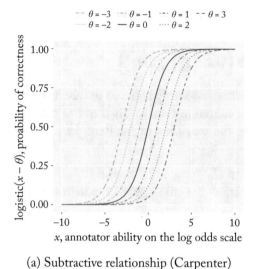

(a) Subtractive relationship (Carpenter)   (b) Multiplicative relationship (Whitehill)

Figure 5.2: The effects of item difficulty on the ability of an annotator. Green corresponds to easy items, black to borderline difficulty, and red to hard items.

certain difficulty it is required an annotator of the same ability to get a borderline probability of correctness; the difficulty of the items and the ability of the annotators are thus directly relatable to each other.

The difficulty parameter from the model of Whitehill et al. (2009), on the other end, (see Figure 5.2), keeps the borderline probability of correctness fixed, and flattens the logistic curve along the y-axis: the greater the difficulty, the flatter the response curve. In item-response theory (IRT) the parameter from Whitehill et al. (2009) is referred to as a **discrimination parameter**, controlling the slope of the logistic curve: on easy items the response curve is highly discriminatory, essentially separating the annotators into two groups, those with positive ability producing correct answers and those with negative abilities making mistakes; as the items get harder, the discrimination level is reduced, the annotators reaching random behaviour in the limit.

Extension to Multiclass Annotations

The models of difficulty we discussed so far were specified for binary tasks. Although most annotation tasks are multiclass, there is very little literature on estimating the difficulty of the items in such cases. One solution is proposed by Bachrach et al. (2012). Conceptually, it may be easier to think of their model as involving a two-step process: one where the annotators decide whether they know or not the true class of the items they are presented with, and another responsible for generating the multiclass annotations. For the first step, they borrow the same modelling concepts from item-response theory we saw in the work of Carpenter (2008) and Whitehill et al. (2009)[5]:

$$p(z_{i,n} = 1) = \Phi \left(\sqrt{\beta_i} \left(\alpha_{jj[i,n]} - \theta_i \right) \right)$$

In the equation above we find the familiar relationship between the ability of the annotator α_j, the difficulty of the item θ_i, and its discrimination rate β_i. Then comes the second step of the generative process. If a coder recognizes the true class of the item, i.e., $z_{i,n} = 1$, they are assumed to annotate correctly:

$$y_{i,n} = c_i$$

In contrast, when the coder does not know the true class of the item they are presented with, they adopt a random behaviour:

$$y_{i,n} \sim \text{Categorical} \left(\frac{1}{K} \right)$$

Practical Application

To offer further insights into the models from Carpenter (2008) and Whitehill et al. (2009), we fit them using Stan (Carpenter et al., 2017) to the by now familiar Recognizing Textual Entailment (RTE) dataset used as running example in this chapter. Assessing the difficulty of the items is not easy (pun intended). Klebanov and Beigman (2014) suggest the degree of difficulty of an item is proportional to the level of disagreement present in the annotations. But the disagreements between the coders have many sources besides difficulty; they can also occur, iter alia, due to chance, attention slips, coder bias, some limitation of the coding scheme, or genuine cases of ambiguity (Klebanov et al., 2008, Poesio et al., 2019, Uma et al., 2021b). All these other interfering sources of disagreement make it hard for a precise identification and quantification of difficulty. Nevertheless, the coders' dissent, at least on average, should be a good indicator of difficulty.

In Table 5.3 we illustrate the relation between the values of the difficulty parameter in the two models and the extent of disagreement. In the table we cluster together the items with the same disagreement patterns and report the average difficulty of each cluster as estimated by both the model of Carpenter (2008) and that of Whitehill et al. (2009).

The two models correctly adjudicate the annotations (checked against a gold standard) on a similar number of items, so the difference between these models, in this case, is made by their difficulty estimates. In this example, the difficulty estimates from the Carpenter (2008) model capture an important property regarding how we perceive difficulty w.r.t. disagreement: that is, the more disagreement among coders we have, the more difficult the items should be considered on average. We can observe both negative and positive instances of textual entailment that the coders find easy to spot—e.g., the first three and the last two rows of the table—more borderline

---

[5]Notation: $\Phi()$ is the cumulative distribution function of the standard normal distribution.

Table 5.3: The average difficulty estimated by the models of Carpenter (2008) (difficulty parameterized with θ_i) and Whitehill et al. (2009) (parameterized with β_i) for items with a certain amount of disagreement

Positive Annotations	No. Items	Positive Items (Gold)	Carpenter (2008)		Whitehill et al. (2009)	
			Avg. θ_i	Pos. Items	Avg. β_i^{-1}	Pos. Items
0	5	0	−1.55	0	0.48	0
1	25	0	−1.03	0	0.32	0
2	90	0	−0.58	0	0.29	0
3	105	3	−0.14	4	0.32	2
4	103	11	0.27	7	0.52	3
5	65	15	0.65	13	0.78	12
6	62	44	0.78	40	0.96	39
7	59	48	0.58	47	0.73	51
8	108	105	0.10	106	0.45	108
9	105	101	−0.36	105	0.25	105
10	73	73	−0.91	73	0.15	73

cases—e.g., those with 3 or 8 positive annotations—and hard cases, e.g., the sentence pairs with 4 to 7 positive annotations. According to the Carpenter model, the items from the easiest bin can be correctly labeled even by coders whose ability is just above 0.18 ($\approx$ logistic(-1.55)) while those deemed the hardest require coders of an ability above 0.69 ($\approx$ logistic(0.78)).

The difficulty estimates provided by the model of Whitehill et al. (2009) do not correlate as well with the level of agreement present in the annotations. In fact, based on the authors' interpretation of the difficulty parameter, all the items, on average, should be considered easy ($\beta_i^{-1} < 1$).

A parallel with item-response theory may be helpful to understand the difference between these difficulty parameters. The difficulty parameter used in the model of Carpenter (2008) is a difficulty estimate, whereas the parameter in Whitehill et al. (2009) is a discrimination parameter. Under this interpretation, the results in the table suggest that for this dataset, the model of Whitehill et al. (2009) simply finds that all items, on average, are good discriminators for the ability of the annotators, i.e., the items allow the model to nicely separate between the different abilities the annotators have on the continuum.

5.5   HIERARCHICAL STRUCTURES

We started the chapter with a simple model of annotation which assumed all coders have the same annotation behaviour. That was an example of a completely pooled model. The models subsequently introduced relaxed that assumption assigning to each annotator their own ability parameters, and introduced a model for item difficulty effects. These latter models are often referred to as unpooled models, i.e., models with individual structures (e.g., annotator level parameters, item level parameters). Although unpooled models are highly effective in practice, one downside to having an unpooled model structure is that it typically requires more observations to properly fit some of the parameters, e.g., fitting the accuracy and bias of the annotators. This requirement can be satisfied in some crowdsourcing settings—e.g., when using microtask platforms where you can control for the number of annotations per annotator and per item, and for tasks where sufficient numbers of workers are available. In other settings however, such as labelling tasks where workers with the appropriate skills are not easy to find, or in environments such as in games with a purpose where the data collection process relies on player engagement, sparsity becomes an important factor. Sparsity also plays a role in the early days of a crowdsourcing campaign and, more generally, alleviating its effects can reduce the time that is necessary to achieve the desired level of annotation quality and cut down the costs of the project.

Partially Pooled Structure

One solution to the problem of sparsity is to develop models with a **hierarchical structure**, also referred to as a **partially pooled structure**. This type of structure improves (regularizes) the estimates of the lower level parameters using information about the hierarchy; it does so by pooling the individual estimates toward the mean of the hierarchical prior. The level of pooling is as strong as evidenced by the data: when enough observations are available, the partially pooled and the unpooled models should perform similarly; when sparsity is present, the lack of observations is compensated using hierarchical information through parameter pooling as just described.

For example, Paun et al. (2018a) describe a simple hierarchical extension of the annotation model from Dawid and Skene (1979). The extension includes an overarching hierarchical prior over the annotator-level parameters. To accommodate the hierarchical structure the annotator parameters are expressed on the log-odds scale. Let $\beta_{j,k}$ be the annotation behaviour of coder $j \in \{1, ..., J\}$ on items whose true class is $k \in \{1, ..., K\}$, we have[6]:

$$\beta_{j,k} \sim \mathsf{MultiNormal}(\zeta_k, \Omega_k)$$

The class-specific annotation behaviour of the coders is drawn from a class-specific population behaviour expressed in terms of a location parameter ζ_k and a covariance Ω_k. The location parameter, on the logs-odds scale, captures the average annotator behaviour on items of a specific class, while the covariance controls the level of pooling exerted by the hierarchical prior on

---

[6]Notation: MultiNormal is the multivariate normal distribution.

the annotator parameters. In conditions of sparsity, the prior informs more strongly the posterior of the annotator estimates; when plenty of observations are available, the likelihood of the annotations will dominate over the prior and have a bigger say in the annotator estimates.

The parameters for the population-wide annotation behaviour can be given fixed priors for regularization. For example, assuming no correlation in the behaviour of the annotators (i.e., a diagonal covariance matrix), we would have:

$$\zeta_{k,k'} \sim \text{Normal}(0, 1), \forall k, k' \in \{1, ..., K\}$$
$$\Omega_{k,k'} \sim \text{Normal}_+(0, 1), \forall k, k' \in \{1, ..., K\}$$

The generative process of the annotations is similar to that from Dawid and Skene (1979) described earlier in the chapter. The only difference is that the annotator behaviour parameters need now to be mapped to the simplex:

$$y_{i,n} \sim \text{Categorical}(\text{softmax}(\beta_{jj[i,n],c_i}))$$

Community Models

A more flexible partially pooled structure can be found in the so called **community models**. Simpson et al. (2011, 2013) identified, after fitting an unpooled model of annotation, distinctive clusters in the annotation behaviour of the coders; more generally, typical annotator communities found in a crowdsourcing setup include spammers, adversarial, biased, average, or high-quality players. Knowledge of these communities would allow to regularize the annotation behaviour of the coders toward the profile of the community they are part of instead of assuming a single hierarchical prior as previously discussed. Venanzi et al. (2014) provide such a model; assuming there are C communities in the pool of annotators, and θ encodes their prevalence, the model begins by assigning each coder $j \in \{1, ..., J\}$ a community profile:

$$z_j \sim \text{Categorical}(\theta)$$

Annotators have their class behaviour drawn from the community profile they were assigned to previously:

$$\beta_{j,k} \sim \text{MultiNormal}(\zeta_{z_j,k}, \Omega_{z_j,k}), \forall k \in \{1, ..., K\}$$

Similar to the hierarchical model introduced beforehand, the community profiles are parameterized in terms of a location parameter $\zeta_{c,k}$ encoding the average annotation behaviour of the coders assigned to them, and a covariance parameter $\Omega_{c,k}$ whose role is to capture the level of pooling exerted by the community on its members. Fixed priors can be added to these parameters for regularization; again, assuming no correlation in the behaviour of the annotators, we have:

$$\zeta_{c,k} \sim \text{Normal}(0, 1), \forall c \in \{1, ..., C\}, \forall k \in \{1, ..., K\}$$
$$\Omega_{c,k} \sim \text{Normal}_+(0, 1), \forall c \in \{1, ..., C\}, \forall k \in \{1, ..., K\}$$

Table 5.4: The communities inferred by the model of Venanzi et al. (2014) on the RTE (Snow et al., 2008) dataset

Community	Prevalence	Confusion Matrix
"good annotators"	0.88	$\begin{pmatrix} 0.92 & 0.08 \\ 0.13 & 0.87 \end{pmatrix}$
"annotators biased towards the second class"	0.12	$\begin{pmatrix} 0.37 & 0.63 \\ 0.18 & 0.82 \end{pmatrix}$

The generative process of the annotators in the model of Venanzi et al. (2014) is governed by a finite mixture. As always in such cases, when the number of mixture components is unknown, determining their optimum is cumbersome: choosing a small number means potentially distinctive groups of annotators will end up being merged together, while choosing a large number will introduce noise (overly fine-grained clusters get created that should otherwise be merged together). The solution Venanzi et al. (2014) settle for is to fit multiple instances of the model with different number of communities and choose the one with the largest marginal likelihood. While effective, one can see why the solution can be inefficient.[7] A more principled approach would be to use a nonparametric (unbounded) mixture, letting the number of communities be determined by the data. The details of such a model can be found in Moreno et al. (2015). It is also relatively straightforward to amend the model of Venanzi et al. (2014) to use an unbounded mixture with the help of a stick-breaking process (Blei and Jordan, 2006).

Practical Application

We will now illustrate the benefits of a hierarchical model in conditions of sparsity with a concrete example. We use for this purpose the community model of Venanzi et al. (2014) and its unpooled counterpart, the model from Dawid and Skene (1979). Venanzi et al. (2014) provide an implementation for both of these models in Infer.NET (Minka et al., 2018), a framework for running Bayesian inference in graphical models. We use these implementations and carry out the analysis on the already familiar RTE dataset.

Both the community model of Venanzi et al. (2014) and its unpooled counterpart Dawid and Skene (1979) have a similar accuracy w.r.t. the gold standard on the RTE dataset, about 0.93. The communities inferred by the hierarchical model can be seen in Table 5.4. The vast majority of coders, 88% of them, are clustered together and have an average specificity of 0.92 and an average sensitivity of 0.87; the rest of the coders are grouped together in a second cluster, found on average to be strongly biased toward positive entailment, having a false positive rate of 0.63 and a true positive rate of 0.82.

---

[7]In practice, the number of annotator communities found in a dataset is often small, thus such a solution is acceptable.

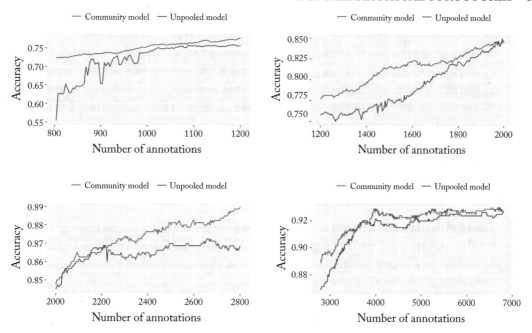

Figure 5.3: The accuracy of a community model Venanzi et al. (2014) and its unpooled counterpart Dawid and Skene (1979) in an adaptive learning setting simulating a sparse environment. Number of annotations increases from top left to right and from top to bottom.

The benefits of the partially pooled model over its unpooled counterpart arise in conditions of sparsity. To show that, we simulate a sparse environment using adaptive learning, following Venanzi et al. (2014): we start with each item having one annotation and progressively select three more items for which the uncertainty found in the posterior of their true label (measured using entropy) is the highest; for these items we randomly select one annotation from the pool of annotations, fit again the models on the new data, and report their accuracy w.r.t. gold standard. The results, which can be seen in Figure 5.3, are in line with the theory discussed earlier in the section: the gains in performance of the community model over the unpooled model are the largest when the level of sparsity is high (see the first three graphs); and the gap in performance between the two models narrows as more annotations become available (see the last graph in the bottom right corner). To reiterate, this is because in an unpooled model the annotation behaviour of the coders is estimated solely based on their annotations (and some fixed priors which usually are either noninformative, or weakly informative to identify the mixture). When the data is sparse, it may be difficult to properly profile the annotators simply because there are not enough observations available to get a good estimate, and the fixed priors are not very helpful. In a partially pooled model, however, the annotations of a coder influence both the estimates of their annotation behaviour and, indirectly, the estimates of the other annotators that share the same hierarchical prior: an annotator's annotations influence their behaviour which informs the overall behaviour of the community, which influences in turn the behaviour of all its members. This sharing of information helps the partially pooled model in conditions of sparsity. When sufficient annotations became available, the likelihood of these annotations will dominate the prior in the estimation of the posterior of the annotators' behaviour, and thus the partially pooled and the unpooled models can end up performing similarly. The conclusion of this analysis is that the partially pooled model is a more versatile model, adapting better to conditions of sparsity in comparison with its unpooled counterpart.

5.6   ADDING FEATURES

The models discussed up to this point only rely for adjudication on the annotations provided by the coders. But some research suggests that making the models **data-aware** (Felt et al., 2015a)— i.e., using, in addition to annotations, features to characterize the items—can enhance their adjudication capabilities (Felt et al., 2014, 2015b, Kamar et al., 2015, Raykar et al., 2010, Simpson et al., 2015, Yan et al., 2010, 2014). Features can be good discriminators for the true class of the items, but can also be used to specify a richer model of accuracy and bias for the annotators that adapts to the characteristics of the items. We shall discuss both aspects in this section.

Raykar et al.'s Discriminative Model
Raykar et al. (2010) used features to enrich the simple categorical model of prevalence proposed by Dawid and Skene (1979). As a reminder, in Dawid and Skene's model the prior probability of an item's true class is given by the class's prevalence in the corpus:

$$p(c_i = k) = \pi_k, \forall i \in \{1, ..., I\}$$

This simple specification of prevalence implies that all items have the same prior probability for a true class. However, it may be that items with certain features are more likely to belong to a class than others. For instance, thinking back to the examples of use of the DAMSL annotation schemes for dialogue act classification discussed in Chapter 2, a classification as an `info-request` is extremely unlikely for certain types of utterances. This preference for certain interpretations can be captured with the help of a softmax classifier. For item i with feature vector x_i, we have[8]:

$$p(c_i = k | x_i) = \mathsf{softmax}\left(b + x_i W^T\right)_k$$

With just a bias term b the prevalence above is equivalent to a log-odds reparamerization of the one from Dawid and Skene (1979), while with non-zero weights W, the features became additional discriminators for the true class of the items. The newly introduced parameters can

---

[8]Notation: softmax$( )_k$ refers to the k-th element of the output vector returned by the softmax( ) function.

be given appropriate priors; for example, assuming F uncorrelated features, we have:

$$b_k \sim \text{Normal}(0, 1), \forall k \in \{1, ..., K\}$$
$$W_{k,f} \sim \text{Normal}(0, 1), \forall k \in \{1, ..., K\}, \forall f \in \{1, ..., F\}$$

The model from Raykar et al. (2010) jointly trains a discriminative classifier and infers a ground truth from noisy labels. Similar work has also been carried out in (Liu et al., 2012, Raykar et al., 2009, Yan et al., 2010, 2014).

A Generative Model

Others employed a naïve Bayes classifier instead of a discriminative classifier (Felt et al., 2014, Simpson et al., 2015). In this latter line of work, the true class of an item has the same prior probability as in Dawid and Skene (1979), and is followed by an additional generative step of the features, assumed to be mutually independent (the naïve part) when conditioned on the true class:

$$p(x_i|c_i) = \prod_{f=1}^{F_i} p(x_{i,f}|c_i) = \prod_{f=1}^{F_i} \theta_{c_i, x_{i,f}}, \forall i \in \{1, 2, ..., I\}$$

The θ_k parameter captures the distribution of the features for class k and it can be given appropriate priors for regularization, e.g.,

$$\theta_k \sim \text{Dirichlet}(1), \forall k \in \{1, 2, ..., K\}$$

Using Features to Specify Annotator Ability

Features can also be used to specify a more flexible model of annotator ability, one that adapts to the characteristics of the items they were asked to annotate. As previously discussed, in the model from Dawid and Skene (1979) coders annotate based on their annotation behaviour associated with the true class of the items they are presented with. For example, for an annotation $y_{i,n}$ on some item i whose true class is c_i we have:

$$p(y_{i,n} = k|c_i) = \beta_{jj[i,n],c_i,k}$$

The parameterization above allows capturing the class-level accuracy and bias of the coders, but it does not consider the effect the difference in characteristics between the items has on their annotation behaviour. Yan et al. (2010, 2014) showed how such an effect can be modelled[9]:

$$p(y_{i,n} = k|x_i, c_i) = \text{softmax}\left(b_{jj[i,n],c_i} + x_i W_{jj[i,n],c_i}^T\right)_k$$

With just a bias term, the model of annotator behaviour introduced above is equivalent, on the log-odds scale, to that from Dawid and Skene (1979), while with non-zero feature weights, the softmax classifier learns to adapt its predictions to the characteristics of the items.[10]

---

[9]We modify the original binary specification to multiclass annotations, to match the rest of the section.

[10]There is an interesting connection here with the difficulty models discussed earlier in the chapter. While those do assume the items have an affect on the annotation behaviour of the coders, they do not model it w.r.t. specific traits these items have.

One problem with this approach is the large number of parameters it introduces: there may not be enough annotations available from each coder to sufficiently cover the feature-space and ensure the model fits properly. Kamar et al. (2015) notice this and propose an annotation model where only one such feature-based model of ability is included, which the annotators can turn to and annotate with in addition to their standard cross-class confusion. This keeps the parameter space manageable, while still allowing the model to capture the bias in annotation induced by the coders' perception of the items depending on their characteristics. Formally, for the generation of every annotation, a decision is made whether to use the annotators' class-confusion, or the feature-based model of ability:

$$z_{i,n} \sim \text{Bernoulli}(\theta_{jj[i,n]})$$

Each annotator is fitted with a weight θ_j to encode how much their own annotation behaviour is used to generate the annotations over the feature-based model of ability accessible to all coders. When the annotator's own behaviour is used (when $z_{i,n} = 1$), the annotation is produced as in Dawid and Skene (1979); when the feature-based model of accuracy and bias is used instead ($z_{i,n} = 0$), we have:

$$p(y_{i,n} = k | x_i, c_i) = \text{softmax}\left(b_{c_i} + x_i W_{c_i}^T\right)_k$$

As usual, we conclude with an example of priors for the newly introduced parameters:

$$\theta_j \sim \text{Beta}(1, 1), \forall j \in \{1, ..., J\}$$
$$b_{k,k'} \sim \text{Normal}(0, 1), \forall k, k' \in \{1, ..., K\}$$
$$W_{k,k',f} \sim \text{Normal}(0, 1), \forall k, k' \in \{1, ..., K\}, \forall f \in \{1, ..., F\}$$

Discussion: Joint vs. Separate Aggregation and Training, Discriminative vs. Generative
Raykar et al. (2010) were the first to show that jointly training a classifier and inferring a ground-truth from noisy labels may lead to improvements in both areas. Up to that point, aggregation and training were handled separately (e.g., Smyth et al., 1994). Raykar et al., however, argued that jointly aggregating and training is beneficial in that the classifier gets regularized by the multiple labels, improving its performance, while the ground-truth labels leverage not only the annotation patterns produced by the coders, but also the knowledge of the task accumulated by the model, which boosts their quality. We discuss in Chapter 6 a number of proposals of this type, some of which do result in improved performance over carrying out aggregation and model training separately.

In addition to the model from Raykar et al. (2010) which uses a discriminative classifier as a model of prevalence for the true class of the items, we also presented in this section the fully-generative model from Felt et al. (2014). A comparison between these two models was carried out by Felt et al. (2015a). Their work was inspired by an earlier study on discriminative vs. generative classifiers by Ng and Jordan (2001) which showed that the former performs better on small datasets, but fails to keep up as the size of the training data increases. The conclusions Felt et al. (2015a) reached, *mutatis mutandis*, are similar to those from Ng and Jordan (2001): the model employing a naïve Bayes classifier (Felt et al., 2014) outperforms the model using a logistic classifier (Raykar et al., 2010) when the number of annotations is low.

Practical Application

We conclude this section discussing in more detail the application of the model proposed by Felt et al. (2015b) for a document categorization task. We include this model as an example that even richer feature-based models of annotation can be formulated, at the expense of generality however, the model being task-specific. We begin the presentation of the model with the generative process of the documents, for which Felt et al. (2015b) use a topic model (Blei et al., 2003). Formally, each document d in the corpus gets assigned certain topic proportions from some prior—for example:

$$\theta_d \sim \text{Dirichlet}(1)$$

Then follows the generation of the words. In the process of that, topic indicators are generated first based on the topic proportions associated with the document:

$$z_{d,n} \sim \text{Categorical}(\theta_d)$$

The words finally follow up from the topic distributions indicated by the aforementioned topic indicators:

$$w_{d,n} \sim \text{Categorical}(\lambda_{z_{d,n}})$$

The distributions that represent the topics are unigram distributions (probability distributions over the vocabulary space) and can be given, for example, uniform priors; assuming, say T topics, we have:

$$\lambda_t \sim \text{Dirichlet}(1), \ \forall t \in \{1, 2, ..., T\}$$

With topics assigned to the words of a document, their frequency is used as a predictor in a softmax classifier for the true class of the document:

$$p(c_d = k | z_{d,1:N_d}) = \frac{\exp(\eta_k \bar{z}_{d,k})}{\sum_{k'=1}^{K} \exp(\eta_{k'} \bar{z}_{d,k'})}, \quad \bar{z}_{d,k} = \frac{1}{N_d} \sum_{n=1}^{N_d} \mathbf{1}(z_{d,n} = k) \ \ ^{11}$$

In the equation above a prior can be put on the weights η for regularization. Last, the annotations of a document for its category follow the same generative process as in Dawid and Skene (1979). Felt et al. (2015b) compared their model with the models from Dawid and Skene (1979), Felt et al. (2014), and Raykar et al. (2010) and found it more robust in conditions of sparsity: using a richer model for the features, a topic model in this case, helps over a naïve Bayes classifier (Felt et al., 2014), a logistic classifier (Raykar et al., 2010), or compared to using no features at all (Dawid and Skene, 1979). A similar model can be found in Rodrigues et al. (2017).

---

[11]Notation: $\mathbf{1}()$ is an indicator function.

5.7   MODELLING SEQUENCE LABELLING TASKS

Many core NLP tasks, from language modelling to part of speech tagging to named entity recognition, can be viewed as **sequence labelling** tasks. What sets such cases apart are **inter-label dependencies**, e.g., in the case of part-of-speech tagging, that a determiner is not typically followed by a verb. But the models of adjudication built for standard classification data, such as those described earlier in the chapter, ignore such dependencies. This shortcoming was recognized and addressed by new models of annotation built specifically for sequence tagging tasks.

Nguyen et al. (2017) extend the model from Dawid and Skene (1979) by replacing the categorical model of prevalence for the true class of the items with a hidden Markov model to capture their inter-dependencies. Remember that in Dawid and Skene (1979) the true class $c_{s,i}$ (e.g., the part-of-speech tag), for an item i in a sequence s (such as a word from a sentence), is selected according to π, the classes' prevalence in the corpus:

$$c_{s,i} \sim \mathsf{Categorical}(\pi)$$

However, the formulation above assumes independence among the true classes. To allow for dependencies, Nguyen et al. (2017) model the true class of the items as hidden states in a first-order hidden Markov model. This makes the generation of a true class dependent on the true class of the previous item in the sequence, an aspect modelled by a transition matrix π:

$$c_{s,i} \mid c_{s,i-1} \sim \mathsf{Categorical}(\pi_{c_{s,i-1}})$$

As its name suggests, the transition matrix π encodes the probability of transitioning from one state to another. For example, $\pi_{k,k'}$ is the probability of going from some state k to state k', such as the probability of having a noun followed by a verb. Once a state has been selected according to the transition matrix, an emission distribution θ controls the generation of the item from the sequence, e.g., generate the token of a verb. Formally, item i from sequence s is produced as follows:

$$x_{s,i} \mid c_{s,i} \sim \mathsf{Categorical}(\theta_{c_{i,s}})$$

The transition matrix and the emission distributions can be encoded with prior information. This is where we specify any knowledge we have about the annotation task, e.g., express any unwanted transitions, such as making it unlikely for a determiner to be followed by a verb. We include below generic uniform priors for regularization, but keep in mind the recommendation about informative priors:

$$\pi_k \sim \mathsf{Dirichlet}(1), \forall k \in \{1, ..., K\}\ ^{12}$$
$$\theta_k \sim \mathsf{Dirichlet}(1), \forall k \in \{1, ..., K\}$$

---

[12]Unwanted transitions can be specified here. For example, if state k stands for 'determiner', then π_k is a probability distribution governing the transitions from a determiner to another part-of-speech tag. Let k' be the state corresponding to a verb. If we want to make it unlikely for a verb to follow a determiner we can set the k'-th component of the Dirichlet() to a value near zero.

The rest of the model is similar to that proposed by Dawid and Skene (1979): annotators are parameterized with a confusion matrix and the annotations are produced following their annotation behaviour associated with the true class of the items they are presented with. For example, the nth annotation of an item i from a sequence s has the following probability[13]:

$$p(y_{s,i,n} = k | c_{s,i}) = \beta_{jj[s,i,n], c_{s,i}, k}$$

The model of coder behaviour expressed above assumes an annotation is produced in relation to the true class of the item only. But in sequence labelling tasks, just as the true class of the items have inter-dependencies, so do the annotations produced by coders. Simpson and Gurevych (2019) further build on the model from Nguyen et al. (2017) and make the annotator behaviour also depend on the label they produced for the previous item in the sequence, allowing now for sequential dependencies in their annotation. Let $y_{s,i-1,j}$ be the label produced by coder j for a previous $i-1$ item, the annotation probability for the current item is:

$$p(y_{s,i,j} = k | c_{s,i}, y_{s,i-1,j}) = \beta_{j, c_{s,i}, y_{s,i-1,j}, k}$$

Practical Application

In this practical section we illustrate the benefits brought by a model of annotation built specifically for sequence tagging data over a standard annotation model for categorical data which ignores the inter-dependencies between the items. To this purpose, we compare the model from Dawid and Skene (1979), the model from Nguyen et al. (2017) which replaces the simple categorical model of prevalence from Dawid and Skene (1979) with an HMM to capture item inter-dependencies, and the model from Simpson and Gurevych (2019) which builds on the Nguyen et al. (2017) model by further allowing for sequential dependencies between the annotations. For completeness we also throw in a majority vote heuristic. Implementations of these models, all using variational inference, are publicly available (to access the code see Simpson and Gurevych (2019)).

The data used for the experiments come from three annotated corpora, covering named entity recognition, information extraction, and argument mining. In the named entity annotation task (Tjong Kim Sang and De Meulder, 2003) the annotators were given news articles and were asked to identify the names of people, organizations and locations; an additional 'miscellaneous' category was introduced to label those names which do not fit into any of these categories. The annotations, once collected, were transformed into sequence labels using a BIO scheme, where the tokens in the text are labeled as Beginning or Inside of a particular type of named entity (e.g., Inside location), or Outside of a named entity. In the information extraction annotation (Nguyen et al., 2017) the coders were given biomedical abstracts about randomized controlled trials and were asked to identify the spans of text which describe the population of patients enrolled in these trials—for example, "we recruited and enrolled [diabetic patients]".

---

[13]Notation: $jj[s, i, n]$ returns the index of the coder who produced the $y_{s,i,n}$ annotation.

Table 5.5: Various statistics about the sequence labelling datasets

Dataset	No. Sequences			No. Annotators		No. Gold Spans	Avg. Span Length
	Total	Dev	Test	Total	Avg/Seq		
News named entity recognition	6,056	2,800	3,256	47	5	21,612	1.51
Biomedical information extraction	9,480	191	191	312	6	700	7.74
Multitopic argument mining	8,000	60	100	105	5	73	17.52

Again, a BIO scheme is used to convert the annotations into sequence labels. Finally, in the argument mining annotation (Trautmann et al., 2020) the annotators were presented with sentences discussing various topics, e.g., minimum wage, gun control, and were asked to mark the spans of text which contain supportive or opposing arguments. The same transformation scheme as before is applied to the annotations for the sequence labels. Table 5.5 presents a few statistics about these datasets.

We used the development set that comes with each dataset to find a good set of hyperparameters (the fixed priors) for each model, and their test set for evaluation; being unsupervised, we trained the models on all of the sequences. In terms of evaluation metrics, we followed Nguyen et al. (2017) and Simpson and Gurevych (2019), and compared the inferred and gold spans using Precision, Recall and F1 score. We used both a strict version of these metrics (the CoNLL 2003 metrics) which assume an exact match between the predicted and the gold spans, and a relaxed version which partially credits overlapping spans (as in Nguyen et al., 2017). The strict metrics may be better suited for the named entity recognition task, considering the average span length in this case is small, and incomplete named entities may not be very useful down an NLP pipeline, while the relaxed metrics may be more appropriate for the tasks with longer spans.

The results are shown in Table 5.6. Notice the models from Nguyen et al. (2017) and Simpson and Gurevych (2019) which model the sequential dependencies between the items perform equally well or better with these types of annotation tasks than the model from Dawid and Skene (1979) where such dependencies are ignored. The model by Simpson and Gurevych (2019), encoding also the sequential dependencies between the annotations produced by the coders, performs best on two of the three datasets. But although more flexible, the richer model of annotation behaviour from Simpson and Gurevych (2019) introduces significantly more parameters compared with the one used in Nguyen et al. (2017). Because of that, there may not always be enough annotations available to properly fit this model, especially in conditions of sparsity, which can affect its performance. As a final note, we found the performance of both

Table 5.6: Results of probabilistic models and baselines for three sequence labelling tasks. The strict version of the metrics require exact matches between the spans for credit, while the relaxed version (partially) credits all overlapping spans.

Dataset	Method	Strict Match			Relaxed Match		
		P	R	F1	P	R	F1
News named entity recognition	Majority vote	0.80	0.55	0.65	**0.85**	0.58	0.69
	Dawid and Skene (1979)	0.80	0.70	0.75	0.83	0.74	0.78
	Nguyen et al. (2017)	0.80	0.72	0.76	0.84	0.75	0.79
	Simpson and Gurevych (2019)	**0.81**	**0.74**	**0.77**	0.84	**0.77**	**0.80**
Biomedical information extraction	Majority vote	**0.64**	0.38	0.48	**0.82**	0.53	0.64
	Dawid and Skene (1979)	0.52	0.47	0.49	0.70	0.65	0.68
	Nguyen et al. (2017)	0.49	0.49	0.49	0.70	0.70	0.70
	Simpson and Gurevych (2019)	0.50	**0.56**	**0.53**	0.72	**0.73**	**0.72**
Multitopic argument mining	Majority vote	0.39	0.30	0.34	**0.88**	0.57	0.69
	Dawid and Skene (1979)	0.49	0.50	0.50	0.82	0.74	0.78
	Nguyen et al. (2017)	**0.61**	0.61	**0.61**	0.83	0.79	**0.81**
	Simpson and Gurevych (2019)	0.55	**0.67**	0.60	0.72	**0.85**	0.78

the sequential models (Nguyen et al., 2017, Simpson and Gurevych, 2019) to be strongly dependent on the choice of hyperparameters. This made the availability of a development set crucial for obtaining good results.

5.8   AGGREGATING ANAPHORIC ANNOTATIONS

In this section we discuss aggregating annotations for the task of identifying and resolving anaphoric references to discourse entities (also known in NLP as coreference resolution), a key aspect of language interpretation which however raises problems for the aggregation methods discussed earlier in this chapter. Anaphoric references, or **mentions**, include pronouns, named entities, and other nominal phrases (Poesio et al., 2016). In standard anaphoric annotation, the mentions are predetermined so the coders can focus exclusively on making anaphoric judgements, rather than also having to decide on the mention boundaries, a difficult task in itself (Madge et al., 2019). The most basic annotation schemes for coreference ask coders to label mentions as **discourse new** if they introduce new entities into the discourse, or as **discourse old**, if they refer to previously introduced entities. When a mention refers to a previously introduced entity it is called an **anaphor**, and the entity it refers to is called **antecedent**. In this case, coders are also asked to specify which entities a mention refers to. The set of mentions referring to the same entity is called a **coreference chain**; coreference chains and entities are typically considered interchangeable. One way for coders to specify the antecedent of an anaphor is to link the anaphor to the most recent mention of its antecedent; the coreference chain can then be constructed a posteriori from the annotations from the links between the anaphors and their antecedent. Alternatively, annotators may be able to see the current coreference chains and link an anaphor directly to those. Richer annotation schemes also exist (Chamberlain et al., 2016, Uryupina et al., 2020) which further allow annotators to mark other types of noun phrases—e.g., expletives and predicative noun phrases. Consider the following example:

(9)   [John], [a colleague from work], said [it] will rain later today. [He] was right.

In the example the annotators should mark the proper noun "John" as discourse new as it introduces a new entity into the discourse, and the pronominal mention "he" as discourse old as it refers to an entity already present into the discourse. In this second case, the annotator should also mark the most recent antecedent of anaphor "he", which is "John". Mentions "John" and "he" refer to the same entity, thus form a coreference chain. More complex schemes also require coders to mark the mention "a colleague from work" as a predicative noun phrase, and mention "it" as an expletive.

As discussed back in Section 3.4.1, the challenge with anaphoric annotation is that whereas in standard NLP classification tasks the class space is fixed, in anaphoric annotation *the set of classes* the coders can choose from *changes depending on the mentions* they annotate (Passonneau, 2004). Some of the classes the coders can choose are predetermined (e.g., discourse new, expletive, predicate), but for discourse old mentions the class is the coreference chain (or, equivalently, the most recent mention of the antecedent). For this reason, standard models of annotation such as those described in the first part of this chapter are not immediately applicable to aggregate anaphoric judgements.

Paun et al. (2018b) addressed this issue by developing the **mention-pair model** of annotation (MPA). This model assumes a preprocessing step where the annotations are transformed into mention-pair judgements. A **mention-pair**—the terminology is borrowed from the model of coreference popularized by Soon et al. (2001)—is a ⟨mention, interpretation⟩ pair. Consider for example the pronoun "he" in Example (9), and let us assume we collect one annotation from 3 different coders, two of which provide the right interpretation—that "he" is a discourse old mention, coreferent with mention "John"—whereas the third annotator, a spammer, labels the mention as discourse new. Two mention-pairs can be extracted from these annotations: they are shown in Table 5.7. For each mention-pair we have a **type** (e.g., discourse old) and a number of binary judgments (in this case, three).

MPA models these mention-pair judgements as the result of the sensitivity (the true-positive rate) and the specificity (the true-negative rate) of the annotators. Formally, for every mention $m \in \{1, 2, ..., M\}$ and their interpretation $i \in \{1, 2, ..., I_m\}$, the generative process assumed by the model starts by assigning each of these mention-pairs an indicator which encodes

Table 5.7: An example illustrating how three annotations are transformed into mention-pair judgements. The annotations, two of which are correct, are for the pronoun "he" from the text from Example (9).

Mention-Pair	Type	Coder 1	Coder 2	Coder 3
("he", "John")	Discourse old	1	1	0
("he", discourse new)	Discourse new	0	0	1

whether they are correct or not[14]:

$$c_{m,i} \sim \text{Bernoulli}(\pi_{z_{m,i}})$$

The indicators c are drawn from priors π that represent the prevalence of the correct mention-pairs for each type. If a mention-pair is considered correct ($c_{m,i} = 1$) then the binary judgements are assumed to be the result of the annotators' sensitivity for that type of mention-pairs[15]:

$$y_{m,i,n} \sim \text{Bernoulli}(\alpha_{jj[m,i,n],z_{m,i}}), \forall n \in \{1, 2, ..., N_m\}$$

When the mention-pair is incorrect ($c_{m,i} = 0$), however, the binary judgements are assumed to be produced according to the specificity of the coders:

$$y_{m,i,n} \sim \text{Bernoulli}(1 - \beta_{jj[m,i,n],z_{m,i}}), \forall \in \{1, 2, ..., N_m\}$$

As we have seen, the ability of the coders in this model is parameterized in terms of their sensitivity and specificity, one for each type of mention-pairs. Separating between the different types of mention-pairs allows the model to capture, for example, that it is probably easier for the coders to correctly identify the mentions which introduce new entities into the discourse, compared with identifying those mentions of previously introduced entities, for which they also need to get right their most recent antecedent. Or that predicative noun phrases are generally hard to annotate correctly. Pooling the ability of the coders together across the different mention-types would be inappropriate in this case. We conclude the description of the model with an example of conjugate priors for regularization:

$$\pi_k \sim \text{Beta}(1, 1), \forall k \in \{1, ..., K\}$$
$$\alpha_{j,k} \sim \text{Beta}(1, 1), \forall j \in \{1, ..., J\}, \forall k \in \{1, ..., K\}$$
$$\beta_{j,k} \sim \text{Beta}(1, 1), \forall j \in \{1, ..., J\}, \forall k \in \{1, ..., K\}$$

Once the parameters of the model have been estimated, only one mention-pair per mention is kept, the one found most likely to be correct, based on the posterior of the mention-pair

---

[14]Notation: $z_{m,i} \in \{1, ..., K\}$ is the type of the mention-pair.
[15]Notation: $jj[m, i, n]$ returns the index of the coder judgement $y_{m,i,n}$ belongs to.

Table 5.8: Estimated mention-pairs evaluated against a gold standard built by linguists

	Majority Vote			MPA (Paun et al., 2018b)		
	Precision	Recall	F1	Precision	Recall	F1
Discourse old	**0.94**	0.63	0.75	0.90	**0.87**	**0.89**
Discourse new	0.79	**0.99**	0.88	**0.95**	0.96	**0.95**
Predicative NPs	0.54	0.10	0.16	**0.64**	**0.72**	**0.68**
Expletives	**0.97**	0.71	0.82	0.94	**0.98**	**0.96**
Accuracy	0.83			**0.92**		
Avg. F1	0.66			**0.87**		

indicators. The coreference chains are built afterwards from the links in the mention-pairs. The model can also be used in an analysis of anaphoric ambiguity, by identifying those mentions with more than one likely interpretation, or where no interpretation was found likely (e.g., see Poesio et al., 2019).

Practical Application

The mention-pair model of annotation (MPA) was originally proposed by Paun et al. (2018b) to adjudicate the anaphoric annotations collected over many years using the *Phrase Detectives* game with a purpose (Chamberlain et al., 2008, Poesio et al., 2013).[16] The latest released version of the corpus (Poesio et al., 2019) contains at least 8 anaphoric annotations (with 12 more validations) for over 100,000 mentions from about 540 documents covering 2 main genres, Wikipedia articles and fiction from the Gutenberg collection; 45 of these documents, containing over 6,000 mentions, were annotated by linguists to provide a reliable gold standard for evaluation. The *Phrase Detectives* corpus stands as one of the largest corpora for coreference for English, and one of the largest crowdsourced NLP corpora.

For this practical section we fitted the model from Paun et al. (2018b) to the latest release of the *Phrase Detectives* corpus, 2.1 (Poesio et al., 2019). (Both MPA and *Phrase Detectives* 2.1 are publicly available: see their respective papers for details.) Table 5.8 shows the quality of the mention-pairs inferred by MPA. As a baseline, we also included mention-pairs determined by assigning each mention the interpretation provided most by the *Phrase Detectives* players. The benefits of a model of annotation over a majority vote heuristic, which assumes all annotators have the same ability, are evident. Notice also the results for the different types of mention-pairs, confirming our prior belief that predicative NPs are generally hard to resolve correctly, and that discourse old interpretations, compared with discourse new, are more prone to error. This makes the separation of the ability of the coders between mention-types in Paun et al. (2018b) useful.

---

[16]Continue contributing to science by playing the game at www.phrasedetectives.com.

Table 5.9: The quality of various coreference chains evaluated using standard coreference metrics against expert-annotated chains. MV stands for chains determined from mention-pairs inferred using majority voting, MPA for chains inferred using the Paun et al. (2018b) model, and Stanford for chains produced by the (Lee et al., 2011) deterministic coreference system.

		MUC			BCUB			CEAFE			Avg.
	Method	P	R	F1	P	R	F1	P	R	F1	F1
Singletons included	MV	**96.0**	63.9	76.7	**95.7**	78.7	86.4	77.1	**94.9**	85.1	82.7
	MPA	91.6	82.4	**86.8**	94.8	**87.8**	**91.2**	**92.4**	93.8	**93.1**	**90.3**
	Stanford	65.4	62.4	63.8	78.9	76.1	77.5	78.4	85.2	81.7	74.3
Singletons excluded	MV	**96.1**	64.8	77.4	**93.8**	45.0	60.8	66.3	48.5	56.1	64.8
	MPA	92.2	**89.2**	**90.7**	88.1	**77.8**	**82.6**	**79.5**	**80.2**	**79.8**	**84.4**
	Stanford	65.7	62.1	63.9	50.3	42.5	46.1	42.7	49.8	46.0	52.0

Once the mention-pairs are distilled from noise, we can build the coreference chains, what we were after for from the beginning.[17] The results are shown in Table 5.9. For a broader comparison, we included into the evaluation, in addition to chains constructed from the mention-pairs inferred using MPA (Paun et al., 2018b) and majority voting, chains determined using a rule-based system (Lee et al., 2011). The results indicate a far better quality of the chains produced using MPA over the alternative methods. Another interesting result is that even a simple majority vote baseline performed far better than the system from Lee et al. (2011), highlighting the advantage of crowdsourced annotations for coreference over automatically produced annotations.

5.9 AGGREGATION WITH VARIATIONAL AUTOENCODERS

The probabilistic models of the type discussed so far in the chapter allow us to encode our assumptions about the annotation process when inferring the ground-truth labels, but these assumptions have to be explicitly specified, and manually coming up with good specifications can be both cumbersome and limiting. An alternative, proposed by Yin et al. (2017), is to shift to neural networks to aggregate the annotations, using a **variational autoencoder** (Kingma and Welling, 2013) in which the ground-truth labels act as latent space in an encoding and decoding of the annotations. Turning to neural networks allows autoencoders to learn more complex, non-linear relationships between the annotations and the ground-truth than otherwise possible with

---

[17]We assess the quality of the resulted chains using the extended version of the standard coreference scorer from Poesio et al. (2018) which can do both traditional CoNLL evaluation, excluding singletons, and including singletons in the evaluation. Singletons refer to those entities mentioned only once in the text.

a standard model of annotation. In this section we describe the variational autoencoder model from Yin et al. (2017), the first of its kind in the literature on models of annotation.

The generative process for annotations in the Yin et al. model follows a set of assumptions familiar from earlier sections in this chapter. Given an item i, first generate its true class c_i from a prior distribution $p_\theta(c_i)$, then condition on the true class to generate the annotations, $p_\theta(y_i|c_i)$. The objective is to find the parameters that maximize $p_\theta(y_{1:I})$, the marginal likelihood. For this optimization, Yin et al. (2017) follow Kingma and Welling (2013) and take a variational approximation approach, where the marginal is decomposed as follows:

$$\log p_\theta(y_{1:I}) = \sum_{i=1}^{I} \log p_\theta(y_i) = \sum_{i=1}^{I} D_{KL}\Big(q_\phi(c_i|y_i) \parallel p_\theta(c_i|y_i)\Big) + \mathcal{L}(\theta, \phi | y_i)$$

The first term from the decomposition above measures the Kullback–Leibler divergence between the approximate posterior $q_\phi(c_i|y_i)$ and the true posterior $p_\theta(c_i|y_i)$ of the true class of the items. This term is non-negative, making the second term a lower-bound of the marginal, and the de facto objective function. (The marginal, also known as the evidence, is maximized indirectly in this framework by having its lower-bound maximized instead.) The second term, named the **evidence lower-bound** (ELBO) due to its aforementioned property, has the following form:

$$\mathcal{L}(\theta, \phi | y_i) = \mathbb{E}_{q_\phi(c_i|y_i)}\Big[\log p_\theta(y_i|c_i) \Big] - D_{KL}\Big(q_\phi(c_i|y_i) \parallel p_\theta(c_i)\Big)$$

From a coding theory perspective $q_\phi(c_i|y_i)$ can be seen as a **probabilistic encoder**: given the annotations of an item it describes a probability distribution for its true class. Similarly, $p_\theta(y_i|c_i)$ can be interpreted as a **probabilistic decoder**: given the true class of an item it specifies a distribution for the annotations. In auto-encoder parlance, the first term from the bound measures the expected reconstruction error, while the second term can be interpreted as a regularizer for the parameters of the encoder, encouraging the approximate posterior of the true class of the items to be close to their prior. What is left is to define the functional form of both the encoder and the decoder. Yin et al. (2017) chose one-layer neural networks for both the encoder and the decoder. (The variational framework is not restrictive to any particular architecture for the two components; the authors made their choice experimentally.)

The encoder network is responsible for learning a mapping from the annotations to a latent space corresponding to the true class of the items. The annotations are arranged into a vector representation before being fed to the network. Let y_i be this vector for an item $i \in \{1, 2, ..., I\}$. The vector contains J blocks, one for each coder, of K elements corresponding to their one-hot encoded annotation. Let us look at an example in which 4 coders are asked to label an item with one of 3 classes. Assuming coders 1, 3, and 4 provide labels 1, 2, and 1, respectively, and coder 2 chooses not to annotate the item, we have:

$$y_i = [\, \underbrace{1\,0\,0}_{\text{coder 1}}\ \overbrace{0\,0\,0}^{\text{coder 2}}\ \underbrace{0\,1\,0}_{\text{coder 3}}\ \overbrace{1\,0\,0}^{\text{coder 4}}\,]$$

The encoder-network takes such a vector of annotations as input and learns a distribution over their class space that describes the true class of the item:

$$q(c_i = k|y_i) = \pi_{i,k}, \quad \text{where } \pi_i = \text{softmax}\left(y_i W_q\right)$$

As for the decoder network, it learns to reconstruct the annotations of an item from its (one-hot encoded) true class[18]:

$$\beta_i = \text{softmax}^*\left(c_i W_p\right)$$

The vector of reconstructed annotations β_i has the same structure as the vector containing the actual annotations described above: i.e., it consists of J blocks of K elements, each of which specifies a predicted annotation for a given coder given the true class of the item. For example, the probability for a coder j to annotate an item i whose true class is c_i with class k is[19]:

$$p(y_i^{(j,k)} = 1|\beta_i) = \beta_i^{(j,k)}$$

The weights W_p of the decoder network are responsible for learning the annotation behaviour of the coders depending on the true class of the items. They consist of J successive blocks, one for each coder, of $K \times K$ class-confusion matrices. The weights from the main diagonal of the class-confusion matrices capture the accuracy of the coders for each class of items, while the off-diagonal weights are for learning their bias:

$$W_p = \begin{bmatrix} \underbrace{\begin{matrix} W_{p,1,1,1} & \cdots & W_{p,1,1,K} \\ \vdots & \ddots & \vdots \\ W_{p,1,K,1} & \cdots & W_{p,1,K,K} \end{matrix}}_{\text{coder 1 class confusion weights}} & \cdots & \underbrace{\begin{matrix} W_{p,J,1,1} & \cdots & W_{p,J,1,K} \\ \vdots & \ddots & \vdots \\ W_{p,J,K,1} & \cdots & W_{p,J,K,K} \end{matrix}}_{\text{coder J class confusion weights}} \end{bmatrix}$$

Having introduced the encoder and the decoder, let us now consider how the objective function, the ELBO, is maximized. Again, Yin et al. (2017) follow Kingma and Welling (2013) and approximate the term measuring the expected reconstruction error with Monte Carlo samples. Concretely, to approximate this expectation, at each training step, for each item in the mini-batch a true class is sampled from the distribution described by the encoder:

$$c_i \sim \text{Categorical}(\pi_i)$$

The sample is then used to evaluate the reconstruction error, which turns out to be the negative cross-entropy of the reconstructed annotations given by the decoder relative to the actual annotations:

$$\log p_\theta(y_i|c_i) = \sum_{j,k}^{J,K} y_i^{(j,k)} \log \beta_i^{(j,k)}$$

---

[18]The softmax operator is applied to each successive K-sized block of logits.

[19]Notation: $y_i^{(j,k)}$ returns the kth element of the jth block from the y_i vector.

The other term in the ELBO, the divergence between the approximated posterior and the prior on the true class of the items, can be computed analytically. Yin et al. (2017) suggest using the distributions described by the annotations for the prior on the true class of the items. This concludes all that is necessary to estimate the parameters of the variational autoencoder model. This can be done, e.g., using an off-the-shelf optimizer like Adam (Kingma and Ba, 2015).

We further present two extensions of the model discussed above, also from Yin et al. (2017). In the first extension, the authors include into the modelling of the annotations an effect about the 'ambiguity' of the items. Concretely, a positive scalar is included into both the encoding and the decoding of the annotations:

$$\pi_i = \mathsf{softmax}\left(z_i\left(y_i W_q\right)\right)$$
$$\beta_i = \mathsf{softmax}^*\left(z_i\left(c_i W_p\right)\right)$$

The ambiguity scalar z_i can be best interpreted in terms of its inverse. Small z_i^{-1} values correspond to an unambiguous item: the distribution governing the true class of the item becomes more heterogeneous as the softmax in this case exacerbates any differences between the logits. As z_i^{-1} increases so does the ambiguity of the item, its true class distribution flattening, and reaching maximum entropy (becoming a uniform distribution) in the limit (when $z_i^{-1} \to \infty$). The ambiguity scalar is modelled as a function of the annotations:

$$z_i = \mathsf{softplus}(y_i W_o)$$

Yin et al. (2017) further introduce the concept of 'latent aspects', i.e., unknown item traits, such as the colour, or the shape of an object in an image, that have an impact on the annotation ability of the coders. The overall encoding and decoding of the annotations is modeled in this extension as a mixture of their encoding and decoding at each latent aspect level:

$$\pi_i = \mathsf{softmax}\left(\sum_{l=1}^{L} z_{i,l}\left(y_i W_{q,l}\right)\right)$$
$$\beta_i = \mathsf{softmax}^*\left(\sum_{l=1}^{L} z_{i,l}\left(c_i W_{p,l}\right)\right)$$

In the equation above L is the number of latent aspects, $z_{i,1:L}$ are the latent aspect weights for item i, and $W_{q,1:L}$ and $W_{p,1:L}$ are the encoder and the decoder parameters for learning the annotation behaviour of the coders w.r.t. each latent aspect. The weights for the latent aspects are modeled as a function of the annotations[20]:

$$z_i = [z_{i,1}, \ldots, z_{i,L}] = \mathsf{softplus}(y_i W_a)$$

With only one latent aspect the model is equivalent to the one presented before modelling the ambiguity of the items. About setting the number of latent aspects, this is to be determined

---

[20]The softplus( ) is applied element-wise in this case.

Table 5.10: The accuracy of the variational autoencoder models discussed in this section evaluated against a few baselines. The results are from Yin et al. (2017).

	Bluebirds	Flowers	Web Search
Majority vote	0.76	0.80	0.73
DARE (Bachrach et al., 2012)	0.78	0.81	0.82
BCC (Kim and Ghahramani, 2012)	0.90	0.87	0.86
Yin et al., 2017 (base version)	0.89	0.87	0.90
Yin et al., 2017 (with ambiguity)	0.91	0.88	0.91
Yin et al., 2017 (with 2 latent aspects)	**0.93**	**0.90**	**0.91**

empirically, e.g., by progressively increasing their number until the latent aspect weights show a strong positive correlation, an indication that the additionally introduced aspects are redundant.

Practical Application

Yin et al. (2017) demonstrate the performance of their variational autoencoder models on three crowdsourced datasets. This practical section discusses their findings. Two of the datasets, Bluebirds (Welinder et al., 2010) and Flowers (Tian and Zhu, 2015), contain image classifications: the first dataset contains about 100 bluebird pictures of 2 different breeds annotated by 39 coders, while the second dataset contains 200 positive and negative examples of peach flowers labelled by 36 coders. The third dataset, Web Search (Zhou et al., 2012), contains about 2,700 (query, URL) pairs judged for relevance on a 5-point scale by 177 coders. The authors compare their approach with a majority vote baseline; BCC, a Bayesian version from Kim and Ghahramani (2012) of the Dawid and Skene (1979) model discussed in detail in Section 5.3; and DARE, the multi-class version of an item difficulty from Bachrach et al. (2012) discussed in Section 5.4.

Table 5.10 reports the results of the evaluation from Yin et al. (2017). The lowest performance is reported for majority voting, an unsurprising result considering its assumption that all coders have the same ability. The next lowest is DARE (Bachrach et al., 2012) which does model the individual ability of each coder, but unlike BCC (Kim and Ghahramani, 2012), does not differentiate their ability between different classes. Possibly because of that ability BCC (Kim and Ghahramani, 2012) considerably outperforms DARE (Bachrach et al., 2012) in these experiments.

The performance of the variational autoencoder models discussed in this section is illustrated in the next three lines. Notice that even the base version manages to get strong results, demonstrating the viability of variational autoencoders to aggregate annotations in these domains. The additional layers of complexity, modelling the ambiguity of the items, and latent aspects, bring even more improvement. Yin et al. (2017) find that the ambiguity estimates, on average, correlate with the entropy of the true class distribution of the items. This empirically confirms our explanation given before that unambiguous items have more heterogeneous true class distributions, while the ambiguous items have flatter true class distributions. The unambiguous items also have a higher accuracy compared with the ambiguous ones, another result expected to be confirmed empirically.

The variational autoencoder with latent aspects further improves the performance over the version with ambiguity on two of the three datasets. On Web Search, the dataset where both models perform on par, the estimated latent aspects show a strong positive correlation, an indication just one latent aspect would have been sufficient, making in this case the latent aspect and the ambiguity models equivalent. Yin et al. (2017) also discuss the estimates for the Flowers dataset, one of the datasets where the latent aspect model does best in this evaluation. Here, the latent aspect weights show a slight negative correlation, an indication the images have different dominating traits. An inspection of the images w.r.t. their latent aspects confirms this, showing one latent aspect is prevalent in pink flowers, while the other is mostly found in white flowers.

Similar work to Yin et al. (2017) can also be found in Li et al. (2020) but applied to an information status classification task (Nissim et al., 2004, Riester et al., 2010). One novelty Li et al. (2020) introduce is to also include item embeddings into the input of the encoder network. This provides the encoder network with more information in addition to the annotations to rely on when learning the true class of the items. In our experience with this model we observed mixed results compared to the Yin et al. (2017) model.

5.10 MODELLING COMPLEX ANNOTATIONS

Tracing its roots back to the 1970s with the work on latent structure analysis, the field of probabilistic models of annotation has seen decades of research and wide adoption of its models in multiple domains. But most of the research has been done on categorical annotation tasks; other types of annotation have received significantly less attention. In standard categorical annotation tasks the coders are given a fixed set of classes to choose from when annotating; but there are many annotation tasks where the labels are more **complex**. This makes aggregating these labels challenging as they do not meet the design of standard models traditionally built for categorical tasks. We already saw an example of annotation not involving a finite set of categorical labels when we discussed anaphoric annotations, the labels there being coreference chains. Sequence labels, also covered in this chapter, although categorical, are another example of complex annotation to aggregate because of the inter-dependencies between the labels. In NLP, in particular, there are plenty of complex annotation tasks, e.g., mention detection, relation extraction (where the 'labels' are pairs), parsing, etc.[21]

---

[21]We borrowed the term 'complex annotations' from Braylan and Lease (2020) and use it to refer to annotations that go beyond simple categorical labels from a fixed set: open-set annotations, free-text responses, categorical labels but with certain inter-dependencies, structured responses, etc.

In recent years, efforts have been made to fill this gap in an otherwise well-established field, including a workshop raising this issue (Paun and Hovy, 2019) and a tutorial surveying current work in this area (Paun and Simpson, 2021). However, the literature on aggregating complex annotations, where it exists, consists mainly of specialized models such as those for sequential labels discussed in Section 5.7 and for anaphoric annotation discussed in Section 5.8. These task-specific models are generally very effective; their downside is that a new aggregation model will need to be developed for each complex annotation task, which is not an easy thing to do. Thus, another line of work have also recently been active, aiming to develop methods for modelling complex annotations in general (Braylan and Lease, 2020, Li, 2020, Li and Fukumoto, 2019). This section focuses on this latter line of work.

In particular, we focus on Braylan and Lease (2020), who propose to develop a task-independent model by modelling the **distance** between the annotations instead of the annotations themselves. Although labels differ in different tasks, the distance between them is numeric, making this approach applicable, in theory, to any annotation task. Let us look at the example of translation task from Braylan and Lease (2020):

Coder 1:   Now Hamas and Israel should make peace so that this bloodshed comes to an end.
Coder 2:   Hamas and Israel should reconcile so that this bloodshed comes to an end.
Coder 3:   Now that the Hamas and Israel should be made to compromise, so the blood and evil.

In the example we have three English translations of a sentence originally in Urdu. To compare the coders' responses, Braylan and Lease (2020) used a distance function based on GLEU (Wu et al., 2016), an evaluation metric similar to the standard BLEU metric (Papineni et al., 2002), but appropriate for sentence-level comparisons. The distances between the translations are (coder 1, coder 2) = 0.43, (coder 1, coder 3) = 0.86, and (coder 2, coder 3) = 0.88, and indicate the first translation as the one most similar to the others, followed closely by the translation of the second coder, and somewhere further away we have the third translation.

Formally, Braylan and Lease (2020) propose that each item annotated by the coders has the distances between the annotations stored in a matrix. Let D_i be this matrix of distances for item i, and let j and j' be two coders whose annotations are $y_{i,j}$ and $y_{i,j'}$, respectively, we have:

$$D_{i,j,j'} = f(y_{i,j}, y_{i,j'})$$

The distance function $f()$ is left for the end user to specify. Such distances could be, for instance, the distances for Krippendorff's α metric discussed in Chapters 2 and 3. Braylan and Lease's suggestion is to make use of an existing evaluation metric for the task the annotations were collected for, although the evaluation metric may need to be adapted to satisfy the requirements of a distance function, i.e., non-negativity, symmetry, and the triangle inequality. Here are some common transformations from an evaluation metric to a distance function:

$$f(x, y) = \text{MAE}(x, y) \qquad\qquad\qquad\qquad \text{when the annotations are numerical}$$
$$f(x, y) = 1 - F_1(x, y) \qquad\qquad\qquad\qquad \text{for classifications, or sequences}$$
$$f(x, y) = 1 - 0.5 \times \big(\text{GLEU}(x, y) + \text{GLEU}(y, x)\big) \quad \text{for sentence translation}$$

Notice some evaluation metrics such as the mean absolute error (MAE) can be used straightaway as a distance function. Other metrics such as the F1 score need to be reversed to measure error instead of accuracy, or as the case with GLEU, they need to be made symmetric. When aggregating the labels Braylan and Lease (2020) propose to select as the true class of an item the label produced by the least erroneous coder:

$$c_i = y_{i,j'} \quad , \text{where } j' = \underset{j}{\text{argmin}}\, \beta_{i,j}$$

In their smallest average distance (SAD) approach, the error of a coder j on an item i is computed as the average distance from their annotation to all the other annotations:

$$\beta_{i,j} = \frac{1}{N_i - 1} \sum_{j' \neq j} D_{i,j,j'}$$

It follows that SAD favors for the true class of an item the annotation found in accordance the most with the other annotations. In another approach, the best available user (BAU), Braylan and Lease (2020) quantify the error of a coder slightly different:

$$\beta_{i,j} = \beta_j = \frac{1}{\sum_i (N_i - 1)} \sum_{i, j' \neq j} D_{i,j,j'}$$

In BAU the error of a coder is computed globally, across all their annotations. Unlike SAD, BAU favors the annotations provided by the generally reliable coders, irrespective of the fact these may not follow the local majority. In addition to these approaches, Braylan and Lease (2020) also introduce a probabilistic model for the distances combining elements from standard models of annotation (Whitehill et al., 2009, in particular, which we discuss back in Section 5.4) and multidimensional scaling (Mead, 1992). Their model learns an embedding for each annotation of an item, based on their reliability and the difficulty of the item, and assumes the distances between any two annotations are the result of their proximity in this embedding space. A coder whose annotation has the embedding space estimated closer to the origin is deemed more reliable. As before, the annotations produced by the most reliable coders are selected as the true class of the items.

Braylan and Lease (2020) evaluated their distance-based approaches to aggregating complex annotations on two datasets, crowdsourced translations and sequences, and found encouraging results. Notably, on sequences, their methods have comparable results to the specialized model of Nguyen et al. (2017) which we discussed back in Section 5.7. Similar work was carried out in Li and Fukumoto (2019) and Li (2020) with good results in adjudicating translations. In the current state the methods we discussed may not better the performance of task-specialized models, but they are competitive, and have the advantage of being applicable to many types of annotation which is especially useful for those annotation tasks not supported by the current aggregation models. Having a way now to distill complex annotations from noise furthers also the use of crowdsourcing for more types of annotation which were previously considered suitable only for experts. Complex annotations also raise the issue on how best to design the annotation schemes for maximum validity. The field is just emerging, and there are plenty of challenges ahead.

CHAPTER 6

Learning from Multi-Annotated Corpora

6.1 INTRODUCTION

The advent of crowdsourcing has made the collection of judgements from multiple coders feasible in terms of time, effort, and cost, which has made it possible for resource creators to publish multi-annotated corpora. Nevertheless, the standard practice for corpus creation and use remains to assign a hard, or one-hot, label to each item, either through manual adjudication or using methods such as those discussed in Chapter 5 and to train from that.

This practice however ignores the growing evidence that one-hot labels are an idealization. Disagreements between coders have been documented in any large-scale annotation projects for any type of task, from those dealing with subjective matters where you would expect disagreement, such as in sentiment analysis (Kenyon-Dean et al., 2018), irony and sarcasm, offensive and abusive language detection, or hate speech detection (Akhtar et al., 2019, 2020, Basile, 2020), to tasks concerned with apparently more objective aspects, where disagreements are probably less expected, but prevalent nevertheless, such as in image labelling (Peterson et al., 2019), part-of-speech tagging (Plank et al., 2014b), wordsense disambiguation (Jurgens, 2013, Passonneau et al., 2012), coreference resolution (Poesio and Artstein, 2005, Poesio et al., 2019, Recasens et al., 2011), or semantic role labelling (Dumitrache et al., 2019).

These disagreements have different causes (Poesio et al., 2019, Uma et al., 2021b), but most of the literature on annotation analysis has focused on two. One obvious issue is **imprecise or vague annotation schemes**, and perhaps **problems with the annotation interface**. One of the primary objectives of the reliability tests discussed in Part I of this book was to eliminate or reduce this kind of problem. A second source of disagreement is **annotation error**, whether due to carelessness or lack of understanding of the annotation scheme. The methods discussed in Chapter 5 were designed to address this type of issue, and to produce aggregated labels taking into account annotator abilities.

But while covering those proposals we repeatedly saw that there were other reasons for the annotators disagreeing—reasons generally covered by the 'item difficulty' category. One factor leading to 'difficulty' is **ambiguity** (Poesio, 2020, Poesio et al., 2019). Ambiguity is sometimes deliberate. Humour (Poesio, 2020, Raskin, 1985), poetry (Su, 1994), or political discourse (Winkler, 2015), are among the many genres where ambiguity is deliberately utilized.

But the great majority of cases of ambiguity are unplanned, inherently present in the way we communicate. Take the following example from (Yang et al., 2011):

(10)   [Table data] is dumped into a [delimited text file], which is sent to the remote site where *it* is loaded into the destination database.

The sentence above illustrates an example of anaphoric ambiguity: the pronoun 'it' has two plausible antecedents it can refer to, 'table data' and 'delimited text file', respectively. The annotations collected for this example indicate the coders split evenly between the two interpretations. Both antecedents in this case are easily identifiable so they are not the reason for the coders' disagreement. The disagreement comes from the fact the coders are forced to choose one antecedent over the other when both interpretations apply.

Ambiguity in this sense is often conflated with, but distinct from, item difficulty as in the examples discussed in Section 5.4. There, it is not the plurality of correct interpretations causing disagreement between the coders, but the difficulty in identifying them in the first place. The ability of the coders to annotate correctly is impacted by the difficulty of the items: on easy items the coders are expected to find consensus, but on difficult items their disagreement becomes more prevalent. The impact of difficulty in this sense on disagreement has been highlighted by, among others, Beigman and Klebanov (2009), Beigman Klebanov and Beigman (2009), Klebanov and Beigman (2014), and Reidsma and Carletta (2008).

Both in the case of ambiguous and in the case of difficult data examples, having a single label is inadequate, as a model treats them as clear-cut examples of classification, when they are clearly not. But this limitation is even more serious in the case of tasks where disagreement is due to the **subjectivity** of the tasks. Consider the following item from the Sexism dataset for offensive language detection (Waseem, 2016) reported by Akhtar et al. (2019):

(11)   @ XXX uh... did you watch the video? one of the women talked about how it's assumed she's angry because she's latina.

Different annotators assign very different labels to such items because they have different subjective views on what counts as sexist or not. Using gold labels in these cases would account to instructing the models to take a side.

In the cases of disagreement due to ambiguity, difficulty, or subjectivity, an adjudication of the annotations to a gold standard leads to a loss of important information about the labelling uncertainty of the coders, overlooking the true nature of the tasks we are trying to solve. In the words of Aroyo and Welty (2015), in such cases, *disagreement is information, not noise*. The data examples that we feed to our models may be subjective, hard, ambiguous, and the coders, experts included, have biases, and can make labelling mistakes, sometimes pushed by problems with the interface, or with the annotation scheme. Having only one label to describe each data example takes away all of this complexity and crudely reduces it to unrealistic clear-cut decisions. This chapter presents evidence that training machine learning models using all the annotations, when these are available, can considerably improve their performance over using adjudicated labels.

The sections cover different methods to learning from multi-annotated corpora, from learning from the collective annotations of the coders, i.e., using so-called soft labels (Section 6.2), to learning from the coders' individual labels (Section 6.3), or how to distill the labels from noise during training (Sections 6.4 and 6.5). We conclude the chapter with useful recommendations about when to apply each method depending on the characteristics of the datasets the models are to be trained on (Section 6.6).

6.2   LEARNING WITH SOFT LABELS

Peterson et al. (2019) propose a straightforward method to train classifiers on multi-annotated corpora. They argue for the use of **soft labels**, i.e., distributions described by the collective annotations of the coders. These distributions over the label space offer in their view a richer source of information compared to adjudicated labels, or **hard labels**. Soft labels indicate the strength of the consensus among the coders, approximating the difficulty of the data; they can flag the presence of ambiguity, i.e., when the coders' judgements separate distinctively between different categories; and can also inform the models about how us humans make mistakes, i.e., capturing that some labelling errors are more likely than others.

Clearly, the success of this learning approach is subject to how well these distributions represent the true labelling uncertainty of the coders. To test their proposal, Peterson et al. (2019) collected about 50 annotations for each image from the test set of the popular CIFAR10 corpus (Krizhevsky, 2009). To make sure the right level of annotation quality is maintained throughout they provided training to the coders and included periodic attention checks. The effort paid off: a simple analysis shows the mode of the distributions described by the collected annotations (the category holding the majority vote) matches the gold (expert) label in more than 99% of the cases. So these soft labels contain not only the signal from the gold labels, but also additional information about their uncertainty. Although not all annotation projects can afford such extensive labelling at scale, we will show in the practical section below that this learning approach brings benefits not only when the annotations are abundant and of a high quality, but also on more typical crowdsourced corpora with a smaller number of annotations per item.

The training regime proposed by Peterson et al. is straightforward. Let h_i be a column vector associated with some training example $i \in \{1, 2, ..., I\}$ and corresponding to the output of the last hidden layer of a (deep) neural network with an arbitrary architecture. All that is required is to add a softmax output layer to the existing architecture. The prediction for training example i is as follows:

$$p_i = \mathsf{softmax}\,(W h_i)$$

The loss $\mathcal{L}_i$ for a training example measures the cross entropy of the prediction distribution p_i relative to a target distribution t_i described by the annotations. Assuming K classes, this is expressed as follows:

$$\mathcal{L}_i = H(t_i, p_i) = -\sum_{k=1}^{K} t_{i,k} \log p_{i,k}$$

In Peterson et al. (2019), the target distributions consist of the raw annotation counts normalized to probabilities in standard fashion, i.e., dividing the counts for each class by their total number. Uma et al. (2020), however, who also tested on datasets without high-quality annotations and in such large volumes, additionally experiment with normalizing the raw counts with a softmax. When the annotations are too scarce and/or too noisy to properly represent the true labelling uncertainty of the coders the softmax seems more suitable compared with standard normalization as it both smooths the target distribution for better regularization of the neural network, and it reduces the level of noise by producing a distribution with a lower entropy. When the annotations are abundant, however, and of a high quality, it is the standard normalization that seems like the better choice as it keeps the original class proportions in place, the softmax in this case exacerbating any differences between the raw annotation counts, and losing so the richness of the original representation. This simple normalization trick has important effects on the prediction quality of the network as the practical example introduced below will show.

Evaluation, Hard, and Soft

The advantage of soft labels over hard labels in terms of preserving labelling uncertainty can also be leveraged to provide a richer and more nuanced evaluation compared to the standard practice which makes the assumption of a single, i.e., a 'hard' truth for the test items. We shall refer to the standard evaluation practice based on gold labels as **hard evaluation**, and to the evaluation that uses soft labels as **soft evaluation**. A number of recent papers make the case for complementing a hard evaluation with a soft evaluation when that is possible, i.e., when multiple annotations are available and these have the right quality (Basile, 2020, Basile et al., 2021, Peterson et al., 2019, Uma et al., 2020, 2021a,b).[1] Among the metrics that can be used to judge the predictions of the models relative to the target soft labels, cross entropy seems an obvious choice (see Uma et al., 2021b, for a more comprehensive discussion on soft evaluation metrics).

Practical Application

An illustration of soft-label training with hard and soft evaluation are the experiments by Uma et al. (2020), who complement Peterson et al. (2019) by demonstrating the benefits of training a (deep) neural network with soft labels on a wider variety of datasets. Uma et al. (2020) consider not only datasets with abundant and high-quality annotations, but also datasets more representative in terms of annotation quality and volume of the datasets commonly used. Also,

---

[1]Evaluation metrics accepting multiple answers are, of course, already the norm for NLP tasks such as machine translation—e.g., BLEU (Papineni et al., 2002)—summarization—e.g., ROUGE (Lin, 2004)—or ranking search results with NDCG (Järvelin and Kekäläinen, 2002). In standard classification tasks, however, this idea has scarcely been adopted, and is only getting more attention now as efforts to better understand disagreements in annotation are intensifying.

Table 6.1: Key statistics for the datasets used in the experiments on learning with hard and soft labels

	PoS Tagging	LabelMe	CIFAR10H
Number of items	14,000	10,000	10,000
Number of categories	12	8	10
Mean annotations per item	16.37	2.50	51.10
Median annotations per item	5	3	51
Average observed agreement per item	0.73	0.73	0.92
Majority voting accuracy	0.80	0.77	0.99
Dawid and Skene (1979) accuracy	0.79	0.80	0.99

Table 6.2: The results in terms of accuracy (Acc) and cross entropy (CE) obtained when training neural networks using hard and soft labels

		PoS Tagging	LabelMe	CIFAR10H	
Training Labels		Acc	Acc	Acc	CE
Hard labels	Gold labels	89.22	97.21	65.22	2.61
	Majority voting	77.90	80.36	65.68	2.63
	Dawid and Skene (1979)	77.46	83.43	65.65	2.55
Soft labels	Standard normalization	78.99	83.46	**66.64**	**1.11**
	Softmax normalization	**80.03**	**84.85**	65.50	2.57

the datasets include both datasets from computer vision—the CIFAR10H corpus annotated by Peterson et al. (2019) and the LabelMe dataset from Rodrigues et al. (2017)—and an NLP part-of-speech tagging corpus from Plank et al. (2014b). Table 6.1 presents a few statistics about these datasets showing, among other things, how they vary in the number of annotations per item, and in the accuracy of the labels chosen by the majority of the coders, information indicative of the quality of the distributions that the annotations describe. When the number of annotations is low and the labels that hold the majority have a poor accuracy, as is the case with the PoS Tagging and the LabelMe datasets, the annotations may offer a skewed representation of the true labelling uncertainty of the coders; on the other hand, when those figures are high, as in the CIFAR10H dataset, the annotations offer a good proxy for this uncertainty.

The results of Uma et al.'s experiments are shown in Table 6.2. All evaluated methods for a given task employ the same neural network (see the paper for the details about the architectures); the only thing that changes is the label used to train them. A first observation is that training using soft labels improves a model's performance over training with hard labels aggregated using majority voting or Dawid and Skene. Notice that this is the case even though the mode of the soft labels, i.e., the category holding the majority vote of the coders and the interpretation with the most probability mass under these distributions, matches or it is lower in terms of quality compared to the hard labels (see the accuracy of majority voting and of the (Dawid and Skene, 1979) model from Table 6.1). The regularization coming from the alternative interpretations proves to benefit greatly the network, something hard labels cannot provide.

Training with soft labels only helps over training with gold labels on the CIFAR10H dataset, where their mode matches gold in quality; on the other two datasets, the gap is too big to be made up by the regularization. Also, training with more accurate labels systematically improves performance over training with lower quality ones—for instance, the highest-quality hard labels produced by a probabilistic annotation model (Dawid and Skene, 1979) systematically improve performance over training with the hard labels chosen using the majority voting heuristic. A final point is that when the network is trained using soft labels, the way the annotations are normalized has a significant impact on its prediction performance. As discussed earlier in this section, when the annotations are scarce and noisy, as in the PoS Tagging and the LabelMe datasets, obtaining the distribution via a softmax produces better soft labels compared with a standard normalization of the annotations. This is because the softmax reduces the level of noise in the annotations by producing distributions with a lower entropy, and also smooths these distributions better for a better regularization of the network. The results are the other way around for the CIFAR10H dataset, where the annotations are abundant and of a high quality. In this case a standard normalization produces the better soft labels, as it keeps unaltered the rich representation of labelling uncertainty described by the raw annotations.

The quality of the annotations in the CIFAR10H dataset also makes soft evaluation empirically more grounded as a form of evaluation. Using hard labels during training we cannot recover well the labelling uncertainty of the coders, which turns out to result in lower performance on unseen data (Peterson et al., 2019). With this dataset it pays to keep unaltered the rich representation of labelling uncertainty given by the annotations, and this happens when we produce soft labels for training using the standard normalization. The softmax in this case makes the soft labels resemble hard labels, a point confirmed by the results (see softmax normalization vs. hard labels).

6.3 LEARNING INDIVIDUAL CODER MODELS

In the previous section we saw how training models with soft labels, i.e., using the annotations from all coders as a distribution, improves their generalization capability over training with hard labels which encode only the most likely interpretations of the training examples. Guan et al. (2018) argue that the generalization capability of a model can be further improved by having the model *learn how the coders annotate individually* rather than collectively as with soft labels. At test time, once the network has learned the labelling patterns of each coder, it can be used to make labelling predictions which can afterwards be averaged to get a combined response. Or a further learning phase can be included into the process to infer how best to *weight the coders' predictions* in the averaging to adjust for their reliability. This section discusses this alternative approach to learning with soft labels.

Formally, let h_i be a column vector associated with some training example $i \in \{1, 2, ..., I\}$ and corresponding to the output of the last hidden layer of a (deep) neural network with an arbitrary architecture. The approach involves adding to the hidden layer as many softmax output layers as there are coders. The prediction distribution associated with training example i and some coder $j \in J$ is as follows:

$$p_{i,j} = \mathsf{softmax}\left(W_j h_i\right)$$

The loss for a training example ($\mathcal{L}_i$) accumulates the loss coming from each annotation. The per annotation loss is the cross entropy of the predicted label distribution ($p_{i,j}$) relative to a one-hot encoding of the actual label produced by the coder ($t_{i,j}$). Let $J_i \subseteq J$ be the subset of coders that annotated the training example, we have:

$$\mathcal{L}_i = \sum_{j \in J_i} H(t_{i,j}, p_{i,j})$$

Training the model described above will have it learn the labelling patterns of the coders. As we mentioned before, at test time, in what Guan et al. (2018) refer to as the Doctor Net (DN) approach,[2] the model can be used to make labelling predictions for each coder and then have them averaged for a combined response:

$$p_i = \frac{1}{J} \sum_{j \in J} p_{i,j}$$

A downside to combining the predictions of the coders with a simple average is their individual reliability is neglected. Guan et al. (2018) recognise this and experiment with a few approaches to learn coder-specific weights to better represent their contribution to the overall prediction. These weights are estimated in a separate learning task based on the labelling predictions themselves. Concretely, for some training example i we have:

$$p_i = \frac{\sum_{j \notin J_i} p_{i,j} w_j}{\sum_{j \notin J_i} w_j}$$

$$t_i = \frac{1}{|J_i|} \sum_{j \in J_i} t_{i,j}$$

The weights $w_{1:J}$ are estimated by minimizing a standard cross entropy loss, i.e., $\mathcal{L} = \sum_i H(t_i, p_i)$. In the approached referred to as Weighted DN (WDN) the weights are initialized

---

[2]The reason for the name is that Guan et al.'s coders are doctors.

from some fixed vector. In another approach, called Image-specific WDN (IWDN), the weights are modelled as function of the last last hidden layer of the DN network:

$$w = \text{softmax}\,(W_w h_i)$$

Finally, a third approach is presented, Bottlenecked IWDN (BIWDN), in which Guan et al. (2018) include an additional small layer into the IWDN network above to reduce the number of parameters to prevent overfitting:

$$h_b = \text{ReLU}\,(W_b h_i)$$
$$w = \text{softmax}\,(W_w h_b)$$

Once the reliability weights have been estimated, using either WDN, IWDN, or BIWDN approaches, they can be used to adjust the labelling predictions of the coders when combining them at test time, instead of taking an average as before:

$$p_i = \sum_{j \in J} w_j\, p_{i,j}$$

Practical Application

Guan et al. (2018) evaluate their approaches to learning from multi-annotated corpora on a diabetic retinopathy (DR) classification task. The dataset consists of over 126,000 images sourced from screened patients. The training and validation data were graded by 31 ophthalmologists (or last year residents), while the test data was labeled by 3 retina specialists. The coders used one of 5 grades to label each image: no DR (healthy), mild NPDR (non-proliferative DR), moderate NPDR, severe NPDR, and proliferative DR. In addition to the training methods described in this section, the evaluation includes also the approach to learn using soft labels we introduced in the previous section. The base neural architecture for all neural models is the Inception-v3 architecture (Szegedy et al., 2016). As we have already explained, what changes between all these networks is only the way they learn from the coders' labels.

The results are shown in Table 6.3. A first observation is that by learning to predict the individual labels of the doctors (as proposed by Guan et al., 2018) the models obtain a lower classification error on this dataset compared to learning from their overall labelling distribution (i.e., using soft labels as in Peterson et al., 2019). At least on this dataset the hypothesis of Guan et al. (2018) that this way of training can further improve the generalization capability of a model over learning with soft labels proves to be correct.[3] The results also indicate that when combining the predictions of the coders it is better to adjust for their reliability over taking a simple average (see DN vs. WDN, IWDN, and BIWDN). From the different approaches Guan et

---

[3]We should note that—on other datasets—Uma et al. (2021b) achieved better performance using soft labels than using individual coder model. This raises the issue of the extent to which the results above generalize to other datasets—but we should also point out that Uma et al. did not test the model by Guan et al., but the Deep Learning from Crowds model discussed in the next section. See also the summary section at the end of this chapter.

Table 6.3: Classification error results for a diabetic retinopathy task

Method	Classification Error
Learning with soft labels (Peterson et al., 2019)	23.83
Doctor Net (DN) (Guan et al., 2018)	21.86
Weighted Doctor Net (WDN) (Guan et al., 2018)	**20.58**
Image-specific WDN (IWDN) (Guan et al., 2018)	20.63
Bottlenecked IWDN (BIWDN) (Guan et al., 2018)	20.83

al. (2018) experimented with to weight the doctors, Weighted Doctor Net (WDN) was found to work best on this dataset. Image-specific WDN (IWDN) and Bottlenecked IWDN (BI-WDN), which additionally have the coder weights dependent on the images, did not get the desired boost in performance. Maybe if the doctors had more varying abilities across the images the benefits would have showed up.

6.4   DEALING WITH NOISE

So far we have discussed in this chapter two approaches for learning from multi-annotated corpora: training models with soft labels, i.e., distributions over the label space built from the collective annotations of the coders, or having them learn from the coders' individual labels. Neither approach, however, incorporates specific mechanisms for dealing with noisy labels. The noise in the training data, and in particular that created by systematic coder biases, can misguide a network to incorrect predictions (see, e.g., the study by Reidsma and Carletta, 2008). One way to mitigate this problem is to remove the noise from the labels with the help of a probabilistic model of annotation such as those described back in Chapter 5. But we have already seen that by training the networks with hard labels, such as the labels estimated by an annotation model, we are losing important information about the coders' dissent, information shown to improve the prediction quality of a network. So a good solution would require to keep all the annotations when training the network, but have the network learn additionally to adjust to the accuracy and bias of the coders in order to avoid picking up noisy patterns. The benefits of a *joint approach* where *the network learns to distill the labels from noise while training*, already advocated by Raykar et al. (2010), are twofold. First, as mentioned before, the prediction quality of the network improves now over training with hard labels as it gets regularized by the multiple interpretations. And second, the labels distilled by the network offer a more accurate ground-truth of the training data over one decided using an aggregation method purely on the basis of the annotations. This happens because in this case we are leveraging not only the coders' annotation patterns, but also the knowledge of the task the network had accumulated. In this section we discuss two approaches for training (deep) neural networks on data with multiple noisy interpretations. One of the approaches incorporates a probabilistic model of annotation to learn to distill the labels from noise, while the other has the advantage of being fully neural.

Modelling the Annotations with a Probabilistic Model

Albarqouni et al. (2016) propose an approach that relies on the ability of a probabilistic model of annotation to distill the labels from noise to more accurately train a neural classifier. The approach follows the direction advocated by Raykar et al. (2010), where the classifier and the annotation model are trained jointly (see Section 5.6 for discussion). Albarqouni et al. (2016) develop their approach assuming dichotomous annotations, but it can easily be extended to work with categorical annotations (see, e.g., Isupova et al., 2018, Rodrigues and Pereira, 2018). Here we discuss this multiclass extension.

Let σ_i be a K-dimensional softmax output layer of a neural classifier with an arbitrary architecture, where $i \in \{1, 2, ..., I\}$ indexes the training examples. Following the theory of probabilistic models of annotation (see Sections 5.2 and 5.3 for a primer) each training example i is assumed to have a true class c_i encoding their most likely interpretation among the interpretations provided by the coders. The prior probability for the true class of the training example is given by the aforementioned prediction distribution of the neural classifier:

$$p(c_i = k|\sigma_i) = \sigma_{i,k}$$

The annotations collected for a training example, $y_{i,1:N_i}$, are treated as noisy observations of its (latent) true class and follow the generative process from Dawid and Skene (1979) which we discussed back in Section 5.3. Remember that the generative process assumes conditional independence between the annotations:

$$p(y_{i,1:N_i}|c_i) = \prod_{n=1}^{N_i} p(y_{i,n}|c_i)$$

And that the likelihood of an annotation is given by the annotation behaviour of its coder with respect to the true class of the training example[4]:

$$p(y_{i,n}|c_i) = \beta_{jj[i,n],c_i,y_{i,n}}$$

The annotation behaviour of each coder $j \in \{1, 2, ..., J\}$ is formulated in terms of a confusion matrix β_j. For example, the probability that coder j annotates a training example whose true class is k with label k' is given by the $\beta_{j,k,k'}$ entry. This design choice allows the annotation model to capture the accuracy (the entries from the main diagonal of the confusion matrix) and the bias (the off-diagonal entries) of the coders during training and to appropriately adjust the true class of the training examples to these factors. Consequently, the neural network, which does not learn directly from the annotations as in the approaches we discussed in the previous

---

[4]Notation: $jj[i, n]$ returns the index of the coder who produced the nth annotation for training example i.

sections, but from the true class of the training examples, has a smaller chance of being exposed to noise.

With slight amendments, the approach from Albarqouni et al. (2016) can also be used in regression tasks. The details of the necessary changes are described in Rodrigues and Pereira (2018) and follow a parameterization for continuous annotations from Raykar et al. (2010). In regression tasks σ_i stands now for a real-valued prediction made by a neural regression network. The approach is conceptually the same to that described before for classification tasks: the annotations provided by the coders are assumed to be noisy values of those predicted by the network. Formally, this is specified by a Gaussian noise model with mean h_i and precision β_j:

$$y_{i,n} \sim \mathsf{Normal}\left(\sigma_i, \beta_{jj[i,n]}\right)$$

The accuracy of the coders can be interpreted following their precision estimates: the more 'precise' coders (i.e., when their β_j is bigger) are the ones more likely to annotate with similar values to those predicted by the neural network. During training the network will be incentivized to learn to make accurate predictions such that the probabilistic model can explain well the annotations of the coders w.r.t. their accuracy.

Th Deep Learning from Crowds Approach

Jointly training a neural network and estimating the parameters of a probabilistic annotation model introduces a computational overhead. The technical details for the optimization of the parameters go beyond the scope of this book, but in general terms, the computational overhead is created by the fact that we need to alternate between two learning mechanisms, one for the network, the other for the annotation model (more details in Albarqouni et al., 2016). To overcome this problem, Rodrigues and Pereira (2018) proposed an approach which integrates the mechanism that distills the annotations from noise, i.e., what the annotation model was responsible for in the previous approach, into the architecture of the neural network. The system, now fully neural, can be trained in standard fashion without the aforementioned overhead. Concretely, the approach from Rodrigues and Pereira (2018) involves augmenting an existing neural network with an additional **crowd layer** which takes as input the network's predictions and learns to further predict the coders' annotations. This additional component will observe the annotations of the coders and pick up their accuracy and biases, calibrating in turn the network's predictions.

Formally, let σ_i be the output layer of a neural network with an arbitrary architecture, e.g., a softmax layer for classification tasks, or a linear layer for regression. The prediction distribution for an annotator $j \in \{1, 2, ..., J\}$ on some training example $i \in \{1, 2, ..., I\}$ is a function of the aforementioned output layer:

$$p_{i,j} = f_j(\sigma_i)$$

Rodrigues and Pereira (2018) experiment with different functions to model the annotation behaviour of the coders. For classification tasks they use:

$$f_j(\sigma_i) = \mathsf{softmax}\left(W_j \sigma_i\right) \qquad \text{using a per coder matrix of weights}$$
$$f_j(\sigma_i) = \mathsf{softmax}\left(w_j \odot \sigma_i\right) \qquad \text{a per coder vector of class weights}$$
$$f_j(\sigma_i) = \mathsf{softmax}\left(b_j + \sigma_i\right) \qquad \text{a per coder vector of class biases}$$

The loss associated with a training example ($\mathcal{L}_i$) accumulates the loss coming from the network's predictions for each of the annotations produced by the coders; the loss for a coder's annotation ($\mathcal{L}_{i,n}$) is the cross entropy of the predicted label distribution ($p_{i,jj[i,n]}$) relative to a one-hot encoding of the actual label ($y_{i,n}$):

$$\mathcal{L}_i = \sum_{n=1}^{N_i} \mathcal{L}_{i,n} = -\sum_{n=1}^{N_i} \log p_{i,jj[i,n],y_{i,n}}$$

When the labels are continuous, such as in regression tasks, Rodrigues and Pereira (2018) experiment with the following functions to model the coders' rating behaviour:

$$f_j(\sigma_i) = s_j \sigma_i \qquad \text{using a per coder scale}$$
$$f_j(\sigma_i) = b_j + \sigma_i \qquad \text{a per coder bias}$$
$$f_j(\sigma_i) = s_j \sigma_i + b_j \qquad \text{a per coder scale and bias}$$

In this case the cross entropy loss used before is replaced by a mean squared error (MSE) loss:

$$\mathcal{L}_i = \sum_{n=1}^{N_i} \mathcal{L}_{i,n} = \frac{1}{N_i} \sum_{n=1}^{N_i} \left(y_{i,n} - p_{i,jj[i,n]}\right)^2$$

The approach described in this section allows a network to calibrate its predictions during training to the accuracy and bias of the coders which are learned with the help of an additionally introduced component from observing their annotation patterns: the network makes predictions which the additional component adjusts to best explain the annotation behaviour of the coders. In the approach from Guan et al. (2018) we described in the previous section the network also learns from the annotation patterns of the coders to predict their labels, but without learning to make its own predictions first. These predictions are useful as they allow the network to learn a representation for the true class of the training examples, adjusted to the accuracy and bias of the coders as explained before.

Practical Application

This practical section follows the experiments from Rodrigues and Pereira (2018) covering the two different approaches we introduced above to training (deep) neural networks while also learning to distill the labels from noise. We discuss the results for a classification and a regression task. The experiments for the classification task were conducted on a crowd annotated

Table 6.4: Classification accuracy (results extracted from Rodrigues and Pereira, 2018) for an image labelling task (the LabelMe dataset)

Method	Accuracy
Training on the labels chosen by the majority of coders	76.74
Training on labels aggregated with (Dawid and Skene, 1979)	80.79
Weighted Doctor Net (Guan et al., 2018)	82.41
(Albarqouni et al., 2016) for categorical annotations	82.68
(Rodrigues and Pereira, 2018) with per coder class weights	81.05
(Rodrigues and Pereira, 2018) with per coder class weights and biases	81.89
(Rodrigues and Pereira, 2018) with per coder matrix of weights	**83.15**
Training on gold labels	90.63

version (Rodrigues et al., 2017) of the LabelMe corpus (Russell et al., 2008) which contains about 2,600 images, with 1,000 of them (the training set) labelled on average by 2.5 workers with annotations covering 8 categories. For the regression task Rodrigues and Pereira (2018) used a dataset of 5,000 movie reviews (Rodrigues et al., 2017), with 1,500 of them (again, the training set) rated on average by 5 coders (out of 137) with values from a 10 points scale.

The results for the classification task are presented in Table 6.4. All approaches to learning from multi-annotated corpora evaluated by Rodrigues and Pereira (2018) use the same neural base architecture, i.e., a fairly standard CNN-based architecture (see the paper for the exact details). What changes between the different methods is the way they learn from the labels given by the coders. A first observation is that the methods which use all the annotations during training have a better performance to those learning from hard, aggregated labels (see the results for the last four vs. the first two methods). As we have been reiterating throughout this chapter, keeping all the annotations during training allows for a better regularization of a network as opposed to training with hard labels. About training using hard labels the performance can be improved by using an aggregation method more capable of distilling the labels from noise, e.g., by using the model of Dawid and Skene (1979) vs. a simple majority voting. From the different methods which train with all the annotations, the ones from Albarqouni et al. (2016) and Rodrigues and Pereira (2018) which learn how the coders confuse the (true) class of the images do best. We see there is not much difference, performance-wise, between the method of Rodrigues and Pereira (2018) (with per coder matrix of weights) and that of Albarqouni et al. (2016), but the real benefit of the former is in the speed and simplicity it can be trained with. We remind ourselves the method of Rodrigues and Pereira (2018) is fully neural, while the one from Albarqouni et al. (2016) relies on a probabilistic annotation model to distill the labels from noise. This introduces a computational overhead for the (Albarqouni et al., 2016) method

Table 6.5: Regression results (extracted from Rodrigues and Pereira, 2018) for a movie rating task. The results are reported in terms of the root mean squared error (RMSE) and the mean absolute error (MAE) metrics.

Method	RMSE	MAE
Training on the mean ratings	1.50	1.22
(Albarqouni et al., 2016) adapted for regression	1.48	1.20
(Rodrigues and Pereira, 2018) with per coder scale	1.51	1.23
(Rodrigues and Pereira, 2018) with per coder bias	**1.41**	**1.13**
(Rodrigues and Pereira, 2018) with per coder scale and bias	1.44	1.16
Training on gold ratings	1.33	1.05

resulting in slower training times. The Rodrigues and Pereira (2018) approach, on the other hand, can be trained in standard fashion with an off-the-self optimizer for neural networks. A simpler training objective can also mean a more effective estimation of the parameters and in turn a better network, though further experiments would be needed to confirm there is a significant difference in performance between the two methods. The approach from Guan et al. (2018) which we introduced in the previous section does not do as well in this evaluation compared with those from Albarqouni et al. (2016) and Rodrigues and Pereira (2018) as it lacks the mechanism these other methods have to distill the labels from noise.

Finally, Table 6.5 presents the results for a regression task about predicting movie ratings. Just as in the classification task, the base neural architecture is a standard CNN-based architecture. The results paint a similar picture to those before: training using all the annotations leads to a better performance over training on single annotations (the last four methods vs. the first one). Among the evaluated methods, the one designed by Rodrigues and Pereira (2018) to capture the bias of the coders gets the best results here, although the significance of the differences between the networks in this particular evaluation is unclear.

6.5   POOLING CODER CONFUSIONS

We discussed in the previous section the work by Rodrigues and Pereira (2018) which propose an effective way to train a (deep) neural network on data labeled by multiple noisy annotators. Their approach requires only a simple augmentation of the neural network with an additional component which takes as input the network's predictions and learns to predict the coders' annotations. During training, by observing the coders' annotation patterns, the additional component can pick up their accuracy and biases, and calibrate in turn the network's predictions. In this section we discuss an extension of the way the coders' annotations are modelled by the aforementioned component. In Rodrigues and Pereira (2018) we saw this is done on the basis of their annotation behaviour relative to the network's predictions, i.e., an encoding of their accuracy and biases. Chu et al. (2021) argue that although the coders do have their own accuracy and biases when they annotate, they also *share common confusions*. For example, the authors analyse the annotations collected for a dataset of songs belonging to different genres (Rodrigues et al., 2014) and find large percentages of coders had mistakenly labeled metal songs as rock songs, or disco songs as pop. Similarly, prevalent collective mistakes were also observed in the annotations from the LabelMe corpus (Rodrigues et al., 2017, Russell et al., 2008). Chu et al. (2021) hypothesize that coders make the decision to annotate following their own judgements, or to use the common perception depending on their confidence. If the coders are more skilled, and/or the items they are presented with are easier, they are more likely to annotate according to their own accuracy and biases. On the other hand, if their expertise is lower, and/or the items are hard, they will more likely choose the labels following a collective perception of the phenomenon they were asked to annotate. Formally, Chu et al. (2021) model the prediction distribution for a coder $j \in \{1, 2, ..., J\}$ on some training example $i \in \{1, 2, ..., I\}$ as follows:

$$p_{i,j} = w_{i,j} \times f_g(\sigma_i) + (1 - w_{i,j}) \times f_j(\sigma_i)$$

The label is predicted using either the collective annotation behavior of the coders $f_g(\sigma_i)$ or the coder's own annotation behaviour $f_j(\sigma_i)$. Both the collective and the coder's own annotation behaviour are modeled as in Rodrigues and Pereira (2018) as a function of the network's prediction σ_i, encoding their accuracy and biases with a matrix of weights:

$$f_g(\sigma_i) = \mathsf{softmax}\left(W_g \sigma_i\right)$$
$$f_j(\sigma_i) = \mathsf{softmax}\left(W_j \sigma_i\right)$$

The weight $w_{i,j}$ encodes the decision about which model of annotation behaviour the network should use to predict the annotation, and it is determined on the basis of an embedding of the coder (u_j), and another of the training example (v_i) the annotation is predicted for:

$$w_{i,j} = \mathsf{logistic}\left(u_j^T v_i\right)$$

Notice that when the weight is set to zero the approach we are discussing becomes equivalent to that from Rodrigues and Pereira (2018) which uses only the coders' own accuracy and biases to predict the annotations. The embeddings for each coder are learned from any features we have available for them, or from their one-hot encoding otherwise. The embeddings for the training examples are learned in a similar fashion. Let e_j and x_i be the features for a coder, and for a training example, respectively; the embeddings are learned as follows:

$$u_j = W_u e_j + b_u$$
$$v_i = W_v x_i + b_v$$

Large values in the embedding space of the coders and in that of the training examples will have the network choose the coders' collective annotation behaviour to predict the labels

Table 6.6: Classification accuracy results

Method	LabelMe	Music
Training on the labels chosen by the majority of coders	79.83	72.53
Training on labels aggregated with (Whitehill et al., 2009)	83.12	77.82
(Albarqouni et al., 2016)	84.75	81.92
(Rodrigues and Pereira, 2018) with per coder matrix of weights	83.27	81.46
(Chu et al., 2021)	**87.12**	**84.06**

while lower values will have the network use the coders' own annotation behaviour. It is unclear whether the network actually learns with these embeddings a representation for the coders' ability and for the difficulty of the training examples, respectively, as Chu et al. (2021) hypothesize, or it simply produces representations on the basis of their features that allow it to best explain the annotation patterns of the coders, whichever interpretation these may have. What is clear, however, as the experiments from the practical example below will show, is that by separating during training between the two different sources of labelling confusion among coders, collective and individual, the network improves its prediction capabilities.

Practical Application

This practical example follows the experiments from Chu et al. (2021) to show the benefits of separating between the collective and the individual accuracy and biases of the coders when using their labels to train a (deep) neural network. The experiments were conducted on two datasets, the LabelMe corpus (Rodrigues et al., 2017, Russell et al., 2008) we have seen already in previous sections (see Section 6.2 for some statistics about this dataset), and a dataset on classifying songs by their genre (Rodrigues et al., 2014). The latter dataset, called Music, contains 1,000 song samples, 700 of which (the training set) were labeled on average by 4.2 crowd workers with annotations about their genre from 10 categories; the rest of 300 song samples were gold annotated using experts and used for testing.

The results can be found in Table 6.6. In the previous sections of this chapter the reader can find, described in detail, all the approaches to learning from multi-annotated corpora Chu et al. (2021) include in their evaluation. Lower results are obtained when the network is trained using hard labels, i.e., using either the labels chosen by the majority of the coders, or the labels from a probabilistic annotation model (Whitehill et al., 2009). Note the annotation model can distill the labels from noise better compared with a simple majority vote, and this gets reflected in the quality of the network's predictions. But the noise distillation and the training of the classifier are performed separately with these methods. In Section 6.4, we discussed how jointly training a classifier and learning to distill the labels from noise improves the network's predictions and this is reflected in the results from this evaluation as well (the last three vs. the first two methods). We have here another comparison between the Albarqouni et al. (2016) and Rodrigues and Pereira (2018) methods and again there is not much difference between the two, the latter having a slightly better accuracy, though it remains unclear if that is significant. We remind ourselves the two methods are equivalent conceptually, the difference being in the execution: the method from Albarqouni et al. (2016) uses a probabilistic annotation model to distill the labels from noise, while the Rodrigues and Pereira (2018) method is fully neural. The method from Chu et al. (2021) that made the subject of this section, and which builds on the Rodrigues and Pereira (2018) method, gets the best performance in this evaluation by an important margin. The additional complexity introduced by Chu et al. (2021) is to model the coders' annotations not only following their own accuracy and biases as in Rodrigues and Pereira (2018), but also on the basis of a collective annotation behaviour. This extension in the modelling of the way the coders annotate proved to be highly beneficial for the learning, and consequently for the prediction capability of the network.

6.6   SUMMARY

In this chapter we discussed a number of ways to augment an existing (deep) neural network to allow it to learn from multi-annotated corpora. We conclude with some useful lessons we learned from our experience with these methods over the years, and more recently from a survey which covers a wide range of datasets from different domains and with varying annotation quality (Uma et al., 2021b).

Aggregate or Keep All the Annotations?
The experiments reported in this chapter provide substantial evidence that keeping all the annotations during training is at least as good if not better compared to learning from aggregated labels. We distinguish here aggregated labels—labels produced by an automatic aggregation method such as those we discussed in Chapter 5—from gold labels—labels produced by experts following the tradition of gold standard annotation—which we discuss separately in the section below. The body of literature we surveyed suggests it is feasible to drop the standard practice to train on aggregated labels and start using all the annotations available. The regularization brought by the additional interpretations can significantly improve the performance of the networks, something we do not get from aggregated labels. We also take the opportunity to call the resource creators out to publish their corpora including in addition to the adjudicated labels the other interpretations they have collected, a practice we noticed is not always followed.

Among the methods to learning from multi-annotated corpora we presented, in our experience (see Uma et al., 2021b, for detailed results), we did not always observe a significant difference between those learning with soft labels (discussed in Section 6.2) and those learning the accuracy and bias of the coders to reduce the effect of the noise from the annotations (as discussed in Section 6.4). Although we did not compare using soft labels against the more capable method discussed in Section 6.5. In principle, if the annotations are too noisy, the soft labels will also be noisy; in this case, the methods that allow the network to adjust its learning to the accuracy and bias of the coders look advantageous.

Crowdsourced Labels versus Gold Labels

Crowdsourced labels have the advantage of being easier and cheaper to collect compared to gold labels which traditionally have been produced through more intensive and often expensive labour. What they lack in terms of scale and cost, gold labels can make up in quality. Although not without problems (they are subject to all the issues we identified in the Introduction that hard labels suffer from), gold labels typically are more accurate compared to those produced by the crowds. When the gap in quality between the gold and the crowd labels is too large, the performance brought by the regularization from the additional interpretations provided by the crowds cannot be made up to surpass the performance we get when training using gold labels, irrespective of the way the crowd labels are used to train the network. The results we discussed in this chapter confirm this aspect, as do those from Uma et al. (2021b) which consider many more datasets.

When the crowd labels have a quality comparable to the gold labels, however, they are a richer source of information for the network, containing not only the learning signal offered by the gold labels, but also additional information about the labelling uncertainty of the coders. In this case, training with crowdsourced labels overperforms training using gold labels (see Section 6.2, but also Uma et al., 2021b). Having access to high quality crowdsourced labels challenges also the current evaluation paradigm on the basis of gold labels. The advantage they have in terms of preserving labelling uncertainty can also be leveraged to provide a richer evaluation, more representative for the difficulty, ambiguity, and subjectivity of the tasks we are trying to solve.

In the event both crowdsourced labels and gold labels are available we found it is generally useful to combine both sources of information. The recommendation applies if the crowdsourced labels do not have the quality to overperform the gold labels during training as explained above in which case we should stick to using the crowdsourced labels (Uma et al., 2021b). The method to combine the gold and the crowdsourced labels, proposed by Fornaciari et al. (2021), takes a multi-task approach, where in one task, called the main task, the network is learning from gold labels as per standard practice, and in another task, called the auxiliary task, it is using soft labels. The authors argue the auxiliary task acts as a regularizer for the main task which is how it improves its predictions.

Mixed Results and What Did Not Work for Us

In addition to the methods described in this chapter which bring conclusive advantages to learning from multi-annotated corpora, granted, not throughout the board, but depending on the training conditions as we discussed above, there are a number of other methods we have experimented with and found limited, or no success. One of these methods is filtering out training examples with a low agreement in their annotations. Previously argued as a way to improve training (Jamison and Gurevych, 2015), we found this approach quite detrimental. We also experimented with the method from Plank et al. (2014c) where the loss for each training example is weighted by how unlikely the coders find the networks' predictions vis-à-vis the gold labels. For this particular method we got mixed results compared to simply training on gold labels (without the weighting). Finally, another method we experimented with comes from Sheng et al. (2008), and involved repeating the training examples in the corpus, one for each annotation, and carrying out the training of the network as usual. Simple as it is, this method showed encouraging results, but it quickly became unfeasible for the datasets with a larger number of annotations. For the details and the results in support of these observations please consult Uma et al. (2021b).

Bibliography

Alan Agresti. *Categorical Data Analysis*. John Wiley & Sons, 2003. DOI: 10.1002/0471249688 1

Luis von Ahn. Games with a purpose. *Computer*, 39(6):92–94, June 2006. DOI: 10.1109/MC.2006.196 105

Mikel Aickin. Maximum likelihood estimation of agreement in the constant predictive probability model, and its relation to Cohen's kappa. *Biometrics*, 46(2):293–302, 1990. DOI: 10.2307/2531434 1, 79, 82, 83, 84, 85, 86, 87, 88, 89, 90, 91

Sohail Akhtar, Valerio Basile, and Viviana Patti. A new measure of polarization in the annotation of hate speech. *AI*IA—Advances in Artificial Intelligence*, pages 588–603, Springer International Publishing, Cham, 2019. DOI: 10.1007/978-3-030-35166-3_41 147, 148

Sohail Akhtar, Valerio Basile, and Viviana Patti. Modeling annotator perspective and polarized opinions to improve hate speech detection. *Proc. of the AAAI Conference on Human Computation and Crowdsourcing*, 8(1):151–154, October 2020. https://ojs.aaai.org/index.php/HCOMP/article/view/7473 147

Shadi Albarqouni, Christoph Baur, Felix Achilles, Vasileios Belagiannis, Stefani Demirci, and Nassir Navab. AggNet: Deep learning from crowds for mitosis detection in breast cancer histology images. *IEEE Transactions on Medical Imaging*, 35(5):1313–1321, May 2016. DOI: 10.1109/TMI.2016.2528120 2, 156, 157, 159, 160, 162, 163

Paul S. Albert and Lori E. Dodd. A cautionary note on the robustness of latent class models for estimating diagnostic error without a gold standard. *Biometrics*, 60(2):427–435, 2004. DOI: 10.1111/j.0006-341X.2004.00187.x 106, 108

James Allen and Mark Core. DAMSL: Dialogue act markup in several layers. *Draft Contribution for the Discourse Resource Initiative*, October 1997. http://www.cs.rochester.edu/research/cisd/resources/damsl/ 13, 53

Omar Alonso. *The Practice of Crowdsourcing*. Synthesis Lectures on Information Concepts, Retrieval, and Services. Morgan & Claypool, 2019. DOI: 10.2200/s00904ed1v01y201903icr066 2

Jacopo Amidei, Paul Piwek, and Alistair Willis. Agreement is overrated: A plea for correlation to assess human evaluation reliability. *Proc. of the 12th International Natural Language Generation Conference (INLG)*, pages 344–354, Tokyo, Japan, 2019. https://aclanthology.org/W19-8642/ DOI: 10.18653/v1/w19-8642 16

Lora Aroyo and Chris Welty. Truth is a lie: Crowd truth and the seven myths of human annotation. *AI Magazine*, 36(1):15–24, 2015. DOI: 10.1609/aimag.v36i1.2564 148

Ron Artstein. Inter-annotator agreement. *Handbook of Linguistic Annotation*, pages 297–313, Springer, Dordrecht, 2017. DOI: 10.1007/978-94-024-0881-2_11 52, 73

Ron Artstein and Massimo Poesio. Bias decreases in proportion to the number of annotators. *Proc. of FG-MoL*, pages 141–150, Edinburgh, August 2005. http://web.stanford.edu/group/cslipublications/cslipublications/FG/2005/artstein.pdf 39, 77

Ron Artstein and Massimo Poesio. Identifying reference to abstract objects in dialogue. *Brandial: Proceedings of the 10th Workshop on the Semantics and Pragmatics of Dialogue*, pages 56–63, Potsdam, Germany, September 2006. 69

Ron Artstein and Massimo Poesio. Inter-coder agreement for computational linguistics. *Computational Linguistics*, 34(4):555–596, 2008. https://aclanthology.org/J08-4004 DOI: 10.1162/coli.07-034-R2 xvii, 1, 10, 77

Sue Atkins. Tools for computer-aided lexicography: The Hector project. *Papers in Computational Lexicography: COMPLEX*, Budapest, 1993. 73

Anna Babarczy, John Carroll, and Geoffrey Sampson. Definitional, personal, and mechanical constraints on part of speech annotation performance. *Natural Language Engineering*, 12(1):77–90, 2006. DOI: 10.1017/s1351324905003803 52

Yoram Bachrach, Tom Minka, John Guiver, and Thore Graepel. How to grade a test without knowing the answers: A Bayesian graphical model for adaptive crowdsourcing and aptitude testing. *Proc. of the 29th International Conference on Machine Learning, ICML*, pages 819–826, Omnipress, Madison, WI, 2012. 119, 141

John J. Bartko and William T. Carpenter, Jr. On the methods and theory of reliability. *Journal of Nervous and Mental Disease*, 163(5):307–317, 1976. DOI: 10.1097/00005053-197611000-00003 15, 22

Valerio Basile. It's the end of the gold standard as we know it. On the impact of pre-aggregation on the evaluation of highly subjective tasks. *Proc. of the AIXIA Workshop*. Università di Torino, 2020. 3, 80, 147, 150

Valerio Basile, Michael Fell, Tommaso Fornaciari, Dirk Hovy, Silviu Paun, Barbara Plank, Massimo Poesio, and Alexandra Uma. We need to consider disagreement in evaluation. *Proc. of the 1st Workshop on Benchmarking: Past, Present and Future*, pages 15–21, Association for Computational Linguistics, August 2021. https://aclanthology.org/2021.bppf-1.3 DOI: 10.18653/v1/2021.bppf-1.3 150

Petra Saskia Bayerl and Karsten Ingmar Paul. What determines inter-coder agreement in manual annotations? A meta-analytic investigation. *Computational Linguistics*, 37(4):699–725, 2011. https://www.aclweb.org/anthology/J11-4004 DOI: 10.1162/COLI_a_00074 47

Doug Beeferman, Adam Berger, and John Lafferty. Statistical models for text segmentation. *Machine Learning*, 34(1–3):177–210, 1999. DOI: 10.1023/A:1007506220214 65

Eyal Beigman and Beata Beigman Klebanov. Learning with annotation noise. *Proc. of the Joint Conference of the 47th Annual Meeting of the ACL and the 4th International Joint Conference on Natural Language Processing of the AFNLP*, pages 280–287, Association for Computational Linguistics, Stroudsburg, PA, 2009. http://dl.acm.org/citation.cfm?id=1687878.1687919 DOI: 10.3115/1687878.1687919 80, 105, 148

Beata Beigman Klebanov and Eyal Beigman. From annotator agreement to noise models. *Computational Linguistics*, 35(4):495–503, 2009. https://aclanthology.org/J09-4005 DOI: 10.1162/coli.2009.35.4.35402 xvii, 79, 80, 89, 148

Edward M. Bennett, Renee Alpert, and A. C. Goldstein. Communications through limited questioning. *Public Opinion Quarterly*, 18(3):303–308, 1954. 16, 92

Christopher M. Bishop. *Pattern Recognition and Machine Learning*. Information Science and Statistics, Springer New York, 2016. https://books.google.ro/books?id=kOXDtAEACAAJ 3, 83, 109

David M. Blei and Michael I. Jordan. Variational inference for Dirichlet process mixtures. *Bayesian Analysis*, 1(1):121–143, March 2006. https://doi.org/10.1214/06-BA104 DOI: 10.1214/06-BA104 124

David M. Blei, Andrew Y. Ng, and Michael I. Jordan. Latent Dirichlet allocation. *The Journal of Machine Learning Research*, 3:993–1022, March 2003. http://dl.acm.org/citation.cfm?id=944919.944937 DOI: 10.1109/asru.2015.7404785 129

Daniel A. Bloch and Helena Chmura Kraemer. 2×2 kappa coefficients: Measures of agreement or association. *Biometrics*, 45(1):269–287, March 1989. DOI: 10.2307/2532052 48

Thorsten Brants and Oliver Plaehn. Interactive corpus annotation. *Proc. of the 2nd International Conference on Language Resources and Evaluation (LREC)*, European Language Resources Association (ELRA), Athens, Greece, May 2000. http://www.lrec-conf.org/proceedings/lrec2000/pdf/334.pdf 51

Alexander Braylan and Matthew Lease. Modeling and aggregation of complex annotations via annotation distances. *Proc. of the Web Conference, WWW*, pages 1807–1818, Association for Computing Machinery, New York, 2020. https://doi.org/10.1145/3366423.3380250 DOI: 10.1145/3366423.3380250 142, 143, 144

Robert L. Brennan and Dale J. Prediger. Coefficient kappa: Some uses, misuses, and alternatives. *Educational and Psychological Measurement*, 41(3):687–699, 1981. DOI: 10.1177/001316448104100307 18, 38

Hermann Brenner and Ulrike Kliebsch. Dependence of weighted kappa coefficients on the number of categories. *Epidemiology*, 7(2):199–202, March 1996. https://www.jstor.org/stable/3703036 DOI: 10.1097/00001648-199603000-00016 29

Ross Brownson, James R. Davis, Jian C. Chang, Thomas M. DiLorenzo, Thomas J. Keefe, and John R. Bagby. A study of the accuracy of cancer risk factor information reported to a central registry compared with that obtained by interview. *American Journal of Epidemiology*, 129(3):616–624, March 1989. https://doi.org/10.1093/oxfordjournals.aje.a115174 DOI: 10.1093/oxfordjournals.aje.a115174 86

Rebecca Bruce and Janyce Wiebe. Word-sense distinguishability and inter-coder agreement. *Proc. of the 3rd Conference on Empirical Methods for Natural Language Processing*, pages 53–60, Association for Computational Linguistics, Palacio de Exposiciones y Congresos, Granada, Spain, June 1998. https://aclanthology.org/W98-1507 2, 9, 18, 73, 80, 93, 100, 106

Rebecca F. Bruce and Janyce M. Wiebe. Recognizing subjectivity: A case study in manual tagging. *Natural Language Engineering*, 5(2):187–205, June 1999. DOI: 10.1017/s1351324999002181 xvii, 1, 2, 60, 61, 62, 73, 80, 93, 106, 110

Jeska Buhmann, Johanneke Caspers, Vincent J. van Heuven, Heleen Hoekstra, Jean-Pierre Martens, and Marc Swerts. Annotation of prominent words, prosodic boundaries and segmental lengthening by non-expert transcribers in the Spoken Dutch Corpus. *Proc. of the 3rd International Conference on Language Resources and Evaluation (LREC)*, European Language Resources Association (ELRA), Las Palmas, Canary Islands, Spain, May 2002. http://www.lrec-conf.org/proceedings/lrec2002/pdf/96.pdf 65, 66

Paul Buitelaar. CoreLex: Systematic polysemy and underspecification. Ph.D. thesis, Brandeis University, February 1998. 73

Harry C. Bunt. Dynamic interpretation and dialogue theory. *The Structure of Multimodal Dialogue II*, pages 139–166, John Benjamins, Amsterdam, 2000. DOI: 10.1075/z.99.10bun 53, 56

Harry C. Bunt. A framework for dialogue act specification. *Proc. of the Joint ISO-ACL Workshop on the Representation and Annotation of Semantic Information*, Tilburg, 2005. 56

Harry C. Bunt.   The DIT++ taxonomy for functional dialogue markup.   *Proc. of EDAML@AAMAS Workshop Towards a Standard Markup Language for Embodied Dialogue Acts*, pages 13–24, Budapest, Hungary, 2009. 53

Harry C. Bunt, Jan Alexandersson, Jae-Woong Choe, Alex Chengyu Fang, Koiti Hasida, Volha Petukhova, Andrei Popescu-Belis, and David Traum.   ISO 24617-2: A semantically-based standard for dialogue annotation. *Proc. of the 8th International Conference on Language Resources and Evaluation (LREC)*, pages 430–437, European Language Resources Association (ELRA), Istanbul, Turkey, May 2012. http://www.lrec-conf.org/proceedings/lrec2012/pdf/530_Paper.pdf 53

Donna K. Byron. Resolving pronominal reference to abstract entities. *Proc. of the 40th Annual Meeting of the Association for Computational Linguistics*, pages 80–87, Association for Computational Linguistics, Philadelphia, PA, July 2002. DOI: 10.3115/1073083.1073099 69

Ted Byrt, Janet Bishop, and John B. Carlin.   Bias, prevalence and kappa. *Journal of Clinical Epidemiology*, 46(5):423–429, 1993. DOI: 10.1016/0895-4356(93)90018-v 20, 37, 39

Chris Callison-Burch. Fast, cheap, and creative: Evaluating translation quality using Amazon's mechanical turk. *Proc. of the Conference on Empirical Methods in Natural Language Processing*, 2009. https://aclanthology.org/D09-1030 DOI: 10.3115/1699510.1699548 105

Jean Carletta. Assessing agreement on classification tasks: The kappa statistic. *Computational Linguistics*, 22(2):249–254, 1996. https://aclanthology.org/J96-2004 1, 9, 14, 22, 47, 48, 50, 63

Jean Carletta, Amy Isard, Stephen Isard, Jacqueline C. Kowtko, Gwyneth Doherty-Sneddon, and Anne H. Anderson. The reliability of a dialogue structure coding scheme. *Computational Linguistics*, 23(1):13–32, March 1997. https://aclanthology.org/J97-1002.pdf 2, 9, 14, 18, 53, 54, 62, 63, 64

Lynn Carlson, Daniel Marcu, and Mary Ellen Okurowski. Building a discourse-tagged corpus in the framework of rhetorical structure theory. *Current Directions in Discourse and Dialogue*, volume 22 of *Text, Speech, and Language Technology*, pages 85–112, Kluwer, 2003. DOI: 10.1007/978-94-010-0019-2_5 9, 63, 76

Bob Carpenter.   Multilevel Bayesian models of categorical data annotation.   Unpublished manuscript, 2008. https://lingpipe.files.wordpress.com/2008/11/carp-bayesian-multilevel-annotation.pdf xvii, 1, 2, 106, 107, 108, 116, 117, 118, 120, 121

Bob Carpenter, Andrew Gelman, Matt Hoffman, Daniel Lee, Ben Goodrich, Michael Betancourt, Michael A. Brubaker, Jiqiang Guo, Peter Li, and Allen Riddell.   Stan: A probabilistic programming language. *Journal of Statistical Software*, 76(1):1–32, 2017. DOI: 10.18637/jss.v076.i01 3, 112, 120

Jon Chamberlain, Massimo Poesio, and Udo Kruschwitz. Phrase Detectives: A web-based collaborative annotation game. *Proc. of I-Semantics*, 2008. https://www.semanticscholar.org/paper/Phrase-Detectives-A-Web-based-collaborative-game-Chamberlain-Poesio/dd3f843f5c34259ad6cd9c44e1259fc7d52aec11 136

Jon Chamberlain, Massimo Poesio, and Udo Kruschwitz. Phrase Detectives corpus 1.0: Crowd-sourced anaphoric coreference. *Proc. of the International Conference on Language Resources and Evaluation (LREC)*, Portorož, Slovenia, 2016. https://aclanthology.org/L16-1323/ 134

Nancy Chinchor. MUC-7 named entity task definition. *Proc. of the 7th Message Understanding Conference (MUC)*, 1997a. https://www-nlpir.nist.gov/related_projects/muc/proceedings/ne_task.html 59

Nancy Chinchor. MUC-7 test scores introduction. *Proc. of the 7th Message Understanding Conference (MUC)*, 1997b. https://www-nlpir.nist.gov/related_projects/muc/proceedings/muc_7_proceedings/muc7_score_intro.pdf 59

Zhendong Chu, Jing Ma, and Hongning Wang. Learning from crowds by modeling common confusions. *Proc. of the AAAI Conference on Artificial Intelligence*, 35(7):5832–5840, May 2021. https://ojs.aaai.org/index.php/AAAI/article/view/16730 2, 161, 162, 163

Domenic V. Cicchetti and Alvan R. Feinstein. High agreement but low kappa: II. Resolving the paradoxes. *Journal of Clinical Epidemiology*, 43(6):551–558, 1990. DOI: 10.1016/0895-4356(90)90159-m 22, 40

Philipp Cimiano and Siegfried Handschuh. Ontology-based linguistic annotation. *Proc. of the ACL Workshop on Linguistic Annotation*, pages 14–21, Sapporo, Japan, 2003. https://aclanthology.org/W03-1903 DOI: 10.3115/1119296.1119299 60

Jacob Cohen. A coefficient of agreement for nominal scales. *Educational and Psychological Measurement*, 20(1):37–46, 1960. DOI: 10.1177/001316446002000104 1, 9, 10, 14, 15, 16, 19, 22, 28, 40, 49, 77, 82, 85, 86, 87, 88, 90, 91, 92, 93, 100

Jacob Cohen. Weighted kappa: Nominal scale agreement with provision for scaled disagreement or partial credit. *Psychological Bulletin*, 70(4):213–220, 1968. DOI: 10.1037/h0026256 25, 28, 29

Shay Cohen. *Bayesian Analysis in Natural Language Processing*. Synthesis Lectures on Human Language Technology, Morgan & Claypool, 2016. DOI: 10.2200/s00719ed1v01y201605hlt035 3, 110

Seth Cooper, Firsas Khatib, Adrien Treuille, Janos Barbero, Jeehyung Lee, Michael Beenen, Andrew Leaver-Fay, David Baker, Zoran Popovic, and the Foldit Players. Predicting protein structures with a multiplayer online game. *Nature*, 466:756–760, 2010. DOI: 10.1038/nature09304 105

Mark G. Core and James F. Allen. Coding dialogs with the DAMSL scheme. *Working Notes of the AAAI Fall Symposium on Communicative Action in Humans and Machines*, Boston, MA, November 1997. https://www.semanticscholar.org/paper/Coding-Dialogs-with-the-DAMSL-Annotation-Scheme-Core-Allen/ac2b71f9dbafb5678334a41a05cdf928e2dac447 9, 18, 54, 56, 58

Richard Craggs and Mary McGee Wood. A two-dimensional annotation scheme for emotion in dialogue. *Proc. of AAAI Spring Symposium on Exploring Attitude and Affect in Text*, Stanford, March 2004. 9, 60

Richard Craggs and Mary McGee Wood. Evaluating discourse and dialogue coding schemes. *Computational Linguistics*, 31(3):289–295, September 2005. https://aclanthology.org/J05-3001 DOI: 10.1162/089120105774321109 9, 10, 11, 20, 37, 38, 39, 48, 77, 78

Ido Dagan, Oren Glickman, and Bernardo Magnini. The PASCAL recognising textual entailment challenge. *Machine Learning Challenges. Evaluating Predictive Uncertainty, Visual Object Classification, and Recognising Textual Entailment*, pages 177–190, Springer Berlin Heidelberg, Berlin, Heidelberg, 2006. DOI: 10.1007/11736790_9 106

Mark Davies and Joseph L. Fleiss. Measuring agreement for multinomial data. *Biometrics*, 38(4):1047–1051, December 1982. DOI: 10.2307/2529886 22, 24, 30, 61

Alexander Philip Dawid and Allan M. Skene. Maximum likelihood estimation of observer error-rates using the EM algorithm. *Applied Statistics*, 28(1):20–28, 1979. DOI: 10.2307/2346806 1, 2, 80, 94, 105, 106, 107, 110, 111, 112, 113, 114, 115, 117, 122, 123, 124, 125, 126, 127, 128, 129, 130, 131, 132, 133, 141, 151, 152, 156, 159

A. P. Dempster, N. M. Laird, and D. B. Rubin. Maximum likelihood from incomplete data via the EM algorithm. *Journal of the Royal Statistical Society, Series B*, 39(1):1–38, 1977. DOI: 10.1111/j.2517-6161.1977.tb01600.x 61, 111

Barbara Di Eugenio. On the usage of kappa to evaluate agreement on coding tasks. *Proc. of the 2nd International Conference on Language Resources and Evaluation (LREC)*, 1:441–444, Athens, 2000. https://aclanthology.org/L00-1155/ 9, 49, 56

Barbara Di Eugenio and Michael Glass. The kappa statistic: A second look. *Computational Linguistics*, 30(1):95–101, 2004. https://aclanthology.org/J04-1005 DOI: 10.1162/089120104773633402 10, 14, 18, 20, 22, 37, 38, 40, 41, 76, 77, 78

Barbara Di Eugenio, Pam W. Jordan, Johanna D. Moore, and Richmond H. Thomason. An empirical investigation of collaborative dialogues. *Proc. of the 36th Annual Meeting of the Association for Computational Linguistics (ACL)and the 17th International Conference on Computational Linguistics (COLING)*, Montreal, 1998. https://aclanthology.org/C98-1051 54

Lee R. Dice. Measures of the amount of ecologic association between species. *Ecology*, 26(3):297–302, 1945. DOI: 10.2307/1932409 67, 72

George Doddington, Alexis Mitchell, Mark Przybocki, Lance Ramshaw, Stephanie Strassel, and Ralph Weischedel. The automatic content extraction (ACE) program—tasks, data, and evaluation. *Proc. of the 4th International Conference on Language Resources and Evaluation (LREC)*, European Language Resources Association (ELRA), Lisbon, Portugal, May 2004. http://www.lrec-conf.org/proceedings/lrec2004/pdf/5.pdf 59

Allan Donner and Michael Eliasziw. Sample size requirements for reliability studies. *Statistics in Medicine*, 6:441–448, 1987. DOI: 10.1002/sim.4780060404 49

Christine Doran, John Aberdeen, Laurie Damianos, and Lynette Hirschman. Comparing several aspects of human-computer and human-human dialogues. *Proc. of 2nd SIGDIAL Workshop*, 2001. https://aclanthology.org/W01-1607/ DOI: 10.3115/1118078.1118085 53, 56

Anca Dumitrache, Lora Aroyo, and Chris Welty. A crowdsourced frame disambiguation corpus with ambiguity. *Proc. of the Conference of the North American Chapter of the Association for Computational Linguistics: Human Language Technologies, Volume 1 (Long and Short Papers)*, pages 2164–2170, Minneapolis, MN, June 2019. https://www.aclweb.org/anthology/N19-1224 DOI: 10.18653/v1/N19-1224 147

Miriam Eckert and Michael Strube. Dialogue acts, synchronizing units, and anaphora resolution. *Journal of Semantics*, 17(1):51–89, 2000. DOI: 10.1093/jos/17.1.51 69

Alvan R. Feinstein and Domenic V. Cicchetti. High agreement but low kappa: I. The problems of two paradoxes. *Journal of Clinical Epidemiology*, 43(6):543–549, 1990. DOI: 10.1016/0895-4356(90)90158-1 22, 40

Christiane Fellbaum, Ed. *WordNet: An Electronic Lexical Database*. MIT Press, 1998. DOI: 10.7551/mitpress/7287.001.0001 72

Christiane Fellbaum, Joachim Grabowski, and Shari Landes. Analysis of a hand-tagging task. *Proc. of ANLP Workshop on Tagging Text with Lexical Semantics*, pages 34–40, Washington, DC, April 1997. https://aclanthology.org/W97-0206 18

Paul Felt, Robbie Haertel, Eric K. Ringger, and Kevin D. Seppi. MOMRESP: A Bayesian model for multi-annotator document labeling. *Proc. of the International Conference on Language Resources and Evaluation (LREC)*, Reykjavik, 2014. https://aclanthology.org/L14-1107/ 126, 127, 128, 129

Paul Felt, Kevin Black, Eric Ringger, Kevin Seppi, and Robbie Haertel. Early gains matter: A case for preferring generative over discriminative crowdsourcing models. *Proc. of the Conference of the North American Chapter of the Association for Computational Linguistics: Human Language*

Technologies, 2015a. https://aclanthology.org/N15-1089/ DOI: 10.3115/v1/n15-1089 126, 128

Paul Felt, Eric K. Ringger, Jordan Boyd-Graber, and Kevin Seppi. Making the most of crowd-sourced document annotations: Confused supervised LDA. *Proc. of the 19th Conference on Computational Natural Language Learning*, pages 194–203, 2015b. https://aclanthology.org/K15-1020/ DOI: 10.18653/v1/k15-1020 126, 129

Joseph L. Fleiss. Measuring nominal scale agreement among many raters. *Psychological Bulletin*, 76(5):378–382, 1971. DOI: 10.1037/h0031619 9, 22, 23, 24, 27, 30, 33, 49

Joseph L. Fleiss. Measuring agreement between two judges on the presence or absence of a trait. *Biometrics*, 31(3):651–659, 1975. DOI: 10.2307/2529549 20, 37

Joseph L. Fleiss and Jacob Cohen. The equivalence of weighted kappa and the intraclass correlation coefficient as measures of reliability. *Educational and Psychological Measurement*, 33(3):613–619, October 1973. DOI: 10.1177/001316447303300309 29

Anton K. Formann. Measurement errors in caries diagnosis: Some further latent class models. *Biometrics*, 50(3):865–871, 1994. http://www.jstor.org/stable/2532801 DOI: 10.2307/2532801 80, 94, 106

Tommaso Fornaciari, Alexandra Uma, Silviu Paun, Barbara Plank, Dirk Hovy, and Massimo Poesio. Beyond black & white: Leveraging annotator disagreement via soft-label multi-task learning. *Proc. of the Conference of the North American Chapter of the Association for Computational Linguistics: Human Language Technologies*, pages 2591–2597, June 2021. https://aclanthology.org/2021.naacl-main.204 DOI: 10.18653/v1/2021.naacl-main.204 2, 164

Karën Fort, Bruno Guillaume, and H. Chastant. Creating Zombilingo, a game with a purpose for dependency syntax annotation. *Proc. of the 1st International Workshop on Gamification for Information Retrieval (GamifIR)*, pages 2–6, ACM, 2014. https://hal.inria.fr/hal-00969157/en DOI: 10.1145/2594776.2594777 105

W. Nelson Francis and Henry Kucera. *Frequency Analysis of English Usage: Lexicon and Grammar*. Houghton Mifflin, Boston, 1982. 2, 9, 51, 105

Jeroen Geertzen and Harry Bunt. Measuring annotator agreement in a complex hierarchical dialogue act annotation scheme. *Proc. of the 7th SIGdial Workshop on Discourse and Dialogue*, pages 126–133, Association for Computational Linguistics, Sydney, Australia, July 2006. https://aclanthology.org/W06-1318 DOI: 10.3115/1654595.1654619 56, 57, 58

Andrew Gelman and Jennifer Hill. *Data Analysis Using Regression and Multilevel/Hierarchical Models*. Analytical Methods for Social Research. Cambridge University Press, 2007. https://books.google.co.uk/books?id=lV3DIdV0F9AC DOI: 10.1017/cbo9780511790942 116, 117

Andrew Gelman, John B. Carlin, Hal S. Stern, David B. Dunson, Aki Vehtari, and Donald B. Rubin. *Bayesian Data Analysis*, 3rd ed., Chapman & Hall/CRC Texts in Statistical Science. Taylor & Francis, 2013. https://books.google.co.uk/books?id=ZXL6AQAAQBAJ DOI: 10.1201/b16018 3, 4, 114

Leo A. Goodman. The analysis of systems of qualitative variables when some of the variables are unobservable. Part I—a modified latent structure approach. *American Journal of Sociology*, 79(5):1179–1259, March 1974a. DOI: 10.1086/225676 61

Leo A. Goodman. Exploratory latent structure analysis using both identifiable and unidentifiable models. *Biometrika*, 61(2):215–231, 1974b. http://www.jstor.org/stable/2334349 DOI: 10.1093/biomet/61.2.215 80, 94

Patrick Graham and Rodney Jackson. The analysis of ordinal agreement data: Beyond weighted kappa. *Journal of Clinical Epidemiology*, 46(9):1055–1062, September 1993. DOI: 10.1016/0895-4356(93)90173-x 29

Derek Gross, James F. Allen, and David R. Traum. The Trains 91 dialogues. *TRAINS Technical Note 92-1*, University of Rochester Computer Science Department, July 1993. http://hdl.handle.net/1802/1132 DOI: 10.21236/ada301012 54

Barbara J. Grosz and Candace L. Sidner. Attention, intention, and the structure of discourse. *Computational Linguistics*, 12(3):175–204, 1986. https://aclanthology.org/J86-3001 62, 63

William M. Grove, Nancy C. Andreasen, Patricia McDonald-Scott, Martin B. Keller, and Robert W. Shapiro. Reliability studies of psychiatric diagnosis: Theory and practice. *Archives of General Psychiatry*, 38(4):408–413, April 1981. DOI: 10.1001/archpsyc.1981.01780290042004 81

Melody Guan, Varun Gulshan, Andrew Dai, and Geoffrey Hinton. Who said what: Modeling individual labelers improves classification. *AAAI Conference on Artificial Intelligence*, 2018. https://aaai.org/ocs/index.php/AAAI/AAAI18/paper/view/16970/16653 2, 152, 153, 154, 155, 158, 159, 160

Irene Guggenmoos-Holzmann. The meaning of kappa: Probabilistic concepts of reliability and validity revisited. *Journal of Clinical Epidemiology*, 49(7):775–782, 1996. http://www.sciencedirect.com/science/article/pii/089543569600011X DOI: https://doi.org/10.1016/0895-4356(96)00011-X 1, 79, 82, 89, 90, 91, 92, 93

Irene Guggenmoos-Holzmann and Richard Vonk. Kappa-like indices of observer agreement viewed from a latent class perspective. *Statistics in Medicine*, 17(8):797–812, 1998. https://onlinelibrary.wiley.com/doi/abs/10.1002/%28SICI%291097-0258%2819980430%2917%3A8%3C797%3A%3AAID-SIM776%3E3.0.CO%3B2-G

DOI: 10.1002/(SICI)1097-0258(19980430)17:8<797::AID–SIM776>3.0.CO;2-G 79, 89, 90, 92

Kilem L. Gwet. *Handbook of Inter-Rater Reliability: The Definitive Guide to Measuring the Extent of Agreement Among Raters.* Advanced Analytics, LLC, 2014. xvii, 1, 79, 81, 82, 86

Kilem Li Gwet. Computing inter-rater reliability and its variance in the presence of high agreement. *British Journal of Mathematical and Statistical Psychology*, 61(1):29–48, 2008. DOI: https://doi.org/10.1348/000711006X126600 82, 89, 90

Ivan Habernal and Iryna Gurevych. What makes a convincing argument? Empirical analysis and detecting attributes of convincingness in web argumentation. *Proc. of the Conference on Empirical Methods in Natural Language Processing*, pages 1214–1223, 2016. https://aclanthology.org/D16-1129 DOI: 10.18653/v1/d16-1129 106, 111

Siegfried Handschuh. Creating ontology-based metadata by annotation for the semantic web. Ph.D. thesis, Universität Karlsruhe, 2005. 60

Andrew F. Hayes and Klaus Krippendorff. Answering the call for a standard reliability measure for coding data. *Communication Methods and Measures*, 1(1):77–89, 2007. DOI: 10.1080/19312450709336664 49

Marti A. Hearst. TextTiling: Segmenting text into multi-paragraph subtopic passages. *Computational Linguistics*, 23(1):33–64, 1997. 9, 62, 63, 64, 78

Dirk Hovy, Taylor Berg-Kirkpatrick, Ashish Vaswani, and Eduard Hovy. Learning whom to trust with MACE. *Proc. of the Conference of the North American Chapter of the Association for Computational Linguistics: Human Language Technologies*, pages 1120–1130, 2013. https://aclanthology.org/N13-1132 1, 2, 93, 106, 107, 111, 112, 113, 114

Eduard H. Hovy, Mitchell P. Marcus, Martha Palmer, Lance Ramshaw, and Ralph Weischedel. OntoNotes: The 90% solution. *Proc. of the Human Language Technology Conference of the NAACL, Companion Volume: Short Papers*, pages 57–60, Association for Computational Linguistics, New York, June 2006. https://aclanthology.org/N06-2015 DOI: 10.3115/1614049.1614064 47, 75, 105

Louis M. Hsu and Ronald Field. Interrater agreement measures: Comments on kappa$_n$, Cohen's kappa, Scott's π, and Aickin's α. *Understanding Statistics*, 2(3):205–219, 2003. DOI: 10.1207/s15328031us0203_03 14, 17, 18, 37, 38, 89

Nancy Ide and James Pustejovsky. *Handbook of Linguistic Annotation*, 1st ed., Springer Publishing Company, Incorporated, 2017. DOI: 10.1007/978-94-024-0881-2 1, 105

Olga Isupova, Yunpeng Li, Danil Kuzin, Stephen J. Roberts, Katherine Willis, and Steven Reece. BCCNet: Bayesian classifier combination neural network. *ArXiv Preprint ArXiv:1811.12258*, 2018. 156

Paul Jaccard. The distribution of the flora in the Alpine zone. *New Phytologist*, 11(2):37–50, 1912. DOI: 10.1111/j.1469-8137.1912.tb05611.x 67

Emily Jamison and Iryna Gurevych. Noise or additional information? Leveraging crowdsource annotation item agreement for natural language tasks. *Proc. of the Conference on Empirical Methods in Natural Language Processing*, pages 291–297, Association for Computational Linguistics, Lisbon, Portugal, September 2015. https://www.aclweb.org/anthology/D15-1035 DOI: 10.18653/v1/D15-1035 165

Kalervo Järvelin and Jaana Kekäläinen. Cumulated gain-based evaluation of IR techniques. *ACM Transactions on Information Systems*, 20(4):422–446, October 2002. DOI: 10.1145/582415.582418 150

Susanne Jekat, Alexandra Klein, Elisabeth Maier, Ilona Maleck, Marion Mast, and Joachim Quantz. Dialogue acts in VERBMOBIL. *VERBMOBIL-Report 65*, Universität Hamburg, DFKI GmbH, and Universität Erlangen, April 1995. 53

Daniel Jurafsky, Elizabeth Shriberg, and Debra Biasca. Switchboard-DAMSL labeling project coder's manual. *Technical Report 97-02*, University of Colorado at Boulder, Institute for Cognitive Science, Boulder, CO, 1997. http://www.colorado.edu/ling/jurafsky/manual.august1. html 55

David Jurgens. Embracing ambiguity: A comparison of annotation methodologies for crowdsourcing word sense labels. *Proc. of the Conference of the North American Chapter of the Association for Computational Linguistics: Human Language Technologies*, pages 556–562, Atlanta, GA, June 2013. https://www.aclweb.org/anthology/N13-1062 147

Prathyusha Jwalapuram, Shafiq Joty, Irina Temnikova, and Preslav Nakov. Evaluating pronominal anaphora in machine translation: An evaluation measure and a test suite. *Proc. of the Conference on Empirical Methods in Natural Language Processing and the 9th International Joint Conference on Natural Language Processing (EMNLP-IJCNLP)*, pages 2964–2975, Association for Computational Linguistics, Hong Kong, China, November 2019. https://aclanthology. org/D19-1294 DOI: 10.18653/v1/D19-1294 89

Ece Kamar, Ashish Kapoor, and Eric Horvitz. Identifying and accounting for task-dependent bias in crowdsourcing. *3rd AAAI Conference on Human Computation and Crowdsourcing (HCOMP)*, 2015. https://www.aaai.org/ocs/index.php/HCOMP/HCOMP15/paper/ viewFile/11600/11431 126, 128

Sin-Hwa Kang, Jonathan Gratch, Candy Sidner, Ron Artstein, Lixing Huang, and Louis-Philippe Morency. Towards building a virtual counselor: Modeling nonverbal behavior during intimate self-disclosure. *11th International Conference on Autonomous Agents and Multiagent Systems (AAMAS)*, Valencia, Spain, June 2012. https://dl.acm.org/doi/pdf/10.5555/2343576.2343585 36

Kian Kenyon-Dean, Eisha Ahmed, Scott Fujimoto, Jeremy Georges-Filteau, Christopher Glasz, Barleen Kaur, Auguste Lalande, Shruti Bhanderi, Robert Belfer, Nirmal Kanagasabai, Roman Sarrazingendron, Rohit Verma, and Derek Ruths. Sentiment analysis: It's complicated! *Proc. of the Conference of the North American Chapter of the Association for Computational Linguistics: Human Language Technologies, Volume 1 (Long Papers)*, pages 1886–1895, New Orleans, LA, June 2018. https://www.aclweb.org/anthology/N18-1171 DOI: 10.18653/v1/N18-1171 147

Adam Kilgarriff. 95% replicability for manual word sense tagging. *9th Conference of the European Chapter of the Association for Computational Linguistics*, pages 277–278, Bergen, Norway, June 1999. https://aclanthology.org/E99-1046 DOI: 10.3115/977035.977084 72, 76

Hyun-Chul Kim and Zoubin Ghahramani. Bayesian classifier combination. *Proc. of the 15th International Conference on Artificial Intelligence and Statistics*, pages 619–627, La Palma, Canary Islands, April 21–23, 2012. 107, 110, 141

Diederik P. Kingma and Jimmy Ba. Adam: A method for stochastic optimization. *3rd International Conference on Learning Representations, ICLR, Conference Track Proceedings*, San Diego, CA, May 7–9, 2015. http://arxiv.org/abs/1412.6980 140

Diederik P. Kingma and Max Welling. Auto-encoding variational Bayes, 2013. https://arxiv.org/abs/1312.6114 137, 138, 139

Beata Beigman Klebanov and Eyal Beigman. Difficult cases: From data to learning, and back. *Proc. of the 52nd Annual Meeting of the Association for Computational Linguistics (Volume 2: Short Papers)*, pages 390–396, 2014. https://aclanthology.org/P14-2064 DOI: 10.3115/v1/p14-2064 80, 120, 148

Beata Beigman Klebanov, Eyal Beigman, and Daniel Diermeier. Analyzing disagreements. *Proc. of the Workshop on Human Judgements in Computational Linguistics, HumanJudge*, pages 2–7, Association for Computational Linguistics, Stroudsburg, PA, 2008. http://dl.acm.org/citation.cfm?id=1611628.1611630 DOI: 10.3115/1611628.1611630 93, 120

Jacqueline C. Kowtko, Stephen D. Isard, and Gwyneth M. Doherty. Conversational games within dialogue. *Research Paper HCRC/RP-31*, Human Communication Research Centre, June 1992. http://citeseerx.ist.psu.edu/viewdoc/summary?doi=10.1.1.52.5350 62

Klaus Krippendorff. Bivariate agreement coefficients for reliability of data. *Sociological Methodology*, 2:139–150, 1970a. https://www.jstor.org/stable/270787 DOI: 10.2307/270787 15

Klaus Krippendorff.   Estimating the reliability, systematic error and random error of interval data.   *Educational and Psychological Measurement*, 30(1):61–70, 1970b. DOI: 10.1177/001316447003000105 25

Klaus Krippendorff. Reliability of binary attribute data. *Biometrics*, 34(1):142–144, 1978. Letter to the Ed., with a reply by Joseph L. Fleiss. 20, 37

Klaus Krippendorff. *Content Analysis: An Introduction to its Methodology*, chapter 12, pages 129–154, Sage, Beverly Hills, CA, 1980. DOI: 10.2307/2288384 1, 9, 10, 16, 17, 19, 25, 27, 28, 50, 70

Klaus Krippendorff. On the reliability of unitizing contiguous data. *Sociological Methodology*, 25:47–76, 1995. https://www.jstor.org/stable/271061 DOI: 10.2307/271061 36

Klaus Krippendorff. *Content Analysis: An Introduction to its Methodology*, 2nd ed., chapter 11, pages 211–256, Sage, Thousand Oaks, CA, 2004a. DOI: 10.2307/2288384 1, 10, 11, 25, 27, 34, 47, 48, 49, 50, 60, 71, 72, 74, 76, 77, 93

Klaus Krippendorff. Reliability in content analysis: Some common misconceptions and recommendations. *Human Communication Research*, 30(3):411–433, 2004b. DOI: 10.1111/j.1468-2958.2004.tb00738.x 10, 20, 37, 38, 77

Klaus Krippendorff.   Krippendorff's alpha.   *Encyclopedia of Research Design*, chapter 12, pages 669–673, Sage, Thousand Oaks, CA, 2010. DOI: 10.4135/9781412961288.n206 28

Klaus Krippendorff. *Content Analysis: An Introduction to its Methodology*, 3rd ed., chapter 12, pages 267–328, Sage, Thousand Oaks, CA, 2013. DOI: 10.2307/2288384 25, 28, 36, 47

Klaus Krippendorff. *Content Analysis: An Introduction to its Methodology*, 4th ed., chapter 12, pages 277–360. Sage, Thousand Oaks, CA, 2019. DOI: 10.2307/2288384 10, 25, 28, 36, 47

Klaus Krippendorff, Yann Mathet, Stéphane Bouvry, and Antoine Widlöcher. On the reliability of unitizing textual continua: Further developments. *Quality and Quantity*, 50:2347–2364, November 2016. DOI: 10.1007/s11135-015-0266-1 36

Alex Krizhevsky. Learning multiple layers of features from tiny images. *Technical Report*, 2009. 149

John K. Kruschke. *Doing Bayesian Data Analysis: A Tutorial with R, JAGS, and Stan*. Academic Press, 2015. https://books.google.ro/books?id=CsOtoAEACAAJ 3, 83

Mathieu Lafourcade, Alain Joubert, and Nathalie Le Brun. *Games with a Purpose (GWAPs)*. Wiley, 2015. DOI: 10.1002/9781119136309 105

J. Richard Landis and Gary G. Koch. The measurement of observer agreement for categorical data. *Biometrics*, 33(1):159–174, 1977. DOI: 10.2307/2529310 50, 70, 77

Heeyoung Lee, Yves Peirsman, Angel Chang, Nathanael Chambers, Mihai Surdeanu, and Dan Jurafsky. Stanford's multi-pass sieve coreference resolution system at the CoNLL-2011 shared task. *Proc. of the 15th Conference on Computational Natural Language Learning: Shared Task, CONLL Shared Task*, pages 28–34, Association for Computational Linguistics, Stroudsburg, PA, 2011. http://dl.acm.org/citation.cfm?id=2132936.2132938 137

Geoffrey Leech, Roger Garside, and Michael Bryant. CLAWS4: The tagging of the British National Corpus. *COLING Volume 1: The 15th International Conference on Computational Linguistics*, 1994. https://aclanthology.org/C94-1103 DOI: 10.3115/991886.991996 9, 47, 51, 76, 105

James A. Levin and James A. Moore. Dialogue games: Metacommunication strategies for natural language interaction. *Cognitive Science*, 1(4):395–420, 1978. DOI: 10.1207/s15516709cog0104_2 63

Jiyi Li. Crowdsourced text sequence aggregation based on hybrid reliability and representation. *Proc. of the 43rd International ACM SIGIR Conference on Research and Development in Information Retrieval, SIGIR*, pages 1761–1764, Association for Computing Machinery, New York, 2020. DOI: 10.1145/3397271.3401239 143, 145

Jiyi Li and Fumiyo Fukumoto. A dataset of crowdsourced word sequences: Collections and answer aggregation for ground truth creation. *Proc. of the 1st Workshop on Aggregating and Analysing Crowdsourced Annotations for NLP*, pages 24–28, Association for Computational Linguistics, Hong Kong, November 2019. https://aclanthology.org/D19-5904 DOI: 10.18653/v1/D19-5904 143, 145

Maolin Li, Hiroya Takamura, and Sophia Ananiadou. A neural model for aggregating coreference annotation in crowdsourcing. *Proc. of the 28th International Conference on Computational Linguistics*, pages 5760–5773, International Committee on Computational Linguistics, Barcelona, Spain, December 2020. https://aclanthology.org/2020.coling-main.507 DOI: 10.18653/v1/2020.coling-main.507 2, 142

Chin-Yew Lin. ROUGE: A package for automatic evaluation of summaries. *Text Summarization Branches Out*, pages 74–81, Association for Computational Linguistics, Barcelona, Spain, July 2004. https://aclanthology.org/W04-1013 70, 150

Chin-Yew Lin and Eduard Hovy. Automatic evaluation of summaries using n-gram co-occurrence statistics. *Proc. of HLT-NAACL*, pages 71–78, Edmonton, May–June 2003. https://aclanthology.org/N03-1020/ DOI: 10.3115/1073445.1073465 70

Qiang Liu, Jian Peng, and Alexander T. Ihler. Variational inference for crowdsourcing. In F. Pereira, C. J. C. Burges, L. Bottou, and K. Q. Weinberger, Eds., *Advances in Neural Information Processing Systems 25*, pages 692–700, Curran Associates, Inc., 2012. http://papers.nips.cc/paper/4627-variational-inference-for-crowdsourcing.pdf 127

Malcolm Maclure and Walter C. Willett. Misinterpretation and misuse of the kappa statistic. *American Journal of Epidemiology*, 126(2):161–169, August 1987. DOI: 10.1093/aje/126.2.161 29

Chris Madge, Juntao Yu, Jon Chamberlain, Udo Kruschwitz, Silviu Paun, and Massimo Poesio. Crowdsourcing and aggregating nested markable annotations. *Proc. of the 57th Annual Meeting of the Association for Computational Linguistics*, pages 797–807, Florence, Italy, July 2019. https://aclanthology.org/P19-1077 DOI: 10.18653/v1/P19-1077 60, 133

Christopher D. Manning. Part-of-speech tagging from 97% to 100%: Is it time for some linguistics? In Alexander F. Gelbukh, Ed., *Computational Linguistics and Intelligent Text Processing*, pages 171–189, Springer Berlin Heidelberg, Berlin, Heidelberg, 2011. DOI: 10.1007/978-3-642-19400-9_14 76

Christopher D. Manning and Hinrich Schuetze. *Foundations of Statistical Natural Language Processing*. MIT Press, 1999. 67

Daniel Marcu, Estibaliz Amorrortu, and Magdalena Romera. Experiments in constructing a corpus of discourse trees. *Towards Standards and Tools for Discourse Tagging*, pages 71–78, Association for Computational Linguistics, 1999. https://aclanthology.org/W99-0307 9

Mitchell P. Marcus, Beatrice Santorini, and Mary Ann Marcinkiewicz. Building a large annotated corpus of English: The Penn Treebank. *Computational Linguistics*, 19(2):313–330, 1993. https://aclanthology.org/J93-2004/ DOI: 10.21236/ada273556 2, 9, 47, 76, 100, 105

Rodger Marion. The whole art of deduction. unpublished manuscript, 2000–2012. https://smithcreekstudios.com/wad/correlat.htm 50

Yann Mathet. The agreement measure γ_{cat} a complement to γ focused on categorization of a continuum. *Computational Linguistics*, 43(3):661–681, September 2017. https://www.aclweb.org/anthology/J17-3006 DOI: 10.1162/COLI_a_00296 34, 36, 37

Yann Mathet, Antoine Widlöcher, and Jean-Philippe Métivier. The unified and holistic method gamma (γ) for inter-annotator agreement measure and alignment. *Computational Linguistics*, 41(3):437–479, September 2015. https://www.aclweb.org/anthology/J15-3003 DOI: 10.1162/COLI_a_00227 36

Tony McEnery and Andrew Wilson. *Corpus Linguistics*, 2nd ed., Edinburgh Texbooks in Empirical Linguistics, Edinburgh University Press, 2019. 1

Al Mead. Review of the development of multidimensional scaling methods. *Journal of the Royal Statistical Society: Series D (The Statistician)*, 41(1):27–39, 1992. https://rss.onlinelibrary.wiley.com/doi/abs/10.2307/2348634 DOI: https://doi.org/10.2307/2348634 144

I. Dan Melamed and Philip Resnik. Tagger evaluation given hierarchical tagsets. *Computers and the Humanities*, 34(1–2):79–84, April 2000. https://arxiv.org/abs/cs/0008007 73, 74

Margot Mieskes and Michael Strube. Part-of-speech tagging of transcribed speech. *Proc. of the 5th International Conference on Language Resources and Evaluation (LREC)*, European Language Resources Association (ELRA), Genoa, Italy, May 2006. http://www.lrec-conf.org/proceedings/lrec2006/pdf/345_pdf.pdf 9, 52

Rada Mihalcea, Timothy Chklovski, and Adam Kilgarriff. The SENSEVAL-3 English lexical sample task. *Proc. of SENSEVAL-3, the 3rd International Workshop on the Evaluation of Systems for the Semantic Analysis of Text*, pages 25–28, Association for Computational Linguistics, Barcelona, Spain, July 2004. https://aclanthology.org/W04-0807 72

Eleni Miltsakaki, Aravind Joshi, Rashmi Prasad, and Bonnie Webber. Annotating discourse connectives and their arguments. *Proc. of the Workshop Frontiers in Corpus Annotation at HLT-NAACL*, pages 9–16, Association for Computational Linguistics, Boston, MA, May 2–7, 2004. https://aclanthology.org/W04-2703 75

Tom Minka, John M. Winn, John P. Guiver, Yordan Zaykov, Dany Fabian, and John Bronskill. /Infer.NET 0.3, 2018. http://dotnet.github.io/infer Microsoft Research Cambridge. 124

Mike Mintz, Steven Bills, Rion Snow, and Daniel Jurafsky. Distant supervision for relation extraction without labeled data. *Proc. of the Joint Conference of the 47th Annual Meeting of the ACL and the 4th International Joint Conference on Natural Language Processing of the AFNLP*, pages 1003–1011, Association for Computational Linguistics, Suntec, Singapore, August 2009. https://aclanthology.org/P09-1113 DOI: 10.3115/1690219.1690287 105

Pablo G. Moreno, Antonio Artés-Rodríguez, Yee Whye Teh, and Fernando Perez-Cruz. Bayesian nonparametric crowdsourcing. *Journal of Machine Learning Research*, 2015. https://jmlr.org/papers/volume16/moreno15a/moreno15a.pdf 93, 107, 124

Megan Moser and Johanna D. Moore. Toward a synthesis of two accounts of discourse structure. *Computational Linguistics*, 22(3):409–419, 1996. https://aclanthology.org/J96-3006/ 63

Megan Moser, Johanna D. Moore, and Erin Glendening. Instructions for coding explanations: Identifying segments, relations and minimal units. *Technical Report 96-17*, University of Pittsburgh, Department of Computer Science, 1996. 63

Christine H. Nakatani, Barbara J. Grosz, David D. Ahn, and Julia Hirschberg. Instructions for annotating discourses. *Technical Report TR-25-95*, Harvard University Center for Research in Computing Technology, 1995. 63

Costanza Navarretta. Abstract anaphora resolution in Danish. *Proc. of the 1st SIGdial Workshop on Discourse and Dialogue*, Hong Kong, October 2000. http://www.sigdial.org/workshops/workshop1/proceedings/ DOI: 10.3115/1117736.1117743 69

Ani Nenkova and Rebecca Passonneau. Evaluating content selection in summarization: The pyramid method. *Proc. of the Human Language Technology Conference of the North American Chapter of the Association for Computational Linguistics: HLT-NAACL*, pages 145–152, Boston, MA, May 2–7, 2004. https://aclanthology.org/N04-1019 9, 10, 70, 71

Kimberly A. Neuendorf. *The Content Analysis Guidebook*. Sage, Thousand Oaks, CA, 2002. DOI: 10.4135/9781071802878 50, 77

Andrew Y. Ng and Michael I. Jordan. On discriminative vs. generative classifiers: A comparison of logistic regression and naive Bayes. *Proc. of the 14th International Conference on Neural Information Processing Systems: Natural and Synthetic, NIPS*, pages 841–848, MIT Press, Cambridge, MA, 2001. https://papers.nips.cc/paper/2001/hash/7b7a53e239400a13bd6be6c91c4f6c4e-Abstract.html 128, 129

An Thanh Nguyen, Byron Wallace, Junyi Jessy Li, Ani Nenkova, and Matthew Lease. Aggregating and predicting sequence labels from crowd annotations. *Proc. of the 55th Annual Meeting of the Association for Computational Linguistics (Volume 1: Long Papers)*, pages 299–309, Vancouver, Canada, July 2017. https://www.aclweb.org/anthology/P17-1028 DOI: 10.18653/v1/P17-1028 106, 130, 131, 132, 133, 145

Malvina Nissim, Shipra Dingare, Jean Carletta, and Mark Steedman. An annotation scheme for information status in dialogue. *Proc. of the International Conference on Language Resources and Evaluation (LREC)*, 2004. https://aclanthology.org/L04-1402/ 142

Stefanie Nowak and Stefan Rüger. How reliable are annotations via crowdsourcing: A study about inter-annotator agreement for multi-label image annotation. *Proc. of the International Conference on Multimedia Information Retrieval (MIR)*, pages 557–566, Association for Computing Machinery (ACM), 2010. DOI: 10.1145/1743384.1743478 105

Martha Palmer, Hoa Trang Dang, and Christiane Fellbaum. Making fine-grained and coarse-grained sense distinctions, both manually and automatically. *Natural Language Engineering*, 13(2):137–163, June 2007. DOI: 10.1017/s135132490500402x 47, 72, 73, 75

Kishore Papineni, Salim Roukos, Todd Ward, and Wei-Jing Zhu. Bleu: A method for automatic evaluation of machine translation. *Proc. of the 40th Annual Meeting of the Association for Computational Linguistics*, pages 311–318, Philadelphia, PA, July 2002. https://aclanthology.org/P02-1040 DOI: 10.3115/1073083.1073135 143, 150

Rebecca Passonneau. Measuring agreement on set-valued items (MASI) for semantic and pragmatic annotation. *Proc. of the 5th International Conference on Language Resources and Evaluation (LREC)*, European Language Resources Association (ELRA), Genoa, Italy, May 2006. http://www.lrec-conf.org/proceedings/lrec2006/pdf/636_pdf.pdf 10, 67, 70, 71, 72, 75

Rebecca Passonneau, Nizar Habash, and Owen Rambow. Inter-annotator agreement on a multilingual semantic annotation task. *Proc. of the 5th International Conference on Language Resources and Evaluation (LREC)*, European Language Resources Association (ELRA), Genoa, Italy, May 2006. http://www.lrec-conf.org/proceedings/lrec2006/pdf/634_pdf.pdf 10, 75

Rebecca J. Passonneau. Computing reliability for coreference annotation. *Proc. of the 4th International Conference on Language Resources and Evaluation (LREC)*, European Language Resources Association (ELRA), Lisbon, Portugal, May 2004. http://www.lrec-conf.org/proceedings/lrec2004/pdf/752.pdf 1, 10, 66, 67, 72, 74, 76, 134

Rebecca J. Passonneau and Bob Carpenter. The benefits of a model of annotation. *Transactions of the Association for Computational Linguistics*, 2:311–326, 2014. https://aclanthology.org/Q14-1025 DOI: 10.1162/tacl_a_00185 1, 2, 80, 93, 105, 106, 107, 110, 113

Rebecca J. Passonneau and Diane J. Litman. Intention-based segmentation: Human reliability and correlation with linguistic cues. *Proc. of 31st Annual Meeting of the ACL*, pages 148–155, Association for Computational Linguistics, Columbus, OH, June 1993. https://aclanthology.org/P93-1020 DOI: 10.3115/981574.981594 9, 62, 63, 64

Rebecca J. Passonneau and Diane J. Litman. Discourse segmentation by human and automated means. *Computational Linguistics*, 23(1), 1997. https://aclanthology.org/J97-1005 2, 63

Rebecca J. Passonneau, Vikas Bhardwaj, Ansaf Salleb-Aouissi, and Nancy Ide. Multiplicity and word sense: Evaluating and learning from multiply labeled word sense annotations. *Language Resources and Evaluation*, 46(2):219–252, 2012. DOI: 10.1007/s10579-012-9188-x 2, 108, 147

Silviu Paun and Dirk Hovy, Eds. *Proc. of the 1st Workshop on Aggregating and Analysing Crowdsourced Annotations for NLP*, Association for Computational Linguistics, Hong Kong, November 2019. https://aclanthology.org/D19-5900 143

Silviu Paun and Edwin Simpson. Aggregating and learning from multiple annotators. *Proc. of the 16th Conference of the European Chapter of the Association for Computational Linguistics: Tutorial Abstracts*, pages 6–9, April 2021. https://aclanthology.org/2021.eacl-tutorials.2 DOI: 10.18653/v1/2021.eacl-tutorials.2 143

Silviu Paun, Bob Carpenter, Jon Chamberlain, Dirk Hovy, Udo Kruschwitz, and Massimo Poesio. Comparing Bayesian models of annotation. *Transactions of the Association for Computa-*

tional Linguistics, 6:571–585, 2018a. DOI: 10.1162/tacl_a_00040 1, 2, 93, 107, 108, 112, 113, 122

Silviu Paun, Jon Chamberlain, Udo Kruschwitz, Juntao Yu, and Massimo Poesio. A probabilistic annotation model for crowdsourcing coreference. *Proc. of the Conference on Empirical Methods in Natural Language Processing*, pages 1926–1937, Association for Computational Linguistics, Brussels, Belgium, October–November 2018b. http://www.aclweb.org/anthology/D18-1218 DOI: 10.18653/v1/d18-1218 106, 134, 136, 137

Joshua C. Peterson, Ruairidh M. Battleday, Thomas L. Griffiths, and Olga Russakovsky. Human uncertainty makes classification more robust. *Proc. of the IEEE/CVF International Conference on Computer Vision (ICCV)*, October 2019. https://openaccess.thecvf.com/content_ICCV_2019/papers/Peterson_Human_Uncertainty_Makes_Classification_More_Robust_ICCV_2019_paper.pdf DOI: 10.1109/iccv.2019.00971 2, 108, 147, 149, 150, 151, 152, 154, 155

Lev Pevzner and Marti A. Hearst. A critique and improvement of an evaluation metric for text segmentation. *Computational Linguistics*, 28(1):19–36, 2002. https://aclanthology.org/J02-1002 DOI: 10.1162/089120102317341756 63, 65

Janet Pierrehumbert and Julia Hirschberg. The meaning of intonational contours in English. In J. Morgan, P. Cohen, and M. Pollack, Eds., *Intentions in Communication*, pages 271–312, MIT Press, Cambridge, MA, 1990. DOI: 10.7551/mitpress/3839.003.0016 65

John Pitrelli, Mary Beckman, and Julia Hirschberg. Evaluation of prosodic transcription labelling reliability in the TOBI framework. *Proc. 3rd International Conference on Spoken Language Processing*, 2:123–126, Yokohama, 1994. https://www.isca-speech.org/archive/icslp_1994/pitrelli94_icslp.html 65

Barbara Plank, Dirk Hovy, Ryan McDonald, and Anders Søgaard. Adapting taggers to Twitter with not-so-distant supervision. *Proc. of COLING, the 25th International Conference on Computational Linguistics: Technical Papers*, pages 1783–1792, 2014a. https://aclanthology.org/C14-1168/ 106, 111

Barbara Plank, Dirk Hovy, and Anders Sogaard. Linguistically debatable or just plain wrong? *Proc. of the 52nd Annual Meeting of the Association for Computational Linguistics (Volume 2: Short Papers)*, 2014b. https://aclanthology.org/P14-2083/ DOI: 10.3115/v1/p14-2083 108, 147, 151

Barbara Plank, Dirk Hovy, and Anders Søgaard. Learning part-of-speech taggers with inter-annotator agreement loss. *Proc. of the 14th Conference of the European Chapter of the Association for Computational Linguistics*, pages 742–751, Gothenburg, Sweden, April 2014c. https://www.aclweb.org/anthology/E14-1078 DOI: 10.3115/v1/E14-1078 165

Massimo Poesio. Discourse annotation and semantic annotation in the GNOME corpus. *Proc. of the ACL Workshop on Discourse Annotation*, Barcelona, July 2004a. https://aclanthology.org/W04-0210/ DOI: 10.3115/1608938.1608948 77

Massimo Poesio. The MATE/GNOME proposals for anaphoric annotation, revisited. In Michael Strube and Candy Sidner, Eds., *Proc. of the 5th SIGdial Workshop on Discourse and Dialogue*, pages 154–162, Association for Computational Linguistics, Cambridge, MA, April–May 2004b. http://www.sigdial.org/workshops/workshop5/proceedings/ 62

Massimo Poesio. Ambiguity. In Daniel Gutzmann, Lisa Matthewson, Cécile Meier, Hotze Rullmann, and Thomas Ede Zimmermann, Eds., *The Companion to Semantics*, Wiley, 2020. DOI: 10.1002/9781118788516.sem098 147

Massimo Poesio and Ron Artstein. The reliability of anaphoric annotation, reconsidered: Taking ambiguity into account. *Proc. of the Workshop on Frontiers in Corpus Annotation II: Pie in the Sky*, Association for Computational Linguistics, pages 76–83, Ann Arbor, MI, June 2005. http://www.aclweb.org/anthology/W/W05/W05-0311 DOI: 10.3115/1608829.1608840 2, 33, 40, 66, 68, 75, 77, 108, 147

Massimo Poesio and Natalia N. Modjeska. Focus, activation, and THIS-noun phrases: An empirical study. In A. Branco, R. McEnery, and R. Mitkov, Eds., *Anaphora Processing*, pages 429–442, John Benjamins, 2005. 69

Massimo Poesio and Renata Vieira. A corpus-based investigation of definite description use. *Computational Linguistics*, 24(2):183–216, June 1998. http://www.aclweb.org/anthology/J98-2001 9, 77, 78

Massimo Poesio, Amrita Patel, and Barbara Di Eugenio. Discourse structure and anaphora in tutorial dialogues: An empirical analysis of two theories of the global focus. *Research in Language and Computation*, 4:229–257, 2006. Special Issue on Generation and Dialogue. DOI: 10.1007/s11168-006-9005-z 63

Massimo Poesio, Jon Chamberlain, Udo Kruschwitz, Livio Robaldo, and Luca Ducceschi. Phrase detectives: Utilizing collective intelligence for internet-scale language resource creation. *ACM Transactions on Interactive Intelligent Systems*, 3(1):1–44, April 2013. DOI: 10.1145/2448116.2448119 105, 136

Massimo Poesio, Sameer Pradhan, Marta Recasens, Kepa Rodriguez, and Yannick Versley. Annotated corpora and annotation tools. In Massimo Poesio, Roland Stuckardt, and Yannick Versley, Eds., *Anaphora Resolution: Algorithms, Resources and Applications*, chapter 4, Springer, 2016. DOI: 10.1007/978-3-662-47909-4_4 133

Massimo Poesio, Jon Chamberlain, and Udo Kruschwitz. Crowdsourcing. In Nancy Ide and James Pustejovsky, Eds., *Handbook of Linguistic Annotation*, pages 277–295, Springer, 2017. DOI: 10.1007/978-94-024-0881-2_10 105

Massimo Poesio, Yulia Grishina, Varada Kolhatkar, Nafise Moosavi, Ina Roesiger, Adam Roussel, Fabian Simonjetz, Alexandra Uma, Olga Uryupina, Juntao Yu, and Heike Zinsmeister. Anaphora resolution with the ARRAU corpus. *Proc. of the NAACL Workshop on Computational Models of Reference, Anaphora and Coreference (CRAC)*, pages 11–22, New Orleans, LA, June 2018. https://aclanthology.org/W18-0702/ DOI: 10.18653/v1/w18-0702 137

Massimo Poesio, Jon Chamberlain, Silviu Paun, Juntao Yu, Alexandra Uma, and Udo Kruschwitz. A crowdsourced corpus of multiple judgments and disagreement on anaphoric interpretation. *Proc. of the Conference of the North American Chapter of the Association for Computational Linguistics: Human Language Technologies, Volume 1 (Long and Short Papers)*, pages 1778–1789, Minneapolis, MN, June 2019. https://www.aclweb.org/anthology/N19-1176 DOI: 10.18653/v1/n19-1176 105, 108, 120, 136, 147

Andrei Popescu-Belis. Dialogue acts: One or more dimensions? *Working Paper 62*, ISSCO, Geneva, 2005. 53, 55, 56

Karen L. Posner, Paul D. Sampson, Robert A. Caplan, Richard J. Ward, and Frederick W. Cheney. Measuring interrater reliability among multiple raters: An example of methods for nominal data. *Statistics in Medicine*, 9:1103–1115, 1990. DOI: 10.1002/sim.4780090917 49

Dragomir R. Radev, Simone Teufel, Horacio Saggion, Wai Lam, John Blitzer, Hong Qi, Arda Çelebi, Danyu Liu, and Elliott Drabek. Evaluation challenges in large-scale document summarization. *Proc. of 41st Annual Meeting of the ACL*, pages 375–382, Sapporo, 2003. DOI: 10.3115/1075096.1075144 70

Nageswari Rajaratnam. Reliability formulas for independent decision data when reliability data are matched. *Psychometrika*, 25(3):261–271, 1960. DOI: 10.1007/bf02289730 25

Georg Rasch. *Probabilistic Models for Some Intelligence and Attainment Tests*. ERIC, 1993. 116, 117

Victor Raskin. *Semantic Mechanisms of Humor*. D. Reidel, Dordrecht and Boston, 1985. DOI: 10.1007/978-94-009-6472-3 147

Adwait Ratnaparkhi. A maximum entropy model for part-of-speech tagging. *Conference on Empirical Methods in Natural Language Processing*, 1996. https://www.aclweb.org/anthology/W96-0213 76

Vikas C. Raykar, Shipeng Yu, Linda H. Zhao, Anna Jerebko, Charles Florin, Gerardo Hermosillo Valadez, Luca Bogoni, and Linda Moy. Supervised learning from multiple experts:

Whom to trust when everyone lies a bit. *Proc. of the 26th Annual International Conference on Machine Learning, ICML*, pages 889–896, Association for Computing Machinery, New York, 2009. DOI: 10.1145/1553374.1553488 127

Vikas C. Raykar, Shipeng Yu, Linda H. Zhao, Gerardo Hermosillo Valadez, Charles Florin, Luca Bogoni, and Linda Moy. Learning from crowds. *Journal of Machine Learning Research*, 11:1297–1322, 2010. https://www.jmlr.org/papers/volume11/raykar10a/raykar10a.pdf 2, 106, 107, 110, 126, 127, 128, 129, 155, 156, 157

Marta Recasens, Ed Hovy, and M. Antonia Martí. Identity, non-identity, and near-identity: Addressing the complexity of coreference. *Lingua*, 121(6):1138–1152, 2011. DOI: 10.1016/j.lingua.2011.02.004 108, 147

Dennis Reidsma and Jean Carletta. Reliability measurement without limits. *Computational Linguistics*, 34(3):319–326, 2008. DOI: 10.1162/coli.2008.34.3.319 xvii, 51, 80, 93, 105, 148, 155

Dennis Reidsma and Rieks op den Akker. Exploiting "subjective" annotations. *Coling: Proceedings of the workshop on Human Judgements in Computational Linguistics*, pages 8–16, Coling 2008 Organizing Committee, Manchester, UK, August 2008. https://www.aclweb.org/anthology/W08-1203 DOI: 10.3115/1611628.1611631 80, 93

Tanya Reinhart. Pragmatics and linguistics: An analysis of sentence topics. *Philosophica*, 27(1), 1981. Also distributed by Indiana University Linguistics Club. 62

Jeffrey C. Reynar. Topic segmentation: Algorithms and applications. Ph.D., University of Pennsylvania, IRCS, Philadelphia, PA, 1998. 62, 63, 64

Klaus Ries. Segmenting conversations by topic, initiative and style. *Proc. of ACM SIGIR Workshop on Information Retrieval Techniques for Speech Applications*, New Orleans, LA, 2001. DOI: 10.1007/3-540-45637-6_5 63

Klaus Ries. Segmenting conversations by topic, initiative and style. In Anni R. Coden, Eric W. Brown, and Savitha Srinivasan, Eds., *Information Retrieval Techniques for Speech Applications*, volume 2273 of *Lecture Notes in Computer Science*, pages 51–66, Springer, Berlin, 2002. DOI: 10.1007/3-540-45637-6_5 64

Arndt Riester, David Lorenz, and Nina Seeman. A recursive annotation scheme for referential information status. *Proc. of the International Conference on Language Resources and Evaluation (LREC)*, pages 717–722, 2010. https://aclanthology.org/L10-1528/ 142

Toni Rietveld and Roeland van Hout. *Statistical Techniques for the Study of Language and Language Behavior*. Mouton de Gruyter, 1993. DOI: 10.1515/9783110871609 50

Filipe Rodrigues and Francisco C. Pereira. Deep learning from crowds. *32nd AAAI Conference on Artificial Intelligence*, 2018. https://arxiv.org/abs/1709.01779 2, 156, 157, 158, 159, 160, 161, 162, 163

Filipe Rodrigues, Francisco Pereira, and Bernardete Ribeiro. Gaussian process classification and active learning with multiple annotators. In Eric P. Xing and Tony Jebara, Eds., *Proc. of the 31st International Conference on Machine Learning*, number 2 in *Proc. of Machine Learning Research*, pages 433–441, PMLR, Bejing, China, June 22–24, 2014. https://proceedings.mlr.press/v32/rodrigues14.html 161, 162

Filipe Rodrigues, Mariana Lourenço, Bernardete Ribeiro, and Francisco C. Pereira. Learning supervised topic models for classification and regression from crowds. *IEEE Transactions on Pattern Analysis and Machine Intelligence*, 39(12):2409–2422, 2017. DOI: 10.1109/tpami.2017.2648786 129, 151, 159, 161, 162

Andrew Rosenberg and Ed Binkowski. Augmenting the kappa statistic to determine inter-annotator reliability for multiply labeled data points. *Proc. of the North American Chapter of the Association for Computational Linguistics, Volume Short Papers*, pages 77–80, 2004. https://aclanthology.org/N04-4020/ DOI: 10.3115/1613984.1614004 75

Bryan C. Russell, Antonio Torralba, Kevin P. Murphy, and William T. Freeman. Labelme: A database and Web-based tool for image annotation. *International Journal of Computer Vision*, 77(1):157–173, 2008. DOI: 10.1007/s11263-007-0090-8 159, 161, 162

Marta Sabou, Kalina Bontcheva, Leon Derczynski, and Arno Scharl. Corpus annotation through crowdsourcing: Towards best practice guidelines. *Proc. of the 9th International Conference on Language Resources and Evaluation (LREC)*, pages 859–866, 2014. https://aclanthology.org/L14-1412/ 106, 111

William A. Scott. Reliability of content analysis: The case of nominal scale coding. *Public Opinion Quarterly*, 19(3):321–325, 1955. DOI: 10.1086/266577 1, 9, 13, 16, 18, 22, 24, 30, 45, 81, 91, 92

Satoshi Sekine, Kiyoshi Sudo, and Chikashi Nobata. Extended named entity hierarchy. *Proc. of the 3rd International Conference on Language Resources and Evaluation (LREC)*, European Language Resources Association (ELRA), Las Palmas, Canary Islands, Spain, May 2002. http://www.lrec-conf.org/proceedings/lrec2002/pdf/120.pdf 59

Victor S. Sheng, Foster Provost, and Panagiotis G. Ipeirotis. Get another label? Improving data quality and data mining using multiple, noisy labelers. *Proc. of the 14th ACM SIGKDD International Conference on Knowledge Discovery and Data Mining, KDD*, pages 614–622, Association for Computing Machinery, New York, 2008. https://doi.org/10.1145/1401890.1401965 DOI: 10.1145/1401890.1401965 105, 165

Elizabeth Shriberg, Raj Dhillon, Sonali Bhagat, Jeremy Ang, and Hannah Carvey. The ICSI meeting recorder dialog act (MRDA) corpus. *Proc. of 5th SIGDIAL workshop on discourse and dialogue*, pages 97–100, Cambridge, MA, 2004. DOI: 10.21236/ada460980 56

Sidney Siegel and N. John Castellan, Jr. *Nonparametric Statistics for the Behavioral Sciences*, 2nd ed., chapters 9 and 8, pages 284–291. McGraw-Hill, New York, 1988. 1, 9, 10, 18, 22, 24, 40, 49

Edwin Simpson, Stephen J. Roberts, Arfon Smith, and Chris Lintott. Bayesian combination of multiple, imperfect classifiers. Unpublished manuscript, 2011. https://www.robots.ox.ac.uk/sjrob/Pubs/vbibcc_workshop.pdf 93, 113, 123

Edwin Simpson, Stephen Roberts, Ioannis Psorakis, and Arfon Smith. *Dynamic Bayesian Combination of Multiple Imperfect Classifiers*, pages 1–35. Springer Berlin Heidelberg, Berlin, Heidelberg, 2013. DOI: 10.1007/978-3-642-36406-8_1 93, 106, 113, 123

Edwin D. Simpson and Iryna Gurevych. A Bayesian approach for sequence tagging with crowds. *Proc. of the Conference on Empirical Methods in Natural Language Processing and the 9th International Joint Conference on Natural Language Processing (EMNLP-IJCNLP)*, pages 1093–1104, Association for Computational Linguistics, Hong Kong, China, November 2019. DOI: 10.18653/v1/D19-1101 106, 131, 132, 133

Edwin D. Simpson, Matteo Venanzi, Steven Reece, Pushmeet Kohli, John Guiver, Stephen J. Roberts, and Nicholas R. Jennings. Language understanding in the wild: Combining crowdsourcing and machine learning. *Proc. of the 24th International Conference on World Wide Web, WWW*, pages 992–1002, International World Wide Web Conferences Steering Committee, Republic and Canton of Geneva, CHE, 2015. DOI: 10.1145/2736277.2741689 126, 127

John McHardy Sinclair and Malcolm Coulthard. *Towards an Analysis of Discourse: The English Used by Teachers and Pupils*. Oxford University Press, 1975. DOI: 10.2307/3585455 63

Anders Skrondal and Sophia Rabe-Hesketh. *Generalized Latent Variable Modeling: Multilevel, Longitudinal, and Structural Equation Models*. Chapman & Hall/CRC Interdisciplinary Statistics. Taylor & Francis, 2004. https://books.google.ro/books?id=JjR6AgAAQBAJ 116

A. M. Smith, S. Lynn, M. Sullivan, C. J. Lintott, P. E. Nugent, J. Botyanszki, M. Kasliwal, R. Quimby, S. P. Bamford, L. F. Fortson, K. Schawinski, I. Hook, S. Blake, P. Podsiadlowski, J. Jönsson, A. Gal-Yam, I. Arcavi, D. A. Howell, J. S. Bloom, J. Jacobsen, S. R. Kulkarni, N. M. Law, E. O. Ofek, and R. Walters. Galaxy Zoo Supernovae*. *Monthly Notices of the Royal Astronomical Society*, 412(2):1309–1319, March 2011. DOI: 10.1111/j.1365-2966.2010.17994.x 105

Padhraic Smyth, Usama M. Fayyad, Michael C. Burl, Pietro Perona, and Pierre Baldi. Inferring ground truth from subjective labelling of Venus images. *Advances in Neural Information*

Processing Systems, pages 1085–1092, 1994. https://proceedings.neurips.cc/paper/1994/hash/3cef96dcc9b8035d23f69e30bb19218a-Abstract.html 106, 107, 110, 128

Rion Snow, Brendan O'Connor, Daniel Jurafsky, and Andrew Y. Ng. Cheap and fast—but is it good? Evaluating non-expert annotations for natural language tasks. *Proc. of the Conference on Empirical Methods in Natural Language Processing (EMNLP)*, pages 254–263, 2008. https://aclanthology.org/D08-1027/ DOI: 10.3115/1613715.1613751 xvii, 2, 105, 106, 107, 108, 110, 115, 124

Wee Meng Soon, Hwee Tou Ng, and Daniel Chung Yong Lim. A machine learning approach to coreference resolution of noun phrases. *Computational Linguistics*, 27(4):521–544, December 2001. https://aclanthology.org/J01-4004/ DOI: 10.1162/089120101753342653 134

Alexander Sorokin and David Forsyth. Utility data annotation with Amazon Mechanical Turk. *IEEE Computer Society Conference on Computer Vision and Pattern Recognition Workshops*, pages 1–8, 2008. DOI: 10.1109/cvprw.2008.4562953 105

Amanda Joy Stent. Dialogue systems as conversational partners: Applying conversation acts theory to natural language generation for task-oriented mixed-initiative spoken dialogue. Ph.D. thesis, University of Rochester, Department of Computer Science, Rochester, NY, 2001. 56

Mark Stevenson and Robert Gaizauskas. Experiments on sentence boundary detection. *Proc. of 6th Applied Natural Language Processing Conference*, pages 84–89, Seattle, WA, 2000. https://aclanthology.org/A00-1012/ DOI: 10.3115/974147.974159 9

Andreas Stolcke, Klaus Ries, Noah Coccaro, Elizabeth Shriberg, Rebecca Bates, Daniel Jurafsky, Paul Taylor, Rachel Martin, Carol Van-Ess-Dykema, and Marie Meteer. Dialogue act modeling for automatic tagging and recognition of conversational speech. *Computational Linguistics*, 26(3):339–371, 1997. https://aclanthology.org/J00-3003/ DOI: 10.1162/089120100561737 9, 53, 55

Alan Stuart. A test for homogeneity of the marginal distributions in a two-way classification. *Biometrika*, 42(3/4):412–416, 1955. DOI: 10.1093/biomet/42.3-4.412 37

Soon P. Su. *Lexical Ambiguity in Poetry*. Longman, London, 1994. DOI: 10.2307/416627 147

Ann Syrdal and Julia McGorg. Inter-transcriber reliability of ToBi prosodic labelling. *Proc. of the 6th International Conference on Spoken Language Processing*, 3:235–238, Bejing, 2000. 65, 66

Christian Szegedy, Vincent Vanhoucke, Sergey Ioffe, Jon Shlens, and Zbigniew Wojna. Rethinking the inception architecture for computer vision. *Proc. of the IEEE Conference on Computer Vision and Pattern Recognition (CVPR)*, June 2016. DOI: 10.1109/cvpr.2016.308 154

Yuka Tateisi and Jun-ichi Tsuji. Part-of-speech annotation of biological abstracts. *Proc. of the 4th International Conference on Language Resources and Evaluation (LREC)*, Barcelona, 2004. https://aclanthology.org/L04-1322/ 51

Yuka Tateisi, Tomoko Ohta, Nigel Collier, Chikashi Nobata, and Jun-ichi Tsuji. Building an annotated corpus from biology research papers. *Proc. of COLING Workshop on Semantic Annotation and Intelligent Content*, Luxembourg, 2000. https://aclanthology.org/W00-1704/ 59, 60

Simone Teufel and Marc Moens. Summarising scientific articles—experiments with relevance and rhetorical status. *Computational Linguistics*, 28(4), December 2002. https://aclanthology.org/J02-4002/ DOI: 10.1162/089120102762671936 78

Simone Teufel, Jean Carletta, and Marc Moens. An annotation scheme for discourse-level argumentation in research articles. *9th Conference of the European Chapter of the Association for Computational Linguistics*, pages 110–117, Bergen, Norway, June 1999. https://aclanthology.org/E99-1015 DOI: 10.3115/977035.977051 63

Tian Tian and Jun Zhu. Uncovering the latent structures of crowd labeling. In Tru Cao, Ee-Peng Lim, Zhi-Hua Zhou, Tu-Bao Ho, David Cheung, and Hiroshi Motoda, Eds., *Advances in Knowledge Discovery and Data Mining*, pages 392–404, Springer International Publishing, Cham, 2015. DOI: 10.1007/978-3-319-18038-0_31 141

Erik F. Tjong Kim Sang and Fien De Meulder. Introduction to the CoNLL-2003 shared task: Language-independent named entity recognition. *Proc. of the 7th Conference on Natural Language Learning at HLT-NAACL—Volume 4, CONLL*, pages 142–147, Association for Computational Linguistics, 2003. https://arxiv.org/abs/cs/0306050 DOI: 10.3115/1119176.1119195 131

David R. Traum and Elizabeth A. Hinkelman. Conversation acts in task-oriented spoken dialogue. *Computational Intelligence*, 8(3), 1992. Special Issue on Non-literal Language. DOI: 10.1111/j.1467-8640.1992.tb00380.x 53

Dietrich Trautmann, Johannes Daxenberger, Christian Stab, Hinrich Schütze, and Iryna Gurevych. Fine-grained argument unit recognition and classification. *Proc. of the AAAI Conference on Artificial Intelligence*, 34(05):9048–9056, April 2020. https://ojs.aaai.org/index.php/AAAI/article/view/6438 DOI: 10.1609/aaai.v34i05.6438 132

John Uebersax, William Grove, and Rand Corporation. *Latent Structure Agreement Analysis*. Rand Corporation, 1989. https://books.google.ro/books?id=487qAAAAMAAJ 80, 94, 95, 96, 97, 98, 107, 108, 110

John S. Uebersax. Validity inferences from interobserver agreement. *Psychological Bulletin*, 104(3):405–416, 1988. DOI: 10.1037/0033-2909.104.3.405 2, 80, 94, 106

John S. Uebersax and William M. Grove. Latent class analysis of diagnostic agreement. *Statistics in Medicine*, 9:559–572, 1990. DOI: 10.1002/sim.4780090509 1, 80, 94, 106

Alexandra Uma, Tommaso Fornaciari, Dirk Hovy, Silviu Paun, Barbara Plank, and Massimo Poesio. A case for soft loss functions. *Proc. of the AAAI Conference on Human Computation and Crowdsourcing*, 8(1):173–177, October 2020. https://ojs.aaai.org/index.php/HCOMP/article/view/7478 2, 150, 151

Alexandra Uma, Tommaso Fornaciari, Anca Dumitrache, Tristan Miller, Jon Chamberlain, Barbara Plank, Edwin Simpson, and Massimo Poesio. SemEval-2021 task 12: Learning with disagreements. *Proc. of the 15th International Workshop on Semantic Evaluation (SemEval)*, pages 338–347, Association for Computational Linguistics, August 2021a. https://aclanthology.org/2021.semeval-1.41 DOI: 10.18653/v1/2021.semeval-1.41 150

Alexandra Uma, Tommaso Fornaciari, Dirk Hovy, Silviu Paun, Barbara Plank, and Massimo Poesio. Learning from disagreement: A survey. *Journal of Artificial Intelligence Research*, 2021b. 2, 3, 120, 147, 150, 154, 163, 164, 165

Olga Uryupina, Ron Artstein, Antonella Bristot, Federica Cavicchio, Francesca Delogu, Kepa J. Rodriguez, and Massimo Poesio. Annotating a broad range of anaphoric phenomena, in a variety of genres: The ARRAU corpus. *Natural Language Engineering*, 26(1):95–128, 2020. DOI: 10.1017/S1351324919000056 134

Enric Vallduví. Information packaging: A survey. *Research Paper RP-44*, University of Edinburgh, HCRC, 1993. 62

Matteo Venanzi, John Guiver, Gabriella Kazai, Pushmeet Kohli, and Milad Shokouhi. Community-based Bayesian aggregation models for crowdsourcing. *Proc. of the 23rd International Conference on World Wide Web, WWW*, pages 155–164, ACM, New York, 2014. DOI: 10.1145/2566486.2567989 93, 107, 123, 124, 125

Noortje Venhuizen, Valerio Basile, Kilian Evang, and Johan Bos. Gamification for word sense labeling. *Proc. of the 10th International Conference on Computational Semantics (IWCS)*, 2013. https://hal.inria.fr/hal-01342431 105

Jean Véronis. A study of polysemy judgments and inter-annotator agreement. *Proc. of SENSEVAL*, 1998. http://citeseerx.ist.psu.edu/viewdoc/summary?doi=10.1.1.27.698 9, 18, 72, 73, 75

Yannick Versley. Vagueness and referential ambiguity in a large-scale annotated corpus. *Research on Language and Computation*, 6:333–353, 2008. DOI: 10.1007/s11168-008-9059-1 108

Marc Vilain, John Burger, John Aberdeen, Dennis Connolly, and Lynette Hirschman. A model-theoretic coreference scoring scheme. *Proc. of the 6th Message Understanding Conference*, pages 45–52, Columbia, MD, November 1995. https://aclanthology.org/M95-1005/ DOI: 10.3115/1072399.1072405 67

Andreas Vlachos, Nikiforos Karamanis, Ruth Seal, Ian Lewin, Chihiro Yamada, Caroline Gasperin, and Ted Briscoe. *Annotation Guidelines for Named Entity Recognition in the Fly-SLIP Project*. University of Cambridge, CRL, Cambridge, April 2006. 60

Ellen Voorhees and Donna Harman. Overview of the seventh text retrieval conference (TREC-7). NIST special publication, 1998. http://citeseerx.ist.psu.edu/viewdoc/summary?doi=10.1.1.2.4400 62

Zeerak Waseem. Are you a racist or am I seeing things? Annotator influence on hate speech detection on Twitter. *Proc. of the 1st Workshop on NLP and Computational Social Science*, pages 138–142, 2016. https://aclanthology.org/W16-5618/ DOI: 10.18653/v1/w16-5618 148

Charles L. Wayne. Multilingual topic detection and tracking: Successful research enabled by corpora and evaluation. *Proc. of the 2nd International Conference on Language Resources and Evaluation (LREC)*, European Language Resources Association (ELRA), Athens, Greece, May 2000. http://www.lrec-conf.org/proceedings/lrec2000/pdf/168.pdf 62

Peter Welinder, Steve Branson, Pietro Perona, and Serge J. Belongie. The multidimensional wisdom of crowds. In J. D. Lafferty, C. K. I. Williams, J. Shawe-Taylor, R. S. Zemel, and A. Culotta, Eds., *Advances in Neural Information Processing Systems 23*, pages 2424–2432, Curran Associates, Inc., 2010. http://papers.nips.cc/paper/4074-the-multidimensional-wisdom-of-crowds.pdf 141

Jacob Whitehill, Ting-fan Wu, Jacob Bergsma, Javier R. Movellan, and Paul L. Ruvolo. Whose vote should count more: Optimal integration of labels from labelers of unknown expertise. *Advances in Neural Information Processing Systems 22*, pages 2035–2043, Curran Associates, Inc., 2009. http://papers.nips.cc/paper/3644-whose-vote-should-count-more-optimal-integration-of-labels-from-labelers-of-unknown-expertise.pdf 1, 2, 106, 107, 117, 118, 119, 120, 121, 144, 162

Janyce Wiebe, Teresa Wilson, and Claire Cardie. Annotating expressions of opinions and emotions in language. *Language Resources and Evaluation*, 39(2):165–210, 2005. DOI: 10.1007/s10579-005-7880-9 2, 81

Janyce M. Wiebe, Rebecca F. Bruce, and Thomas P. O'Hara. Development and use of a gold-standard data set for subjectivity classifications. *Proc. of the 37th Annual Meeting of the Association for Computational Linguistics*, pages 246–253, College Park, MD, June 1999. https://www.aclweb.org/anthology/P99-1032 DOI: 10.3115/1034678.1034721 80, 99, 100

Susanne Winkler. *Ambiguity: Language and Communication*. De Gruyter, 2015. 147

Yonghui Wu, Mike Schuster, Zhifeng Chen, Quoc V. Le, Mohammad Norouzi, Wolfgang Macherey, Maxim Krikun, Yuan Cao, Qin Gao, Klaus Macherey, Jeff Klingner, Apurva Shah, Melvin Johnson, Xiaobing Liu, Łukasz Kaiser, Stephan Gouws, Yoshikiyo Kato, Taku Kudo, Hideto Kazawa, Keith Stevens, George Kurian, Nishant Patil, Wei Wang, Cliff Young, Jason Smith, Jason Riesa, Alex Rudnick, Oriol Vinyals, Greg Corrado, Macduff Hughes, and Jeffrey Dean. Google's neural machine translation system: Bridging the gap between human and machine translation, 2016. https://arxiv.org/pdf/1609.08144v2.pdf 143

Yan Yan, Romer Rosales, Glenn Fung, Mark Schmidt, Gerardo Hermosillo, Luca Bogoni, Linda Moy, and Jennifer Dy. Modeling annotator expertise: Learning when everybody knows a bit of something. In Yee Whye Teh and Mike Titterington, Eds., *Proc. of the 13th International Conference on Artificial Intelligence and Statistics*, volume 9 of *Proc. of Machine Learning Research*, pages 932–939, PMLR, Chia Laguna Resort, Sardinia, Italy, May 13–15, 2010. http://proceedings.mlr.press/v9/yan10a.html 126, 127

Yan Yan, Rómer Rosales, Glenn Fung, Ramanathan Subramanian, and Jennifer Dy. Learning from multiple annotators with varying expertise. *Machine Learning*, 95(3):291–327, June 2014. DOI: 10.1007/s10994-013-5412-1 126, 127

Hui Yang, Anne De Roeck, Vincenzo Gervasi, Alistair Willis, and Bashar Nuseibeh. Analysing anaphoric ambiguity in natural language requirements. *Requirements Engineering*, 16:163–189, September 2011. DOI: 10.1007/s00766-011-0119-y 148

Li'ang Yin, Jianhua Han, Weinan Zhang, and Yong Yu. Aggregating crowd wisdoms with label-aware autoencoders. *Proc. of the 26th International Joint Conference on Artificial Intelligence, IJCAI*, pages 1325–1331, 2017. DOI: 10.24963/ijcai.2017/184 2, 137, 138, 139, 140, 141, 142

Dengyong Zhou, Sumit Basu, Yi Mao, and John C. Platt. Learning from the wisdom of crowds by minimax entropy. In F. Pereira, C. J. C. Burges, L. Bottou, and K. Q. Weinberger, Eds., *Advances in Neural Information Processing Systems 25*, pages 2195–2203, Curran Associates, Inc., 2012. http://papers.nips.cc/paper/4490-learning-from-the-wisdom-of-crowds-by-minimax-entropy.pdf 141

Rebecca Zwick. Another look at interrater agreement. *Psychological Bulletin*, 103(3):374–378, 1988. DOI: 10.1037/0033-2909.103.3.374 17, 20, 37, 38

Authors' Biographies

SILVIU PAUN

Silviu Paun got his Ph.D. from the University of Essex in 2017 with a thesis on topic models. Since then he has been at Queen Mary University of London. His research focuses on models of annotation, probabilistic and neural, for creating resources and to more efficiently train machine learning models. His models have been deployed to create the *Phrase Detectives* coreference corpus, one of the largest crowdsourced NLP corpora, created using the *Phrase Detectives* Game-With-A-Purpose.

RON ARTSTEIN

Ron Artstein received his Ph.D. in Linguistics from Rutgers University in 2002, held positions at the Technion–Israel Institute of Technology and the University of Essex, and is presently a research scientist at the Institute for Creative Technologies, University of Southern California. His current research focuses on the collection, annotation, and management of linguistic data for human–machine interaction, analysis of corpora, and the evaluation of implemented dialogue systems; he has published work on theoretical and computational linguistics, conversational dialogue systems, and human–agent and human–robot interaction.

MASSIMO POESIO

Massimo Poesio received his Ph.D. from the University of Rochester in 1994. He is a Professor in Computational Linguistics at Queen Mary University of London and a Turing Institute Fellow. His main interests are in anaphora resolution, disagreements in language interpretation, the use of games-with-a-purpose for creating NLP resources, and semantic interpretation in dialogue.

Printed in the United States
by Baker & Taylor Publisher Services